Latesha Gilchrist

All
I Have

Ovacom Publishing

All I Have
All Rights Reserved.
Copyright © 2020 Latesha Gilchrist
v2.0

The opinions expressed in this manuscript are solely the opinions of the author and do not represent the opinions or thoughts of the publisher. The author has represented and warranted full ownership and/or legal right to publish all the materials in this book.

This book may not be reproduced, transmitted, or stored in whole or in part by any means, including graphic, electronic, or mechanical without the express written consent of the publisher except in the case of brief quotations embodied in critical articles and reviews.

Ovacom Publishing

ISBN: 978-0-578-22958-4

Cover Photo © 2020 www.gettyimages.com. All rights reserved - used with permission.

PRINTED IN THE UNITED STATES OF AMERICA

ACKNOWLEDGEMENTS

I WOULD LIKE to thank my Lord and savior Jesus Christ for giving up his life for me. I would also like to thank Jesus for also going to the father on my behalf. Thank you God for hearing and answering my prayers and for also having people such as my son father Rodrequise L Calhoun Sr, T.D Jake's and Joyce Meyers and I could go on and on with this list but this is just a few for helping me out on my spiritual journey.

Thank you, Lord, for using my platform for your own purpose and I wouldn't take back nothing I've been through in life because that's what made me the woman that I am today. I would like to thank my children Rodrequise Jr, Destiny, and Brianna for their love and understanding. Thank you, Lynda Gilchrist, for loving me and Karen Gilchrist I thank God for choosing you to be my mother, even though we have our moments. I want you to know with time I've learned to truly love your life.

To the Gilchrist family I love you all and by the Grace of God we're going to get it together.

I would also like to thank all my friends and family for loving me and I love you guys!!

God has the wheel! Just know that God is not concerned with what we do, it's why we do it and in time, we're going to see brighter days. Melinda Turner, thank you for helping me type my first manuscript. I would like to give a special shoutout to Rosemary Godwin for her legal assistance with pertaining this book. Thank you, Bridgette Agguire for your legal assistance for many years and for caring. For all the Warriors and fallen soldiers, whether it's being lost to the system or in the afterlife, peace be with you!

TABLE OF CONTENTS

Chapter 1 1

Chapter 2 4

Chapter 3 10

Chapter 4 20

Chapter 5 26

Chapter 6 36

Chapter 7 50

Chapter 8 61

Chapter 9 66

Chapter 10 74

Chapter 11 84

Chapter 12 91

Chapter 13 99

Chapter 14 103

Chapter 15 111

Chapter 16 117

Chapter 17 123

Chapter 18 130

Chapter 19 141

Chapter 20 148

Chapter 21 156

Chapter 22 168

Chapter 23 181

Chapter 24 200

Chapter 25 205

Chapter 26 218

Chapter 27 223

Chapter 28 234

Chapter 29 241

Chapter 30 249

Chapter 31 257

Chapter 32 263

Chapter 33 275

Chapter 34 283

Chapter 35 289

Chapter 36 301

Chapter 37 310

CHAPTER 1

"TINA GO IN the bathroom and get my comb and brush out the cabinet under the sink." My mom said as she was racing through the living room looking for her shoe.

"Here you go. Where are you going tonight?" I asked as I handed my mom May the comb and brush that she asked for.

"We going to the club tonight." My mom said as she was combing her hair while looking at the television show young and the restless. The year was 1986 and I was 6 years old...

My mom, and her sister Nita had a place together on Clover Apartments off South Anders street in Raleigh North Carolina. For as long as I could remember there was always a lot of traffic where people were constantly in and out of the apartment. Nothing fancy. Just the modest two-bedroom apartment where my aunt Nita occupied one side and my mother the other. There were 5 children there also. My mom May had 3 and was pregnant with another and my aunt Nita had 2 and she too was pregnant. My mom had me who was 6, my sister Tonya who was 4 and my brother Lamont who was 3. My aunt kids were Candy who was 4 and her brother Wayne who was 2 also. To me I figured that my mom and Nita was in competition with each other cause they both seemed to get pregnant around the same time. With people at their apartment all the time, one thing that I can say about them, they were very popular. At the time, my mom had a male friend who name was Vick. He was mad cool to me and treated me like he was my dad. Since I never knew

ALL I HAVE

who my dad was, I would always wonder to myself if he was, but I never asked because deep down, I didn't know how to? Eventually I just left it alone. But on this night that my mom May, Nita, Vick and a few others decided to go out, I remember my mom and my aunt Nita putting all the kids in one room together and closing the door. In time I fell asleep and suddenly I'd been woken up by someone who was taking my panties off. Remind you, I'm only 6 years old…

For a second or two, I couldn't make out the face but when I did, it was Reese, Vick brother. He was around 18 at the time. For the life of me, I tried moving my hands and legs `but couldn't because he done put all his weight on me. While screaming and hollering I pleaded with him to get off me but then he slapped me and told me to shut the fuck up. I remember crying uncontrollably as he lay on top of me and unexpectedly, I felt a sharp pain between my legs that words couldn't describe. I pleaded and begged him to stop but he just kept going. The next thing I know, I see my sister Tonya jump on his back to try to get him off me but like a rag doll, he slung her against the wall. While crying, she stood by powerless as he kept going faster and faster inside me, all the while telling me that if I kept hollering, he would kill me. So, I had to take it. I didn't want to die. I can't even remember why he was there actually. I believe he was there to babysit, but with no other adults there, my cries for help was hopeless. I then begun calling for someone to please come help me in my mind, but it was pointless because as he kept going and hurting me more and more, abruptly the guy finally stops. As he exhaled when coming out of me, he told me that if I told anyone, he would kill me and my family. I was petrified… all I kept asking myself is, how could he do this to me? I'm only 6 years old! He had just given me candy, chips, and cookies earlier that day. I thought he was a cool guy. But now after this I hated him for doing this to me. It made me feel nasty. Filthy even. How could he? It made me afraid to move, so I just lie there. But Tonya my sister came and put her arms around me and didn't let go. I soon dozed off and just when I thought that it was over, I hear the room door open and felt the

CHAPTER 1

lights come on. I had my head under the covers because I was scared to move, hoping that he wouldn't come back but he did. Suddenly I was picked up out the bed and carried to the bathroom. I remember him trying to stand me up on my feet, but I was in so much pain that I couldn't. He then took it upon himself to take off my clothes and once done, he sat me in the bathtub. I remember the water being so hot that it felt as if my whole body was burning. Especially between my legs. But at that point I didn't care. I just felt so dirty. So, I took the pain. He then got a rag and soap and begun washing me from head to toe. Even between my legs. I was going through so many stages of pain, but I was too afraid to say anything because as he washed me, he kept telling me that if I told anyone I was good as dead. I couldn't help but keep asking myself why. But then he picked me up out the bathtub, dried me off, put me in a t-shirt and panties and carried me back inside the room and laid me down. I laid there and cried all night long silently hoping that May, somebody would hurry up and come back so I could get some sleep because every time I tried, I couldn't because I was too scared that he'd come back to hurt me again. I was scared to death and then finally I heard a knock on the door, and it was the voice of my aunt Nita and my mom May. That alone made me feel a whole lot safer and it was then I finally went to sleep.

When I woke up the next day I heard my aunt Nita asking me if I was o.k. (now mind you I did hear her beforehand saying to everyone what was wrong with Tina because I had slept all that day.) I tried my best to whisper to her because I knew that Reese was still in the front room because I'd heard him in the background. So, I whispered for her to come follow me and then I grabbed her by the hand and led her to the bathroom. Once inside, she closes the door behind us, but once I pulled my panties down and she saw all the blood, she began crying uncontrollably and hollering. When I told her who had done it, it was right after that I heard a lot of banging, fighting and things being thrown around. The kids ran in the bathroom with me and we all sat up against the wall and from that day forward, my whole life would change forever.

CHAPTER 2

"HEY AUNT MARGARET, I've missed you so much. Where have you been? " I hadn't seen her since I lived in Chester, Pennsylvania. I loved her so much.

My aunt Margaret had long beautiful hair that looked wet with caramel complexioned skin. But as she aged her rheumatoid arthritis had gotten a lot worse than it had the last, I'd saw her. It was so bad that she couldn't even stand up or move around at all. But I missed her a lot so therefore I was glad to see her. Right after that incident that happened with Reese, I was then sent to my great grandma Daisy's house. She has a beautiful 3 story brick house on Carboro road. 121 South Carboro road to be exact. She had a store called the Blue Front. It was run by my Great Grandpa whose name is Eugene. To me they had it going on. He sold fresh fish, hamburger, all kinds of meats, sodas, and dairy products. Pretty much anything you wanted because my great grandpa Eugene had it. People would go around the backyard and down the steps to the basement because that's where the store was. But my grandpa Eugene was a strange dude. I would see him fix a bowl of cereal and literally put the first thing he could get his hands on, whether it be a Sunkist or Coca cola and he would put it in his cereal and eat it. His excuse was always that it all went down the same way! Just plain nasty. EWWW! But one thing I can say about him was that he was about his money. They had a beautiful house on the second floor was the living room and the den was on one side.

CHAPTER 2

With money green carpet, the beautiful furniture was wooden with red roses imprinted in the loveseat and sofa set. There was a recliner chair all the same, a 7 piece dining room set with, 2 tall china cabinets, silver all throughout the house and my great grandmother Daisy made it perfectly clear that no one was to step foot on her green carpet. And if you did, your butt was hers. When leaving the dining room, it led you to the kitchen that had a table and only 2 chairs and for some reason her house always smelled like old people and "mothballs". Once you left the kitchen, to the right you had the bathroom and next to it you had my aunt Margaret's room. With hardwood floors, in the hallway, she had another little table with a chair and a rotor phone on top of it. Right beside my aunt Margaret's room, it was a den. But inside the den, it was a sofa, chair, and a bed but it was also where my great grandma Daisy would sleep. To me their house was a dream house. Now upstairs I never went because that's where my great grandpa Eugene would be and because I didn't trust men after what happened to me with Reese, I kept my distance.

To my knowledge, I can only go back throughout my family tree, to know that my great grandma Daisy and my grandpa Eugene were the parents of my aunt Margaret and my grandma Louise. Louise had passed away in Chester Pennsylvania, but she did have a daughter, Lynda Gilchrist. Lynda had 5 children of her own which were my mom May, my aunt Nita, and my uncles Reggie, Rodney, and Mike. It was my grandma Lynda who brought me to my grandma Daisy house which was Lynda's grandmother.

Staying at my great grandma Daisy's house at 6 years old was boring because all she did was watch TV and cook. A few days had passed away and I was missing my brothers and sisters and because I had heard that my mom May had just had a little boy whom she named David, I was eager to see them because it had been almost a month since I had, so I was ready to go home. When I asked my grandma Daisy could she call my mom so I could leave, her words were, I was never going back over to that place again. To a 6 year old kid, I couldn't understand what I had done wrong. I loved being around my sister Tonya, my mom May and the rest of the family, so I didn't want to be at that house, with no one to play with and my great grandma Daisy telling me, Tina do this and Tina do that, everyday all day. It was as if I was a live in maid because she would never let me go outside and every time I'd ask she would say, Tina sit your grown ass down somewhere like it was my fault that I had got raped!

When I began understanding what was going on, it made me question whether I made the right decision to tell someone what happened to me. I began to think that if I hadn't, I would have still been with my sister, brother, and cousins. As the months went by and because I felt I'd done wrong by telling someone, with each day that went by, I went further and further into a deep depression.

I had just entered the first grade and I hadn't seen a soul. No one came to check on me. There were no happy birthdays. No Merry Christmas. No mom May, no Aunt Nita, no sister Tonya, no one. I told myself that telling someone taught me a valuable lesson. It taught me to keep my mouth closed and I slowly begun hating myself and begun telling myself that I'm a stupid little girl for doing so. Another year had gone by and as time went by, I had built up in my heart by telling myself that no one loved me because no one was showing me that they cared about me. Eventually I got used to being alone. As I've mentioned before, my great grandma Daisy's house was beautiful to me and I never wanted for anything but what I wanted most was the company of some kids my age. But then one day out the blue, my sister Tonya came smiling at the front door with her buck teeth! At 5 years old, with dark pretty skin, I was just so happy to finally have someone that I could play with. I missed her so much! I noticed that she had a suitcase with her. My grandma Lynda bring her as she did me, so I asked my grandma Lynda was she staying with me and she said yes. I was so happy to hear that. But in the back of my mind I had wondered had the same thing happened to her as me? The thought of it made my headache!

CHAPTER 2

So, the first chance I got her alone, I knew that I was going to ask her. Thank God for protecting her!

By the time my sister Tonya came around I was 8 years old and in the second grade going into the third. I was going to Elvie Green Elementary which was located off Six Forms road. I loved going to school because it was the only time that I could get out the house. Looking back on it, I believe that my great grandma Daisy was looking out for me, I know now that she was doing it the wrong way. Or maybe not because it might've been something that could've saved my life. Every day and every time I went to school and came home my sister Tonya would always be so happy to see me. Everywhere I turned, she would be always on my heels asking questions. How was school? What did you do today? So what I did after I finished helping my aunt Margaret clean herself I would check her blood pressure, help her to get on the pot so she could relieve herself since her pot was on her side of the bed and then I'd give her medicine and (yes I was doing this by the age of 8) I'd sit my sister Tonya down every day and play school with her. Because she was a quick learner, I would teach her exactly what I learned, and she enjoyed it. Besides, she'd be starting kindergarten soon so she needed all the help she could get. But back to my great aunt Margaret … With me being around, I became her personal live in nurse. But I didn't mind doing it for my great aunt Margaret because I love her a lot. There was a cot that I slept on that was right next to her bed and she called me so much that I can still hear her saying "Tina". I would jump right up because I knew that she needed something important like helping her use the pot, it would prevent me from getting a lot of butt whippings because I had begun peeing in the bed. So, when my great Aunt Margaret woke me up, I would put her on the pot, and I'd run next door so I could use the restroom myself. A win-win situation.

With no friends, in time, I began not liking school. All I was allowed to do was sit in the house because I couldn't go outside and when I did it was only to go to the neighbor's house and clean their

ALL I HAVE

houses for them. Mrs. Clairece and her husband's house were on the left and I liked her. She paid me $5.00 to clean her house and I had Mrs. Easton to the right but she only paid me $2.00 when her house was way bigger than Mrs. Clairece's. But my great grandma Daisy would make me go do it anyway and her excuse to me was that how she paid for her house. Cleaning white folks' houses! The only other time I would be able to get out of the house was every 3 months we would go and get a curl put in our hair. At that time, Jeri curls were popping but I began not to like it because every time I went to school the other kids would pick on me. My great grandparents' house was downtown Raleigh, right across from the DMV (Department of Motor Vehicles). It was on the wealthy side of downtown Raleigh but if you walked right across the street to Partin St, Harnett St., Bliden St. or Freemon St., there was a lot going on there. It was the hood. I remember that every time I would get on the school bus, when the bus driver would ride that way to go pick the other kids up for school, it was always a lot of people outside in that area. It was also a housing project development over that way with a big park to play at. I would ask my great grandma Daisy could I go to the park and play, but my question fell on deaf ears. "Tina go sit your fast ass down somewhere." Her favorite quote, there went the opportunity to make any friends again. Just so happened, all the girls that rode the school bus was from the same hood except for me. Technically I was, but on the wrong side of the street. Also, I was a big girl. Extra big to be just 8-9 years old and at 180lbs, short and with a curl, it was real! I was also born with asthma and that didn't make my situation any better. I stayed in the hospital due to my health but what aggravated me more was how the kids would always pick on me. At one point I wanted to snap one of their necks. Even to this day I can remember their names which were Kasha, Landa, Endy, Manda and Laresha. There were a few others but today if you saw any of them you would say how dare you? But Landa she turned out to be cool people. She struck me to be not the stuck-up type when the other girls would come for me, she would just put

CHAPTER 2

her head down. Kim who stayed on Bliden street she was cool people also. Landa stayed on Harnett St. and because they were cool, I could relate to them. Their people had money also. But once my sister Tonya started going to school, it made things a whole lot better because I had someone there with me. But things would change for the better when my aunt Nita would turn us on to a lady named Mrs. Pat.

CHAPTER 3

AT THE TIME she was picking up my aunt Nita's kids and was taking them to church and she called one day and asked my great grandma Daisy could me and my sister Tonya go with her to church. She agreed. I was so happy to get out the house I didn't know what to do. I had always been around the word because my great grandma Daisy would hold bible study once a week at the house. There were a lot of people that would come by and sit on the "good side" of the house and study the bible but my sister and myself use to have to sit in the kitchen and listen because for some reason she wouldn't let us join the group. Why I have no clue. When Mrs. Pat asked to take us to church, I was ready to do something else other than cleaning, playing nurse or just sitting in the house. So, when that Sunday came, Mrs. Pat was outside early, Tonya and I went happily to church. She had been going to a nice church that was located on Millsboro St. The pastor name was Mary McKay and for the people that have went to a black Baptist church, well this was one of them. Mrs. Pat would come and pick us up at 8am and we didn't get home until 5pm. Yes, that kind. Sunday school, worship service, singing, preaching. I mean people are literally break dancing, doing the two step, but it was a beautiful thing and I enjoyed every bit of it and was ready for the next time to go. And it happened sooner than I thought because Mrs. Pat had asked me would I like to come to bible study on Tuesday? And it was on from there. I finally had someone that likes me besides my sister Tonya and my great aunt Margaret. She was much older, but I felt we

CHAPTER 3

had so much in common. We both like going to church. So, every chance she got to come and pick me up she did. My sister Tonya didn't go as much. I took it as the service was to long for her. Me; I was trying to find myself. During this time, I was going to church about 4 days out the week and some days I would go twice a day. I loved hearing about Jesus and God. It was very interesting to me. And plus, it got me out the house. All I did there was clean, or I was getting yelled at by my great grandma Daisy, so it always kept me on pins and needles. If any food was left on the plate after I washed the dishes, I got a whipping. Dust left on the table; she would whip me. Sometimes she would call me so much, I would suck my teeth. Guess what? I got a whipping. The crazy part is that it was me she was the hardest on. She barely whipped my sister Tonya. It was always me. Because my sister Tonya was her favorite, it got to the point that Tonya would do slick stuff and run to our great grandma Daisy, stick her tongue out at me and there that switch goes, straight across my legs. My great aunt Margaret use to see what was going on and she would tell me to just stay in the room with her and don't even bother going out. I would try to stay away but my great grandma Daisy would always call me to do something. I did but I would always look sad and she would tell me to straighten my face before she picked up her belt. I did what I was told and went back in my aunt Margaret room. I was going through a lot of emotional issues. I was trying to figure out why I was the one being punished? Why didn't people like me? Was it because I was overweight? I was just a kid; I hadn't had enough time to do anything wrong to anyone. I could just never understand... So what I would do was go in the back yard and try to find as many four leaf clovers I could because I always heard that if you made a wish on the clover and stick them in the bible, that your wish would come true. So that's what I did. I would look for them everywhere I went, and I would collect them. Janet Jackson was my idol and I always wanted to look as pretty as she did because everyone loved Janet. I wished I had her looks and size and maybe then, people would like me. When I went to church, I would hear the pastor say things like prayers answers all

ALL I HAVE

things, you have to give to receive and pay your tithes, so I would save every coin I got, and when I went to church that Sunday, I would put some in Sunday school and then some during offering. I would also save a few coins so I could get some candy from the drugstore but as time went by, and things got worse at home, I would just put that in church also. I still was cleaning my neighbor's house and I would also look on the ground to pick up the coins I saw, but I got tired of being picked on, tired of getting in trouble and it had gotten to the point that I'd begun missing school a lot because I had to stay home to take care of them. By the time I was in the 5th grade, my great grandmother Daisy of course had gotten older. The store had closed, and my great grandpa Eugene was going back and forth to the hospital. It seemed like all their health started deteriorating at the same time and because of that, in my great grandma Daisy eyes I couldn't do anything right. It was so bad, everything I did was under a microscope. When I made a sandwich and cut it into pieces, she would sit there and count how many pieces was on the plate just to make sure I didn't eat a piece. I remember one time I had got some Vienna sausages for my aunt Margaret and cut them up, but I ate one and put the others in a plate and then proceeded to my aunt Margaret's room. But on this particular day she stopped me in the hallway and counted the Vienna's and of course one of them was missing. She then snatched the plate from me, and I was called all types of fat bitches etc.... That was a mean old lady. She terrorized me mentally and I'd gotten fed up with all the abuse I was receiving. Another time she called me to come to her, but my great aunt Margaret told me to stay put. She noticed how she was treating me, and she didn't like it either, so I did what she told me to do and I stayed put. So, my great grandma Daisy comes in the back and try to snatch me off the cot that I usually slept on. I jerked away, but then I made my grandma Daisy fall backwards on my cot. I didn't want that to happen to her, so I jumped up to help her out. She jerked away from me, got up and went to make a phone call. I could hear her calling me all kinds of names. Lord knows that I didn't mean her no harm, but about 35-45

CHAPTER 3

mins later, I heard the doorbell ring. So, I ran in the front room and I saw my mom May get out the cab. Wow I was so excited to see her. It had been a long time since the last time I had saw her and I was wondering what had brought her through these necks of the woods. I was hoping that she would come and get us because I was tired of staying here with this woman, but as she exited the cab, I noticed the cab didn't leave so I'm glad now because I know she had come to get us. So, I ran back in my great aunt Margaret room and she asked me who was at the door, I told her it was my mom May. Next thing I know I hear my mom calling me, so I went running because I was ready to go. My sister Tonya was already up there with my mom May but May told Tonya to go in another room so she could talk to me. With my great grandma Daisy, my mom and me in the hallway, my mom May asked my great grandma Daisy what happened. She told her that I had knocked her down, that I was talking back and being disrespectful. With that my mom May picked up the first thing she could get her hands on which was a phone cord and beat me until I couldn't cry any longer. Every swing stung, and she didn't care where it landed whether it be my face, neck, back, stomach, hands or feet. It seemed like it would never stop. I loved my mom May. I hadn't seen her in a long time, and I couldn't understand why she had done that to me. She didn't say hey, I miss you, I love you, nothing. Just whipped me and got back in the cab and left. But she did warn me that if she had to come back; it would be worse. When I looked at my great grandma Daisy, I could see a smirk on her face and when I looked at my sister Tonya, she didn't even look my way. I didn't talk to anyone. I just went into my aunt Margaret room and laid down on my cot and went to bed thinking to myself why didn't anyone like me? I didn't get it. But out of nowhere I heard my aunt Margaret say, "it's going to be ok Tina". I just closed my eyes and went to sleep. The next morning when I was getting ready for school, I looked in the mirror and I had whips everywhere. On my face, a swollen eye, fat lip and after my grandma Daisy saw how I looked, she didn't allow me to go to school that day. But I did go to church that Sunday. It took a week for things

ALL I HAVE

to get normal and my sister Tonya had stopped by my classroom and got my schoolwork for me so I could make the work up.

But my mom May had been coming around on the regular, so I guess my grandma Daisy was getting tired of us children being around, she would call May on every little thing we did. When whipping us she would try to avoid our upper body neck, and the face but it was fair game anywhere else because we could wear pants, long sleeve shirts and turtlenecks to cover most of the bruises up. Plenty of days my great aunt Margaret couldn't do nothing but point because she couldn't move nothing. She would see me and sometimes she would just break down and cry. I was made to believe that I was the bad child that couldn't do anything right. And I was tired, so the next time I went to church I had talked to Mrs. Pat and explained to her the situation that I was in at home and asked her could she come get me any and every time she could. I explained to her what was going on and showed her some of my bruises with the understanding that she'd keep it between us. But she did look out because sometimes she would come and pick me up just to spend the night at her house and that was cool. I just tried to stay away as much as possible. I had no one to turn to but God. I never knew my father and my mom didn't like me, so all I did was talk to God to try to figure out why people were treating me this way. Now at 9 years old and in the 5th grade with no friends, I thanked Mrs. Pat for taking the time to take me to church because it taught me that God is always there. So, everything that had been bothering me, I would talk to God. I would continue to go to church several times a week until one Sunday, I had and experience that would change the rest of my life. I had received the Lord as my Lord and savior!!! It was a feeling that is indescribable. It felt like 50lbs was lifted off me and I caught myself dancing and crying like the adults. And I didn't care who was looking at me. I didn't know what was really going on at the moment, but later on I realized what had happened. I was saved!!! It was a wonderful feeling. At the time, I really didn't understand the meaning of getting saved until I asked

CHAPTER 3

Mrs. Pat. She the one that told me that I had gave my life to the Lord and he forgave me of all my wrongs that I had done and that was a good feeling to me because I knew something was wrong with me because no one liked me. It was such an honor! Thank you, God. She then told me that I had to get baptized and do communion. My answer was yes because I'd do anything to get this new beginning popping. I was so excited once I left church, I couldn't wait to get home to tell my great aunt Margaret what had happened. Anxious to get there, once we pull up to the house, I saw and ambulance and fire truck. My heart fell to my feet because I knew it wasn't good. I literally jumped out the car before Mrs. Pat could put the car in park. When my grandma Lynda came up to me, she told me that my great grandpa Eugene had died. Sorrow went across my face, but I was so happy that it wasn't my aunt Margaret. I felt bad for thinking that way, but I barely knew him. He lived in the house, but he would always stay to himself and never spoke. So, I couldn't get to know him like that. I asked my grandma Lynda what had happened, and she told me that he sat on the toilet and never got up. I found out that all his insides had come out in the toilet and that kind of threw me off. I couldn't understand how that could of happen. But I did know that since it happened, they had the upstairs bathroom closed off and my great grandma Daisy didn't allow no one to go up there. So now with it only being four of us, my great grandma Daisy, my aunt Margaret, my sister Tonya and myself, the pressure was extra hard on me after my grandpa Eugene passed. My great grandma Daisy was in her 80s and my great aunt Margaret was getting worse. The only time I had seen anyone was when my mom May had come by when my grandma Daisy would call her, and she would come over to whip me and my sister Tonya. She would use anything, the first thing that she got her hands on, curtain rods, extension cords, clothes hangers, curling irons, and after that she would just leave. I had begun to build up a lot of hatred for that lady. The only time we would see her is when she came to beat us and that's when grandma Daisy would call her about something we had done, and it could be the smallest things. Half of the time I thought my grandma Daisy was losing her mind because I know something not right with her. I tried to mention it to my grandma Lynda, but I think it went in one ear and out the other. This was during my last year in elementary school and I had just started the 5th. Oh yea; I thought that I was hot stuff I had just gotten saved and I also had a couple of new friends. One was this guy who name was Charlie Durst. He was a cool dude. He wore glasses and he was light skinned and the crazy thing is that I still remember that his phone number 919-555-5535 to this very day. I also had a friend and her name was Bethany and she stayed in Westwood Apartments. Things were looking a lot brighter and I also liked my 5th grade teacher whose name was Mrs. Stedman. She was a black lady with long pretty red hair and wore glasses which amplified the fact that her eyes were cockeyed, but I loved her because I could talk to her about anything. When I had gotten saved, I told her as soon as it happened, and she congratulated me. I was a child and things were moving so fast for me, I was forced to fill pretty big shoes at such a young age. These little girls around here still running their mouths, and now they also trying to come at Bethany because both of us was big to be our age and they were much smaller and looked better than us in their eyes but right now I wasn't on that type of time enough was enough and I snapped back at these chicks. I didn't want to, but I got fed up with them running their mouths. I had a lot of frustration inside of me. Beatings at home and then go to school and go through more abuse. ENOUGH! "So, what you bitches gonna do? I asked one day in the heat of the moment. And you know what? They did nothing. All that talking and neither one flinched. Oh, they had just messed up now. I got their number! Mrs. Stedman had seen how I changed since I started her class and she pulled me to the side and said "Tina, you just got saved, why are you acting that way?" So, I broke down in tears and explained to her all I was going through, the bullying, the mental, emotional, and physical abuse at home and I'm getting tired! I have no one to help me and the only one I had to help me was my aunt Margaret and she was bed written and couldn't even move. So,

CHAPTER 3

I was beginning to have a I don't give a fuck attitude where anybody could have got it. Mrs. Stedman called home one day to relay her concerns to my grandma Daisy and I knew that her heart was in a good place but what she didn't know was that she had just opened a can of worms. As soon as I got home and opened the front door, I was punched in my face with a two piece and she just kept hitting me like I was a grown woman when I'm only in the 5th grade. Hatred built up to the point that I wanted to kill everybody. My mom May and my grandma Daisy because I hated how they treated me. I would always ask myself Lord why me? And because I needed answers, I prayed harder than ever. Of course, my grandma Daisy told me not to go to school the next day, but you know what? I did anyways and showed Mrs. Stedman what my mom and grandma Daisy had been doing to me for years. I had gotten tired, and the next thing I know the police was at my school and I was telling them everything that was going on with me. I told them why I was missing school and it was because of my mom May who was like a big bully and I looked at her like a total stranger who I hated with all my being because she beat me up all the time. She doesn't even know me!

I had to ask myself, what was going on here? I had just gotten saved not too long ago and now it seemed like my situation was getting worse and worse. But a few things did work out, I didn't have to worry about my mom May anymore because social service had gotten involved and bullying at school stopped also. I wouldn't of never went that way with social services, but things had gotten too far out of hand. There was a way of dealing with a child and she was going about it the wrong way. One thing I did learn was prayer answers all things, so I was still attending church, but I wanted to get more involved in church like singing in the church choir or play instruments. But the kids in church wasn't no different from the kids at school because they picked on me even harder and it caused me to say the hell with them also. So that was out. It made me think that something had went seriously wrong once I'd gotten saved. So, I asked Mrs. Pat,

ALL I HAVE

could someone get unsaved and her answer was yes. She told me that once a person got saved, the devil would try harder to bring that person down and then I began to see what was going on with me and why the devil was coming at me through all forms. Although I was too young to fully comprehend what was going on at the time, I kept going to church. Mrs. Pat continued to come get me, and at the same time my aunt Margaret wasn't getting no better. So, I prayed for her at church. I continued to pay my tithes, hoping that God would reverse her illness. I believe with all my being that God can do anything. Just have faith as much as a mustard seed and in my eyes, God is BIG! Yes, he can do anything! So, I waited and prayed, and I also noticed that I began missing more days than usual at school. I had to make sure my aunt Margaret would get well, and my grandma Daisy wasn't in the position physically to take care of my aunt Margaret and herself. So, I stayed home to make sure they got all their meds. I had to fix the food exactly how it supposed to be. No yoke in her eggs, no salt or sugar. I checked my aunt Margaret heart rate with a stethoscope, checked her blood pressure and yes, I was still in the 5th grade. But of course, a child is limited to the days that they can stay out of school, so I had to get back on track with getting my education. So, my Grandma Lynda had finally helped with setting up a nurse that came by and looked out for them in the daytime. So that made me feel better about leaving them home until I got out of school. But one day as my sister Tonya and myself was getting off the school bus Tonya father Virgil was standing at the bus stop waiting for us to get off. I thought he was there to pick Tonya up as he did often. I can say that he played his position when it comes down to being a father to my sister Tonya. But it was a weekday and he usually didn't come and pick Tonya up until the weekend. So, while we were walking back to the house, he stopped us and said that he had something to tell us and that's when he came out and told us that my aunt Margaret had passed away. When hearing the news, my whole world had come crashing down. First words were God how could you let that happen? I've tried, I've

CHAPTER 3

done everything right. I've prayed, I've tithed, I've believed in you so why God? Mentally I was done. I now had no one. Not even God.

What did I do wrong? Were my thoughts. No one didn't want to talk to me. With that, I ran all the way to the house, bust through the back door and ran straight to her room and she wasn't there. But once I saw all the people at the house, I knew it was true. My love, heart, faith all gone in one incident. It's all over now!

CHAPTER 4

It's Starting To Get Real Around Here!

ONCE I HAD graduated elementary school and started going to Clairol Middle School, it just so happened to be located on the same street as my elementary school. My great grandpa Eugene and my great aunt Margaret had died 2 years apart or maybe less and because my great grandma Daisy couldn't stay at the house by herself, my grandma Lynda which was Daisy's granddaughter came to stay with her. I love my grandma Lynda so much that I called her mom. She treated me just like I was her daughter. She showed me so much love and that's something I felt that a mother should show their children and to this day I still call her mom. Once my grandma Lynda came in things ran smoothly. She allowed my sister Tonya and myself to go over our friend house and she allowed us to go and spend the night at our aunt Nita house. I liked going over there because she was a cool aunt and during that time, she was staying in Hallifax Court. It was a lot going on over there at that time. It was people everywhere. My cousin George nickname Stinky stayed at the top of Hallifax Court and my aunt Nita stayed in the middle of the projects and my uncle Rodney and his girlfriend lived on the back end. So, when I went over there, I was all over the place because all of my cousins were there. It was kids everywhere!!! It's the pjs! My aunt Nita has 4 kids and pregnant as usual. My mom May had 2 more kids, David and Punky with Punky being the youngest. They were a year apart and although

CHAPTER 4

I didn't know them that well, they looked like they could have been identical twins. But I knew one thing, I love going over there, it's always something to do. My aunt Nita house had always been the spot but this time, times were different. It was roaches everywhere because she kept a nasty house. Beer cans and food all over the place. Straight filthy and the kids laid right on top of filth like it didn't even phase them. See I wasn't use to no shit like that, so I was scared to lay down but eventually I did and when I woke up the next day, I would be sick as a dog. I then was sent home and would get rushed straight to the hospital. I'd have an asthma attack. So, after that I couldn't go back to my aunt Nita apartment. I hated my life. It seemed like I couldn't never do nothing right. I felt like no one liked me because no one never came to see me and because I couldn't never do things that normal kids did, I did still go to church and as time went on, I got a better understanding and realized that I always had someone to talk to. So, despite me not having a mother and father, I knew in my heart that I had God. So, guess what I did? I talked his head off! With only my grandma Lynda, my great grandma Daisy, my sister Tonya and myself staying on Carboro rd., my great grandma Daisy health started getting worse and she began going in and out of nursing homes. I had just entered the 6th grade. It was like everyone that I came across didn't stay long. First it was my great grandma Louise, she was Daisy oldest daughter and I remember when I was only in diapers living in Pennsylvania I was crying loud and the memory comes to mind like it was yesterday, but I got up hollering in her face and she didn't move I got off the sofa bed that was in the living room walked into my aunt Margaret room took her by the hand pulled her in the living room and the next thing I know EMS and police was everywhere in the apartment and that's the last time anyone ever saw Louise. Mind drifted a moment next my grandpa Eugene, then my heart, my great aunt Margaret and now my great grandma Daisy now in hospice, and they were saying that she won't be returning home. I refused to see her, but my grandma Lynda made me. I started feeling like I was bad luck, so I wanted to keep my distance, but I eventually went cause I had no choice. She had always taken very good care of me and because of that I never wanted for anything. I remember sitting at the Bryan Center rest home off New Burn Ave. in Raleigh and the first time I saw her there was also the last time I would see her; I gave her a kiss on her forehead. She passed away a few days later. Everyone was gone, everything started changing. Man, its real out here...

Now at 11 years old in the 6th grade, my grandma Lynda had the house and now everyone wanted to come and live with us. My aunt Nita and her 4 kids came and never left. My mom May came with her 3 kids. But my uncle Mike and my uncle Reggie was in college and my uncle Rodney was a lady's man, he stayed gone. With my grandma Lynda working at Dortha Dix Hospital as an LPN, when my grandma Daisy passed away, she left my grandma Lynda with everything. With Lynda being the loving, caring mother and grandmother that she was she allowed her children and grandchildren to come live on Carboro road with us. This was in 1992. At the time it was a lot different for me because I had reached puberty and now, I wanted my privacy. I didn't really know these people like that, but I knew we was related. I figured that I could get to know them better since it was a 3-story home, I thought what could it hurt? Well guess what? It started get real quick around here! All my great grandma's dishes started coming up missing, her silverware and books piece by piece. Things started breaking apart, toilets, bathtub, kitchen sink, water heater in the basement and all the furniture was broke. Man these people was ruthless and my grandma Lynda would walk all the way from Carboro rd. to Dortha Dix Hospital on the regular and that was about a 15 mile walk there she would leave at 6am and get off at 4pm and wouldn't get home until 7pm. And on top of that, my mom May and my aunt Nita would just leave those kids home with me. I'm only 11, my sister Tonya 9, my brother Lamont 7, my other brother David 6, my sister Punky 5. My aunt Nita kids were Takiyah 9, Wayne 7, Chris 6, Chante 4 and Trice 2. Now that's 10 kids on a 11year old that knows nothing about nothing! And what made it worse is that sometimes they didn't even come back until 2 or 3 days later. My grandma Lynda got to the point that she didn't even come back. I didn't blame her because it took less than 2 years for these people to destroy what grandma Daisy and Grandpa Eugene worked their whole lives paying for. It wasn't no need for Lynda to come back home because these people took the roof off the house and the doors off the hinges!!! Literally! It got to the point that we had to cook everything in the microwave. We had to go in the backyard and dig holes to do number 2 and we peed in the bathtub. The basement was flooded so the hot water pump wasn't working and with no hot water or heat, we boiled water in the microwave and washed up in a bucket because sewage water was coming up through the sinks. Man, it seemed like everything was happening so fast. My mom May did come through occasionally, in a cab and gave my brothers Lamont, and David and sister Punky money. She would give them all the ones and five dollar bills she had but she never gave me nothing. Why I don't know. But thinking about it now, it might be because I learned that my cousin Stinky was really my dad. I didn't realize it until now at this very moment. But anyways, I didn't care because I never looked at her like a mother anyways. So, once she left, my brothers would buy 2 tailgates from Bo's Chicken and that would be enough for all of us to eat. We would then go to the corner store and get bread, soda, candy, lunch meat, etc.... I love my brother Lamont. I love all of them, but he is my favorite! But anyways, this was during the summertime and we had to get ready for school soon. It seemed like no one was coming to check on us and it began to be weeks at a time. I took it upon myself to walk and try to find someone. The boys of the house Lamont, David, Wayne, Chris and myself at nighttime sometimes. But the good thing about the whole situation is, that everyone knew who we were. That's those Gilchrist children. That's what they would always say, and they pointed us in the right direction and we always found out where they were at. Hallifax Court! I remembered where that place was but sometimes, we didn't get there until 12-1am in the morning, my aunt Nita and May would get mad at me because I had the kids out that late at night. I know that I was kind of wrong but we hadn't seen an adult in over a week. We had no food, same clothes on and was sleeping in a nasty, filthy house. We were laying on top of clothes and everything else. So now that we finally get to Hallifax Court which took us over 2 hours to walk, they brought us right back to Carboro Road and guess who gets the whipping? Me. Man it was really getting depressing and now you can't go nowhere. But I reasoned that maybe next time, it wouldn't take as long for them to come and if so, I would make sure its daylight. Check what happened the next time, I went in the daytime. The same result. So, what was I to do now? Looking back how my grandma Daisy house was a lil over a year ago that now had rats and roaches everywhere, nothing working, doors off the hinges and a lot of hungry children looking at me asking where were their mom at? It was a sad situation, I wasn't use to this. And I had no answers. During this time Mrs. Pat the lady that was coming to take me to church, well she got sick and I soon found out that she had cancer. So, I had lost touch with her and lost myself in the process. I had never been through anything like this and these were some bad children. No home training at all. But I can say they made sure we kept video games such as Super Mario Brothers and Sonic that went to the Super Nintendo. And that's what calmed the boys down a lot. But we would wear those video games out. We also had a vcr and we would wear those vhs tapes out, we watched the same things repeatedly and recorded over the tapes 1000 times! I couldn't figure out how grown women could just leave their little children at home with an 11-year-old for days at a time. Looking back on things now, I don't blame Lynda for not staying at her own house. These grown women had the nerve to keep sitting around popping babies out and leaving them to fend for themselves. Why? So, they can chase a nigga? Or was it something else? These people just about had my grandma Daisy house like and abandoned house in less than 3 years. Trifling people! And every time I sat back and looked at my grandma Daisy house, it burned me up more and more. These people were sorry… Period! I know I was only 11 years old, but I am far from slow. And on top of that once school started again, it got even realer.

CHAPTER 4

Okay they did make sure the ones that could get in school got in. So that was a plus because at least we got 2 meals a day, but we had gone to school plenty of times with the same clothes on for days. I'm in middle school and it was already real for me just imagine going to school with dirty clothes on and on top of that the same dirty clothes on for days at a time. I'm a young girl so what was I supposed to do? What could I do? I absolutely had no one to turn to. But I did have my friend Bethany so that was a plus. She would let me borrow a shirt here and there, but I kept the same jeans and I worked it out the best way I could. I would always see May come and pick my brothers and sisters up and would take them shopping, give them money but she never showed me any love. Mind boggling, but my best guess is that she never knew me. But was that my fault? I was only 11. But I got use to it. Had no choice...

As for how I was living, I was getting sick and tired of living in filth. I got tired of being mistreated. I wanted things also. I just couldn't see what I had done to get treated the way I did. I already didn't know my father and although I knew my mom's name was May, I didn't know her either. As time went by, I began missing more days out of school because I couldn't leave the kids at home by themselves. It started getting so bad that I had to take my baby sister Punky to school with me, but the guidance counselor got in touch with someone to come and pick her up from school. But boy, why did I do that? Well social services were knocking on the door and I got my butt tore up. That was it for me! I got tired of May putting her hands on me and treating me like I'm trash. I'd made my mind up. I'm outta here!

CHAPTER 5

I HAD BEEN on punishment for a few days and I had asked May could I go to the store? At first, she said no but for some reason she went head and let up but she told me the only way I can go is if I took my sister Punky with me. At the time Punky was only 5 years old. And the store was two blocks from the house. I agreed, but once we headed to the store and got pass Harnett street, I told my sister Punky to go back. I told her to make sure she looked both ways before she crossed the street and to make sure that there were no cars coming. I then watched her as she crossed the first street and then the next and because I knew that the house was 8 houses up, I took off running. I ran as fast as I could and didn't look back. I ran straight up Partin street, went down Freemon street, made a right on Delvie street and went to my friend Bethany house. I knew her mom she was cool because I had gone to her house a few times before and she was a very nice lady. Bethany had a sister whose name was Kosha she was 9 years old and a brother whose name was Harvey 6 years old. I told Bethany's mom my situation, but she was already aware of that because of how I looked. I was dirty, nappy head, 200 plus pound girl who looked like a straight boy. Once in Bethany room, she gave me some clothes to wear and I took a shower and called it a night. I said to myself that night that I would never go back home because if I did, I knew my mom May was going to kill me!

CHAPTER 5

As time had went by, I started seeing that everyone had their own problems. Bethany's mom stayed out a lot and Bethany stayed on the go also. That girl Bethany, she had a lot going on at the age of 12. She knew a lot of people, so we stayed walking from Delvie street to Briggs street back to Candore lane. The apartments we stayed in was Westwood Court apt; right across the street she had a guy friend whose name was Eli and he was 16 and he had his own place. His mother had a room there, but she was never at home. That was a good look also, so most of the time after all the walking we would do, we'd always end up at Eli house. He was a cool dude, tall, dark skinned, but to me at that time, I wasn't interested in boys. Didn't trust them and how I looked, none of them wasn't interested anyways. Bethany was the one for the boys because everywhere we walked to, she knew some boy and she also made that bread. I don't know how she did it but it was done and we would go downtown to McKay's or Rainbows' and snatch her something to wear and I would steal me underwear, socks, bras, some outfits and we would leave. And we did this same routine daily. I can say that we stuck together. I liked Bethany because she never once judged me or looked down on me because of my situation. We were both young and trying to get by the best we could with what we had to work with.

My birthday came and went, I turned 12 years old on the streets, unfortunately. I eventually stop going to school, Bethany no longer went neither and by this time, Bethany left her mom's house to go stay with Eli because he ended up being her boyfriend. So, I went with her to his 2-bedroom apt and I slept on the couch while they slept in Eli room. With his mom's door always locked, shoot we were good. His mom paid for everything while he was there, and she stayed right around the corner with her boyfriend on Cambria street. So, it was just us 3. We did everything together. Cook, wash clothes, chores, and Eli seemed like he just enjoyed our company. I don't think we had to do anything really and he still would have been fine with us just being there. And I did notice that no one ever came to chill with

27

ALL I HAVE

Eli neither. Birds of a feather cause all we had was each other no outsiders no friends, only us. Also, Eli mother rarely came to the house, that was kind of strange to me because she had the house laid smelling fresh and we never had to worry about the lights and water getting turned off she kept the bills paid. I can get use to this!

It had been a while since I left home, I was still scared to death to go anywhere near Carboro road. I had left the summer of 92 at 11 years old and I turned 12 on Dec. 31, 1992. So, it was almost the following summer when I ended up living at Eli house. I have been by Bethany side since I left home.

Bethany was a girl before her time. She was doing everything a grown woman would do. It was none of my business but me I wasn't interested in the line of work she was doing, especially after what had happened to me early on in life. scarred me. But Bethany was young, and the men wanted her because she was willing. Me, I'd go with her sometimes if she asked for a lookout and believe me, she made that paper when she laid down with those men. It was a few of them but most of them was the same ones and because she kept food and clothes coming in, I would lookout for her. She was my friend I didn't care about what she was doing. I never once not judge her. Who am I to judge? I didn't know no better anyways. I'm just trying to survive. We all were. That year I had stayed away from home had been a journey for me. I had met a lot of kids that was in similar situations that I was in. Either their parents were at home and didn't care where their children were, or the parents were never there. But in any case, home was the furthest thing from my mind.

2 years later...

I'm 14 years old now and for some reason I noticed that people had started paying more attention to me suddenly. I know I had lost a little weight but didn't know how much because I didn't have a scale to find out. But what made me notice was I suddenly couldn't wear none of my clothes anymore. As usual we would go out stealing and I would steal a size 18 but now I was stealing a size 11-12. I never paid my weight that much attention. But I was thankful that it was dropping. Within the 2 years since I been out on the streets I had started smoking weed and cigarettes. You couldn't tell me nothing! I hadn't been back to school yet but was thinking about going back. But on this one day after we had gone into Hunsin Belk's and stole us a few outfits, we headed into Jenny's supermarket Downtown Raleigh. For some reason I don't know, I picked up a bottle of orange juice, drunk it and sat the bottle back down. The next thing I know the manager came, strong armed me and locked me in the office until the police came. They sent me to Whitaken Mill Detention center. All for opening a bottle of orange juice. Never again. Thou shall not steal!! And come to find out, they had got Bethany also. They also got the clothes that we stole from Hunsin Belk's but the tags were off so they couldn't charge us with the clothes because they didn't know where to go back to. We didn't stay long because they contacted Bethany mom and she came and got the both of us. Yes, that's my girl. Close call! I learned a valuable lesson that day, but something had to give. Once Cynthia came and picked us up, we left and went back to Eli house. And our people were there when we got there. Doody, Tiny Jim, Alvin and Bobby. We stayed deep. By this time all the hood kids were staying at Eli house. That's when I began to see why Eli mom didn't come back home. It was because he was jumping on her. She came in one day fussing because of all the people he kept in her house and he cussed her ass out and told her to get out of her own house. Man, that alone messed me up because I would have never imagined that a child would talk to their parents that way. I always thought that you should honor thy mother and thy father. But that's none of my business. So, once we were by ourselves, I hollered at him because I had been around awhile and because of that, he often confided in me. I told him that it wasn't right, but everyone had a story to tell and since I had run away from home, things had become interesting for me also. I had broken into some stores, broken into swimming pools after hours and would stay there all night just about. We basically did everything a child heart desired. But after that conversation with Eli I started thinking about the family so One day we had got hungry and I had a few dollars and I felt like walking to Bo's Chicken. I told myself that I was going to walk on the opposite side of Carboro road on the DMV side to see if anyone was sitting on the porch at my grandma Lynda house. So, I walked right by the house and it was a lot of people sitting on the front porch. I looked right over there at them and kept walking, and no one noticed who I was. But once I went and got my chicken, I went back the other way. I just wanted to test the water.

But when I was on the back block, I came across a short stocky dark-skinned dude who was walking a big pit bull. He looked mean but a cute mean! Sounds crazy but it is what it is. He was walking the opposite way I was going, and he stopped me and asked me to walk with him back to Bo's I had literally just walked out but It was cool, I turned around and walked with him. He bought 2 tailgates and before we made it out the parking lot, he gave his dog a whole box of chicken. I asked him what the other box was for and he said it was for his other dog. Must be nice!!! We then walked and talked, and I ended up on Partin and Freemon street. Once we got over that way, everybody out there was waiting on him. All I hear them saying was Kym I got this and that, so I asked him was his name Kym? His reply was, what you don't like it? I just smiled. I then told him that I was about to go and that I'd catch him later. He then asked me to wait for a minute and let him put his dog up. I waited and watched him walk through a cut behind a house and put his dog up. But one thing for sure, it was a lot going on, on that street. It was people everywhere on both sides of Partin street and the surrounding streets. I was feeling very uncomfortable out there, but Kym didn't stay that long. I really didn't have much to do so I went and sat with him on a stoop up under a tree. He asked me what I was doing out there and I said nothing at the moment. But I was heading back to Eli house to chill. He then asked me to chill out with him for a while and I said ok. I had

CHAPTER 5

no problem with that anyways cause I wanted to see what was going on. The few years I had been in the area, I knew that drugs were being sold out there and it was a lot of money to be made. With me looking at him as a chocolate, stocky, thick brother dressed in all black, when I saw how the people was drawn to him, that alone let me know I was at the right place at the right time. Say no more! I'm here witcha pimpin! I ended up staying out there with him a few hours and I sat back and watched his movement. He didn't even know me period but looking back on things now, he knew I was younger than I proclaimed because what would make someone be so comfortable with a person after the 1st time they met? But all I did was sit outside, watch the people come up and hand him money and he handed them something and the people got missing. He seemed like a cool dude but once I found out his age, it kind of threw me off. He was 25 years old. 11 years older than me. I wanted to tell him my real age, but I didn't. He seemed like he would be a good friend later down the road. It started getting dark outside and I was getting tired sitting out there. So, I parted ways and I headed on back towards Eli house. On the way back to Eli house, I couldn't seem to get his face out of my mind. I was smiling the whole way walking and telling myself I knew I had to see him again. But I was glad I left when I did because as soon as I got to Eli house, I saw Bethany in the backyard with her stuff strolled out in the yard and her face was bruised. I asked her what was going on and then I heard Eli calling her all types of fowl names and how he hates he ever messed with her. I'm saying to myself the spot is all over with now. Bethany had called one of her male friends to come and pick her up and he pulled up just in time. I helped her get in the car and I went and picked up her clothes that were strolled out in the yard. She asked me was I coming with her. I told her no because I was going to go back in and talk to Eli. I figured that I'd try to change his mind about the situation, but she told me it wasn't no need because she wasn't coming back to his house. That was the last time I had seen my friend. I missed her a lot. It was just me left out to fend for myself with no one else to turn to. I stayed with Eli a couple days, but it didn't feel right with Bethany gone. I then decided to walk to the top of Partin street to see if Kym was out there. And there he was right there on the corner, posted like a light pole.

He smiled as soon as he saw me. He asked me what I was doing around his way and I told him that I needed to talk to him. I told him that I needed to make some money. I had nowhere to go but Eli place and after I saw how he had treated Bethany and thought about how he disrespected his mother, I didn't feel comfortable with going back to his house and besides, his days are going to be cut short anyways cause he didn't even honor his mother. Also, it didn't feel right without my friend. That was Bethany boyfriend, not mines. Kym then asked me why I didn't go home, and I told him because I didn't want to. Then he asked me who my people were. Mother, aunts, uncles, etc. I told him and he knew exactly who they were. And that was all it took because it was on from there. He had got me a room at one of the rooming houses on Partin street towards Carboro road where I could see my house driveway from where I was at, he gave me a pill bottle and had whatever it was cut up into individual pieces and by the advice of my attorney I can't say the quantity but it was a lot. For me that was good money when all I had to do was sit there as he would send the sales to me and I sold it. Perfect! It was four other tenants in the rooming house that I was staying at but each one of them was smoking this stuff that he had me selling. So that was a win, win situation. The thing is how long will it take to sell all of it? To my amazement it took no time because, whatever Kym had them people on, they were eating that shit up like it was candy I gave him what he asked for and I kept. Now this is something I can get use to! I really didn't have nothing to worry about because as I began to see how he moved, no one bothered him and from hearing how the smokers had talked about him I knew I had lucked up. I worked a week straight and that weekend I had got fresh and clean. Got the hair done and I was on fleet! I informed him I wasn't working that night because a few of my people I had met on the way was going to the club that night. After I showered and got my clothes on, he was looking me up and down and he told me that I looked nice and me with a Kool-Aid smile, I said thank you. I then called a cab at the pay phone and once the cab arrived, I was out. At club Iguanas that night they had a wet t-shirt contest and whoever won got a free photo shoot and $300.00. "why not?" I had platinum blonde hair and I was a 44dd, so I took my bra off and kept my tank top on. They sprayed my t-shirt with water and check this out, I won that contest that night! We were deep up in the club and we all were turned all the way up! Club Iguanas I would never forget. That night I dared a nigga to flinch because we were on 1000 ready to go! And after I got the money, they took me in the back for a photo shoot. Topless but covered up the nipples. I did different poses and killed it. But they did ask me if I was interested in adult entertainment. No! I took my shit and I was out. So out there to this day I might have some pictures of me topless but with my hands covering my nipples. But I was also only 14 at the time so I hope they burned them because someone would be in a lot of trouble!! After the club I dropped my people off in a cab and I headed to my room on Partin street. I was so tired, and I had done a lot of drinking that night unfortunately. See back then they weren't on it with the alcohol like they're now days. I stepped out the cab paid for it and headed in the house. I opened the door to my room, locked it, and flopped on the bed. I was too tired to even turn on the lights. The next thing I know, I hear someone say "Tina"! Damn he messed me up with that one I had jumped so fast... Hey shhh! It's me Kym. My reply was, "damn man u scared me". So, he turned on the lamp and he was sitting right in the chair behind the door. Messed me up! He asked me how was the club? "it was good" I replied I then asked him what was up? He said that he couldn't sleep. So, I came back at him with what was on his mind? And so, he came and sat beside me on the bed. He then kissed me on my lips, and it felt so good to me. I'd never felt the way I did at that moment. I was only 14 and this was something that I didn't mind happening. I had never been with a guy willingly and in that very moment, I was glad it was him. Stocky, thick chocolate brother with a Caesar cut and deep waves. Looking like Meek Mills!! Yessss honey but by me being a virgin at the time I didn't know how to handle it. So, I guess he kind of figured it out because he asked me had I ever been with a guy before? I started to lie and say yes but for what? Maybe he will be gentle since it's my first time. So, I told him the truth. Yes, I'm a virgin. When I told him, he told me not to worry because he was going to take it slow and if at any time, I want him to stop, don't be afraid to say something. So, he started kissing me on my lips then he started using his tongue. I just followed suit because he already knew my position. I couldn't do much but then he started kissing me on my neck. Then he pulls my t-shirt up over my head and takes my pants off and I laid back on the bed. Then he takes his clothes off and he comes and lay on top of me. He then started licking me on my neck and went to my breast. Once he got there, it had done something to my cookies. A tingling sensation had run through my body and I couldn't explain it. He then proceeds down to my belly button and opened my legs wide. Once he started kissing me in between my legs. OMG!!! I didn't know what was going on, but I was twisted. This man was making me feel like I was on top of the world. And suddenly, he just stopped. He then started kissing me again but this time he was trying to get inside of me. I think he thought that I was lying about this being my first time but he tried to put it in but she was tight [cookies] and he said " you won't lying was you ma"? so he took his time started with his head going back and forth but now it was an uncomfortable feeling. But I wanted it to be him. So, I took it until he was all the way inside of me. It felt so good to me. I melted all on him as we were kissing, making love and sweating. Yes, that quick. I had done fell in love. He made me believe that he had done fell in love also because when he kept telling me how good the cookies tasted, how good my cookies were and how I better not give my cookies to no one else. I came back at him with, I won't Daddy it's yours only. We went at it for a while until he fell asleep and I did also. I woke up the next day and he was gone. I just laid there in the bed trying to comprehend what happened the night before. I couldn't

CHAPTER 5

believe I wasn't a virgin anymore and he was a handsome man also. I just couldn't stop smiling. I was on cloud 9.

One thing for certain it was back to that bag of course and he came and gave me what I needed to start work that day. The crazy thing is that we carried on like the night before never happened. My birthday was coming up in a couple of weeks and I was trying to make as much money as possible so I could floss. So, money was on my mind and after that night, it was like we were inseparable because we were always together. I would catch a couple of females hating and talking shit about me, but Kym would always tell me that they was just hating because I had done took the place that they wanted. He did reassure me that none of them will lay a hand on me because if they did, they would have to go through him. And I didn't have to worry about neither one of them either.

CHAPTER 6

MY BIRTHDAY CAME and I'm 15 years old now. Kym and I had been together for a while now and as much as we were together, I would've never thought that this man had a wife and 2 children!

Yes, this lady that looked just like him, comes running up on me one day. But once she laid her eyes on me, the first thing she said was you only a baby and she started crying. I asked her who was she and she said she was Kym wife and she can't even put her hands on me because she would end up in jail. When she said she was his wife it fucked me up because he never not once mentioned anything about this. My whole world had come crashing down. I was raised in church and in my eyes, God didn't play that. At 15 years old I knew that much. And then I saw him come running through the cut. He looked at his wife and called her name "Sandra" then he started fighting her and she got into her car and she left. After that things weren't the same anymore. I looked at him different. How could he play me like that, let alone, your wife? You're married! So, once she left, he pulled in front of the rooming house and told me to get in the truck. I did and he took me to this guy's house name Alvin. We started arguing and fussing over there and then out the blue, the nigga smacks me. Now shit getting real now! I'm pissed and I want to leave but he wouldn't let me. He was way stronger than me, so he overpowers me and throws Alvin his keys and tells him to go get his dogs. While Alvin was gone this nigga started torturing me. He took all my clothes

CHAPTER 6

off by gun point and he literally raped me. Smacking me and telling me that I wasn't going nowhere. I wasn't feeling him anymore after that. His true colors came out and I saw how he had these females in check. They knew how stupid and crazy this nigga could get. The nigga flipped 5000 really quick and I said to myself what had I gotten myself into now! Now the nigga took my clothes off, took my cookies without my consent, and brought 3 big ass pit bulls that weighed 100 pounds each and put them in front of the door just to make sure that I didn't leave the house. This went on for almost a week fighting arguing i was being raped and kidnapped repeatedly in my mind until he finally came and took them dogs' home. But during a week straight, this dude straight terrorized me. He showed me a side of him that I wouldn't have ever imagined. I wanted to leave but he knew where my grandma house was at. He knew who my people were, and he would threaten them if I ever tried to leave. That wasn't the first time he had put his hands on me but in my mind, it was most definitely going to be the last. He didn't even allow me to work anymore. I had to come up with a plan. Think Tina! During this time the guy named Alvin who's house I was at, Kym had him watching me so I wouldn't go nowhere. I tried to think of a way to get him to allow me to get out of his house. I know he always carried a gun on him, and I also knew that he was a flunky I could tell. Then one day I sat in the living room with him. He had a lot of coke on the table. He had a few lines separated on the table and I asked him to let me try some just to befriend him. It had been awhile since I left the rooming house almost a month now. He wasn't even the same man that I first met. Something had changed a lot with him. And where I was at I haven't a clue. He had blind folded me before we left. Yes, this nigga crazy! Now with Alvin, I took a line and that shit went straight to my head. My whole face was numb, and I was high as fuck. WTF was that? I want some more! So, me and Alvin stayed up all night, getting high. I did so much that my nose was hurting to the point I couldn't breathe. I went in the room and laid on my back and fell out. I then woke up to this nigga Kym on top of me kissing me. I was too tired to argue so I just let him

ALL I HAVE

go ahead and I turned over and went back to sleep. When I finally got up all the way, Alvin begged me not to tell Kym that he gave me powder and I didn't because he didn't force anything on me, I could have said no at any moment. I needed help with getting back home. I had been gone for too long now and I wanted to go home because I was tired of this dude. But Alvin would say just go with the flow and tell the doctor, referring to Kym that you want to go back to work. And that's what I did I told him that I was ready to get right because I needed to make some money. It took another week or so, but he gave in and took me to the southside. But he didn't let me out of his sight. The room that I was in he had let that go and he had all my things at this guy named Fred house that stayed on Freemon street. So that's where I was at. Wherever I was at he made sure no one let me out of their eyesight. He had all these people over here shook! This dude had some serious issues and I truly believe that he has a hatred for women in general. Later on, that night Fred and I was sitting outside. It was about 2-3am and we kept hearing a lady screaming and hollering right near the church on the corner of Slate street and Partin street this was in 1996. Fred, myself and Kym was the only ones out there. The lady screams got louder and louder. Me and Fred both knew it was Kym doing but I didn't care as long as it wasn't me. Fred made the comment like the doctor at it again! Then we see him running through the cut coming from behind Mr. James house and he called for Fred to hurry up and go into his house for something and once they ran in the house, I took off running. I ran all the way to Carboro road, and I walked right in my grandma's house because I knew that the door was unlocked, and everyone was asleep. I put the stick up against the front door and the step so no one could get in. I got on the couch and fell right asleep. Everyone woke up the next day and they were so glad to see me. It had been 3 years since I had been there, and my aunt Nita was there also. She said she had been hearing how Kym was treating me, but they couldn't never find us. She was glad I was home. I knew one thing; I didn't want to never go back! The next thing I know we hear a heavy ass knock on the door; it was the Wake

CHAPTER 6

Police Department. Shit! What the fuck do they want? They asked could they talk to Tina Gilchrist. "This is she" I replied They asked me have I read the newspaper this morning. I told them I haven't, and they handed me the front page and it read, Girl Found Dead behind church clothes pantry on the corner of Partin street and Slate street. Then they said they do have a person of interest which stay right across the street from the church... Now they allowed me to read this article and they asked could they ask me a couple of questions. I told them that I don't know anything, and I have nothing to do with that. All I cared about was never going back over there ever because this nigga is crazy, and he needs to stay far away from me as possible. I'm thinking in my head on what the police said that they had a suspect who lived across the street from the crime scene and that's where Kym stay at and with me knowing firsthand what he was capable of doing I most definitely didn't want any part of that. I stayed far away from Partin street as possible. Never wanted to see that man again

One year later...

I'm 16 years old now and a lot has happened. I moved with my grandma Lynda in Washinton Terrace apts. With my uncle Mike and we were sharing a 2-bedroom apartment. They allowed me to sleep on the couch to get me from over that side of town. I met a few new friends on the way. A guy name Applegate and a funny girl by the name of Fatima. Fatima stayed on Flushing street right across the street from Washinton Terrace. Applegate was a guy that I began having a relationship with. He was a cool dude, but he was young, and he just wasn't matured enough for me, so I ended that relationship early with him. Fatima was a cool chick. Her family was deep in that area and Fatima was the same age as me, but she had me by 10 months. We would do everything together. I had picked up a couple of bad habits before I moved to that side of Newburn Avenue. Flushing street was still southeast Raleigh but Partin street was on one side of Newburn Ave. and Flushing street was on the other side. I was so happy to try

ALL I HAVE

to get a new start. New faces, no Kym, I had met a lot of people and I knew most of the smokers that was around. I always listened to what the older people would say because they had already been through a thing or two so I would take heed. I also treated them with respect, and I wanted the same in return. Back to the scriptures, you reap what you sow! I also learned something that was important, you had to keep that fire. It was mandatory. And I kind of had the upper hand because my mom May had it going on. She had a beauty salon "It's You Hair and Nails" had an 8 bedroom house in Idle Village and a house being built in Clanton, N.C. yes girlfriend had it going on and I didn't even know it before. What my mom May use to do was come and pick me up take me to her house once a week to clean up for her. But every time I would go, she would have blocks of cocaine in the basement under concrete blocks. And how I found out was that I overheard her talking to one of her people. So, what I would do is clean up her house spic and span and take me a chunk off and she never noticed. If she did, she must have blamed someone else cause she never said anything to me. Week after week I would go clean. And once I got back with Fatima, she would take me to her uncle Charlie, and he would cook the powder for us. I would take me out a personal stash and he'd cook the rest. I'd give him some and we would hit the block. We would walk on the outskirts of Newburn Ave., Carboro road, make a right on Parkwood Ave down Waldon street. We would try to catch the people before they turned into the red zone. The red zone consisted of Pedigree street, Booster street, Mapel street, Carvey street. On those streets them niggas was going to war and Fatima family was deep. Because we were young, they wouldn't want her out there like that. But she had done got a taste of that fast money and we had some fire, so it was on then. Whatever we made we would split 3 ways. I would tell her we had to re-up which we did, because it would take another 4 days to finish and when I would give her hers, I took the rest. It was so much money out I had bought me a Toyota from a smoker, but I needed someone to put it in their name and my mom May said she would and she had driver's

CHAPTER 6

license also. But she took my shit! I was really beginning to hate that lady with a passion. I was beginning to see how kids could kill their parents. Because of the way I was feeling towards her to this very day I keep my distance. That honor thy mother thing was about to go straight out the window and that's why I stayed the fuck away from that lady, she had some serious issues. I only paid $200 for the car, so it was cool. I'd get another one soon.

One day after I'd finish early and was tired of keep taking from May I had asked myself who could I get something from? A light bulb went off!! My aunt Nita! She then turned me on to her people in Apache Heights and it was on from there. See I didn't know that my aunt Nita was smoking crack until the first time she had went and turned me on to her people and she tried it in front of us. That was it! I had someone out there with me I can trust to a certain extent. But in the back of my mind, I don't even trust myself, so everything is always suspect. Things were moving slow over there on Flusher street side because all the shootings and killings that had been going on lately and the police wasn't allowing nothing over there to move. I had this product and I needed it to move. I was young and didn't understand how important it was to be patient. Partin street came in the back of my mind but at the same time something was telling me not to go in that area because it wasn't long enough since I had left, but it had been a couple of months so why not slide through there to see what I can make pop right quick? I was hearing from the smokers anyways that it was too hot for Kym to be outside because after that girl had ended up dead and he was in the newspaper as being a suspect, the police had turned up the heat on him and he wasn't playing Partin street. So, I went over there to see what was up and sure enough it was the same smokers there and they were more than happy to see me. They knew exactly who I was, and I picked up where I left off. Well during this time, I was a chick out there getting her grind on. I had nothing to worry about because people didn't know if I was out there with Kym or not. But I truly don't think they cared as long as I

ALL I HAVE

had what they wanted. And me at this point in my life, I was never tied down to one nigga. NO MORE FAKE PHONY ASS NIGGAS, I'm tired! I treated them niggas like they treated us women. I fucked Buddy Monday, Applegate Tuesday, Mario Wednesday, Bobby Thursday and did me the rest of the week. I didn't need a nigga for nothing because Kym had scarred me, and I didn't want my heart to be broken again no time soon. I think I was on Partin street 3 weeks before Kym found out that I was over there, and he ran up on me one night and told me to get in his truck. I was skeptical at first, but I did anyways. I was still in love with him, he was my first. He drove into the backyard of a friend's house and I knew exactly where we were so if I wanted to bounce it would have been no problem. He was telling me about him getting locked up and catching another case. He started shedding tears, so I felt sorry for him in a way. And I had learned I was pregnant, and I wasn't sure if he was the father or not. Besides I wasn't interested with sleeping with him anyways. Now a nigga is the furthest thing from my mind. And keeping it real with you Applegate and Buddy could be the father of my child also and how I'm feeling right now I don't want to be bothered with no nigga! I hated them!! I'm not ready for no children and now I'm trying to find a way to get rid of this pregnancy but first I must get to this bag!! Now back to my conversation, "Ok Kym we can work it out. When are you going to be ready?" I said. He said meet me tomorrow night on Freemon street. I caved in that quick! If I can help someone that's just my nature I'm going to try. One day I will learn! The next night came and I met him at Fred's house on Freemon street. He told me to go through the cut behind Mr. James house and he told me the exact spot to go to and dig up the pill bottle that was buried in the backyard. And I did as he told me but when I was walking back out the cut, the police were everywhere. "Drop it and put your hands up, it's the police". They had caught me red handed with a pill bottle full of rocks…

We get to the precinct. They asked me my name and I told them. They said "now you know this is heroin you have this bottle" I'm not saying anything. The police then said "you know who set you up

CHAPTER 6

right?" Still I'm not budging. They asked, "Do you know who Kent Lewis is?" I'm thinking to myself Kent Lewis. The only Kent Lewis I know is the singer. Other than that, I never heard of that name before. They looked at each other and said AKA, Kym! Then the whole scene played back in my head in slow motion. The police said, "how do you think we got you at the right time?" Once it played back completely my heart fell to my feet! It made a lot of sense to me. They had a point because how could they know? And with heroine, he never sold that. It was always crack cocaine. That nigga set me the fuck up that piece of shit!! And with a full bottle of heroin. They said we will look out for you on your bond if you would tell us what we need to know. "Just take me to jail, I need a lawyer I have no more words for you". They told me for the quantity I had the minimum I could get was 10 years and I didn't trust the police. That cops show that came on just about every night that had the song bad boys' bad boys', what you gonna do what you gonna do when they come for you!!! I always looked at them like they are the bad boys! That song is referring to the police but now I know that the bad boys are the people that they are arresting. I thought guilty until proven innocent? Anyways I went to see the magistrate and they set my bond at $10,000 cash bond. I tried to call Kym phone, but he changed his number that quick. The man I trusted and loved, set me up with the police. The biggest baddest muthafucka out here is the fucking police!! I was charged with trafficking of heroin and the minimum are 10 years in prison at the age of 16 years old and pregnant. Man, if it's not one thing it's another. They took me straight to 1034 Briggs street at the women's prison safe keeping because the jail couldn't house me because I was too far along in my pregnancy. So, I was crying my eyes out because I was a 16-year-old and heading to the women prison and couldn't call anyone because I knew no one that had $10,000 cash dollars to spend on me. Now what am I going to do? I would be 26 years old before they would let me out and my child would be 10! So, I turned to someone that I hadn't called on in a while and that was GOD! LORD, PLEASE HELP ME TO GET OUT THIS SITUATION THAT I GOT MYSELF IN. LORD

ALL I HAVE

I WON'T DO THAT AGAIN, I'M SORRY. PLEASE FORGIVE ME. I said that prayer repeatedly. The Sheriff van finally pulled to pick me up from the detention center to transport me to 1034 Briggs street, the women's prison and the officers escorted me out the van to the infirmary. First thing I heard as soon as I got there was fresh meat. Okay automatically my tears dried up I'm only 16 years old and the officer already told me that I was the youngest one housed there. Alone, don't know anyone, I'm lost. After they checked my vitals, asked me a million health questions, gave me a physical basically, they went ahead and took me to single cell b. That's where they kept safe keeping at the time and medical. Once I got in waiting to be housed, I saw all types of men walking around with the same kind of clothes that the women had on. So, I asked one of the officers was this a men and women prison? She said no, those are women you see. My heart melted. I knew one thing though, I was ready to go, and I didn't want to never come back to this place, ever. I wanted to burst out crying right then but I couldn't let them see me sweat. So, they assigned me to a cell all to myself until they tried to figure out where they were going to put me. I stayed in that cell for two weeks and didn't come out to shower or eat anything, it was real! One officer and older black woman came and talked to me. She asked me was I alright and I told her "yes" but mentally I wasn't, and she knew that. I was just ready to go home and that's quite normal! She told me that the other girls are complaining about the odor coming from my cell. She asked me when the last time I had took a shower? I told her the truth, that I hadn't took one since I'd been in over two weeks ago. I hadn't even come out the room, watched TV, read no books, no food and I was pregnant. She said how about this. If you get up and clean your room, take a shower, I will let you use the phone to call your family. I told her that I didn't want to take a shower with no one else, so she allowed me to take one by myself. I mopped and swept my room, had it smelling fresh and I felt a lot better after I cleaned myself up. I didn't have anyone phone number in my family because the house phone was turned off, so I called this guy who name was Steve. He was a

CHAPTER 6

cool guy that was 19 at the time and he was also on Freemon street at his uncle's house Mr. James. Mr. James stayed right behind Kym house and Steve had a crush on me. Before I got locked up, he would buy me shoes and clothes and he was a very sweet guy. So, I called him, and he accepted my call. That's when he finally realized where I was at. I also told him what the police had said what Kym had did, and I asked him could he go and tell my grandma or one of my family members that they had me in safe keeping at the women prison. I felt a whole lot better just knowing that someone on the outside knew where I was at. After the phone call she asked if I wanted to go in the day room to watch TV and to pick out a couple of books to read and I did. I stayed in the day room for about an hour or two then I headed back in my cell. All I did in that cell for the whole two weeks that I was in there was cry and pray. The next day and officer came in and said that they needed my cell to house an inmate that needed to go on lockdown. She said that she found me a bottom bunk in the day room and that's where I would be sleeping at. It had been awhile, and I finally had started coming around a little on the situation I had gotten myself into. I couldn't blame it on no one but myself because if I would of went off my first instincts to stay away from Partin street let alone Kym, I wouldn't even be in this situation. So, I had to humble myself and get ready for what was next. The unknown! This is the year 1997 and Thanksgiving was coming and a couple of days before Thanksgiving, Steve brought my grandma Lynda and my sister Tonya to come see me. During that time, they could bring food from the outside in. Boy my grandma threw down. She brought sweet potato pie my favorite, marble pound cake another one of my favorites, collards, turkey, potato salad, ham, I mean 3 paper bags full of food. I was so happy to see everyone, and I was so thankful for Steve because he took the time out to bring them down here to see me. Like I said he was a good dude and to this day, when I see him, I wonder what life would've been like if we were together. The visit was 1 hour and 30 minutes long, I didn't want to see them go but I had no choice. I told my grandma Lynda to please try to find out when my court date

ALL I HAVE

was because I had been in prison for 2 months now and hadn't heard nothing from no one. And I thanked Steve for bringing them to see me. And Steve continued to come see me on the regular and made sure that money was on my books. SHOUT OUT TO YOU STEVE! When I got back to single cell B with my Thanksgiving, boy we threw down up in there. I was the only one that had Thanksgiving in there, so I looked out for the other girls. The month or so I had spent in the day room I had gotten closer to the ladies that was there. It was 9 other girls in the day room, where there were 5 girls on the top bunk and 5 on the bottom including myself. Everyone that was housed in single cell b had a medical condition except for the ones that had their own cell because they were on lockdown. See in single cell, you couldn't smoke cigarettes then. So every time they would bring the food up to the dorm, they would accidentally crash the cart up to the dayroom window and because it was a hole through the screen in the window, they would accidentally crash the cart up to the dayroom wall near the window and because of the hole we would grab the cigarettes and hand them the money at the same time. And boom! We got our cigarettes. We would have someone watching for the guards and we kept baby powder to mask the smell. We would stand where the hole was at the window and hold the cigarettes out the hole and blew the smoke out also through the hole. I didn't have to buy any cigarettes because this girl whose name was Smooth who looked just like a man and sort of favored the rapper Fabulous. She would always call me 16 and she was the one that told me how to get the cigarettes and what to relay to the girls delivering the food and that's how we also ordered ours also. God was looking out for me even then and I'm just now realizing it. I would have to run them down to her cell and get them to her without getting caught and she would give me 4 cigarettes. She told me how to break them down using toilet paper wrapping and that's how I did it, but then I got to the point of buying my own. Packs were $8.00 and that was a lot when back then they only cost $3.00 on the street. But in there you had to do what you had to do.

CHAPTER 6

Thanksgiving had passed, Christmas and my birthday 12-31 and I turned 17 years old. I had been there for about 3 months by that time and I was 8 months pregnant. I had met a lot of cool females in prison and we all made some bad choices that we fully didn't know the consequences of our actions. I don't know what Smooth did for her to be on lockdown for as long as she did, but she had been there for over a month now and once my birthday came, she changed my name to 17. So, she started calling me seventeen! I also met a few on death row Inmates because single cell A was right next door and they would come through and it was scary knowing that soon they will be dead literally. I know that we all here to die but to know someone about to put you to death is another story. Lanch Ore, the lady that killed her husbands, Blonde. And a few lifers that was there with Smooth that was on lockdown. Amir, Dessa, all had a lengthy sentence. They might not remember me now, but I truly appreciate the kindness they showed me while I was in there. They all treated me like I was their daughter telling me what to do and what not to do on some being helpful tip. In the back of my mind I had to at least have do 10 years. It was a sad situation but the good thing about the whole situation was a church group that came every Sunday to preach to us and did Bible study. I enjoyed that because reading the Bible had always been interesting to me. Maybe because every time I read it, I would open my heart to God and I could always feel his presence come over me. I would ask them to pray for me because I was sitting there with no attorney, no court date, and I hadn't seen a judge in 4 months. NOT ONE TIME.

One day when one of the church members asked if anyone wanted to get saved and I said yes and that day I was born again for the second time. A feeling of relief that weighed 1000 pounds was lifted off my shoulders. But I was still in prison bringing in the New Year.

January of 98 came and it was a bad snowstorm that came with it. The whole city was shut down for days and during that storm the courts lost people files, computers had frozen, the courthouse was broken into and it was terrible. The courts were even closed. In North Carolina, if a couple of sprinkles hit the ground it's a state of emergency. Sad! But this time was different because the power was out for days. To me it couldn't get any worse. Knowing that the longer the courts closed I'm not getting no closer to going home.

January 20, 1998, I was laying down in the dayroom and all a sudden, my water broke. All the girls in the day room started hollering for the guard to come. Everyone was running around like chickens with their heads cut off! Even the guards but they finally got it together and brought me a wheelchair and rolled me to the infirmary where the ambulance was waiting. The midwife was there with me also. My stomach was aching bad and the contractions were hitting me like words I can't even describe the feeling. The contractions were coming every 6 minutes! I tried to act civilized, but I couldn't. That was pain I didn't want to feel let alone back to back! With no loved ones there to support me, I was on my own. See during the time I was at the women's prison, we already had things set up to where my mom May was going to take the baby until I got home. When that was going to be only God knew. Boom! Boom! Boom! My contractions were hitting me left and right. "Please hurry up and get this baby out of me" I said! We finally arrived at Wake Medical Center and I had just enough time to get an epidural where I was numb from the waist down. On January 21, 1998 Destiny Laquanda Michelle Ruth Gilchrist was born 6lbs 8oz. She was and ugly little girl! But I didn't care I love my baby!! Now I am not going to front for no one. Now people keep it 100; when a baby is first born all of them come out funny looking until their color comes in first. So yes, my baby was ugly, but she was mines that's all that mattered. They let me hold her for a couple of hours and they left her at the hospital, and they took me back to the infirmary. Back to prison. I couldn't even spend one night with my child. All that night in the infirmary, I cried and cried wondering how Destiny was doing. These people were cruel. I have been in this prison for 5 months now and I didn't know nothing. No

CHAPTER 6

court date, no lawyer, Nothing! I had to begin applying pressure because I wanted to go home to my child. I needed to know who my lawyer was. I needed someone's help. Lord Please Help Me. PLEASE! A couple more months passed by and in March 1998, My Mom May finally got me a paid lawyer to see what was going on. The reason why I was still locked up is because they had no record of me ever being in the system! So, all of that time I was sitting on Briggs St., It was like I was never there and as soon as she hired the attorney, a couple of weeks later I was in front of a judge and they dismissed all charges. Thank You GOD! That was nobody but God because they had violated my civil rights by not getting me in court within 72hrs of getting locked up and it took 8 months before I went in front of a judge. It went from them saying the minimum of 10 years to case dismissed! Who else could it be? But there is always a lesson to be learned. What was this one?

I get home with my daughter Destiny. My Mom May had everything for her. She went all out for Destiny! Everything she had was new. Matching everything. It kind of shocked me because the last person I expected to be there was the one who had stepped up to the plate. Must be nice! But after I got home it was over for that because she was out, and I did not blame her. That was my responsibility. I had also lost touch with Steve. I'm guessing he found someone else. I didn't blame him either because he deserved better. So now that I'm out of prison and back on Carboro Rd. with a daughter, no job, no pampers or milk, I had to do something and quick! So, I talked to my cousin Candi who was 13 and pregnant (some Tupac shit) and I knew she needed money also. I had a few dollars left so I paid her to babysit with the promise of never going back to Partin St.

CHAPTER 7

What's up Fatima

FATIMA WAS SO happy to see me. Fatima's daughter was 10 months older than my child and she was a pretty chocolate little girl. Her name is Nique. We had said when we first got pregnant that we would be each other God Parent. Fatima was anxious to see Destiny, but I told her that I was not going back to the house until I found out what I needed to know... I had a lil change left and I had to make something shake. I asked Fatima what she had, and she said that her baby daddy was holding her money she took me over to Carvey St. behind a house where they were staying at. They were living in a shed! Jesse was her baby daddy's name, but Jesse was a Mexican and the baby looked nothing like she had any Mexican in her genes, but I kept my mouth closed because that was none of my business. The shed they were staying in was hooked-up. They had extension cords running from the house into the shed for electricity. They had a TV and a bed. It looked nice in there. It was just right for the three of them. Jesse could not speak or understand English well. Just a few words. Fatima had started to speak a little Spanish with being around his people and all and was trying to teach me. Jesse had spent up all the money so all we had to work with is the buck fifty that I had. So, she took me to one of her peeps houses who gave me what I needed to make things shake for what I had and we went to work. We stayed out there all night until we finished because Candi had my baby and

CHAPTER 7

Jesse had hers. I gave her what she was satisfied with and I told her to hold on to her money because tomorrow night we can do it again. I then went home and gave Candi $50 for babysitting and she was loving that. I also told her to hold my money for me and if she would watch Destiny again that night that I would pay her the same. Candi was loving that also! She needed all the money she could get because her baby daddy was only 12 years old. What was he going to do? Teamwork. My daughter Destiny was a good, thick and chunky baby. She looked like a little baby dinosaur because she had so many rolls on her thighs. My chunky baby! Me and Fatima would walk our babies together and everyone fell in love with them. We had a good routine going on. We would put the babies to sleep at night and then we set out to conquer the world! It was a whole nother world at night. The freaks come out at night is an understatement. We had it good because Fatima family was so deep on that side of town and my Mom May name was ringing bells out there. It seemed like everyone knew who I was, but I didn't know them. But I didn't care. How much you got? It seemed like it was 1000 people out on the corners in Lincoln Heights. Lincoln Heights ran from Pool Rd. back towards St. August College. Booming wasn't the word but once you into the heart of Lincoln Heights it was Carvey St., Flushing St., Ponder St., Booster St. niggas was going to war. It Didn't make sense to me everything was so close together. By us knowing that we are not bullet proof we continued to play the outskirts. We would go to the rooming houses to check them out and keep it moving. During this time, I'm still on the nose candy. It wasn't a big thing to me. See I was the type that knew my limits and I would quit. If I had to buy more I wouldn't because what I would do was take a gram out of what I was about to cook and that would last me all night. I would try to hide it from Fatima, but she was so nosy. She bust in on me one night at the rooming house on the corner of Carboro and Booster St. in Mr. Ames room. Us being young and not knowing the consequences of our actions she asked me to hit the bag. At first, I didn't want to do it but then I gave in. She was killing my high! She asked me how to do it and I told her how to get it right.

ALL I HAVE

I tore a piece of the Newport box, folded it and dipped it in the bag. She tried to put damn near the whole bag on one scoop. "No Fatima take your time and besides you aint bout to be taking all of my shit!" So, after she did the first scoop, she wanted another. A few minutes later she was lit! Talking 100mph, OMG! "Fatima please shut up! You are blowing my high." But she went on and on and on! So that night we just chilled out and made our money in the rooming house. But before daylight hits, I would make sure I was at home because I didn't like being out when the sun came up. Okay so now Fatima goes running her mouth about us on the nose candy. So now these MF's running around calling us crackheads because of the nose candy. Now I'm on a mission to get each one of them one by one. I'm pissed!! I'm a very private person and I couldn't understand what made her run her mouth. Fatima had gotten to the point that she was wide open. OMG! What have I done at 17 years of age? We weren't really thinking. I was laid back and chilling when I wasn't on it. It didn't change my character, but it sure has done something to Fatima. I remember one night we were at the rooming house and we walked pass one of the rooms where they were smoking crack. As they blew out the smoke Fatima said, "Tina don't that smell good"? "Hell, no Fatima"! I said, one thing my Mom May told me that sticks with me until this day is "Don't put fire on anything white"! And until this day I tell the kids that. Well we got up out of there. I tell you after that night Fatima hit the bag, she was like the energizer bunny. It was on now! I still had my cousin Candi babysitting at $50 a day and she was still holding my money also. I love my cousin. We had each other back. Me and Fatima were doing big things out there now. The police had cleared Lincoln Heights of all the shooting, and Niggas out there at the time and what the police didn't get, they killed each other off, it was real out there during that time. Bullets was flying everywhere; it was like a battlefield! But there was plenty of money to be made. And me and Fatima moved in slowly eventually posting up on Mapel St. because Carvey St. was hot, and it was the next street over. We knew a couple of people that stayed on Mapel St. so we posted on the corner. With

CHAPTER 7

Fatima being born and raised in that area, I got to know everyone she knew. We had her family house they owned on Flushing St. that we would dip into if the police got hot and during that time we were over there, we started really getting to know people in the area. Her aunt Lacy also stayed on Carvey St. with her cousins Markus and lil Mick an as time went by, I got to know a lot of good people. Harley, he stayed on the corner of Mapel and Ponder St. he was a cool dude, his cousin Kenyatta, she was a pretty girl all the guys was on her, Snow and his wife Mrs. Matlin which stayed right across the street from Harley on Mapel street side. My boy John-John and his cousin Rick which stayed at the top of Mapel going towards Parkwood. Freda, and her sons Jack, New York, and Chuck. It was a lot of cool people that I got to know as time went by and everyone that was out there was on some get money shit. It was more than enough money out there for everyone. Oh, yea I can't forget my queens Calvin and Jamie!! Yes, those are my bitches! Born men but they look better than me on their bad days!! Love them both, you couldn't tell them nothing. And if I had any problem out of a nigga or a bitch, all I had to do was holla at them and the problem was solved. I wasn't the type for arguing, I have a superb talk game. See my motto was to keep it 100 regardless. So, I really didn't see how anything could come back to me. I was laid back and didn't really deal with too many people, only smokers. Fatima was the one that was on the front line because she was a socialite, I played the background.

I remember one day when I was walking towards Carboro Rd to go home and a tall butterscotch handsome guy came up to me and asked me my name. OMG! When I see this cat, it was like I melted all over literally. He was thick, cut, chest, arms and looking like a snack. And he had a good grade of hair on top of his head. "What's up shorty?" he asked. My response was "you". I then asked, "what are you" young we all know how that go, he then said that he was "Guyanese" he lost me with. But shit, he was fine to me. He asked me my name again, "Tina and yours?" "Shamar" was his reply. He asked could he walk with me. I told him sure but not all the way because I didn't want him knowing where I stayed at. I didn't know him, so he walked me up to the Bo's Chicken almost to the house. He asked me my age and he was 25 years old he had me by 9 years but for some reason I always put 2 years on my age because I was a very mature 17-year-old. "19" I replied. I know it was wrong, but it is what it is. He had no kids and I told him I had a daughter and her age. We were just getting acquainted and he asked me could he see me again and I said, "yes no problem". So, he gave me his sisters number and we parted ways. That negro was on my mind all night long. But I told myself, "Tina slow down honey." But that was one fine brother to me. I got home, gave Candy her money and checked on baby girl and I fell asleep.

For some reason the next day I was dragging ass and I couldn't get it together for nothing. Suddenly there was a knock on the door. When I peeped out the window, I didn't recognize the voice. "Who is it"? it's Mrs. Glen from social services. So, I opened the door. I then asked her who was she looking for and she said "Tina Gilchrist". Fucked me up! My reply was "this is she" she then said that she had got a call saying that I was neglecting my daughter. She then asked could she see Destiny and tried to come in. "naw" you can wait outside, hold on and I'll go get her". So, I went upstairs, grabbed her and brought her out. She then started asking me 1000 questions like, did I have everything I needed for her and whether I was working and did I need anything. We didn't want for nothing, but I couldn't tell them how I was getting money. So, I told her if I needed anything, I would most definitely be getting in touch with her. I was pissed that someone could just out the blue call social services and boom they pop right the fuck up at your doorstep!! How could they? I made sure my child was straight and on top of that, I made sure everyone around me was straight! So, who could it be? You know what I told myself that I had too much on my mind to be worried about a hater, so as long as I stay out of her way (social worker), then I'll have nothing to worry about.

CHAPTER 7

But one thing that I knew that needed to be done was get the house spic and span. So, then I went to the block to find a smoker to come get the house right for me, and instead of me turning at Church's Chicken off Newburn Ave. something told me to walk down a little further and there he goes again Shamar. Mum!! And there go his pretty smile. I then asked what he was doing in the neighborhood? He said that he be up on Hills and Ponder street. At the time I have been in that area I'd never saw him. He said that he had just came down from New Jersey with his people. I had walked with him up that way and it was the next street over from where I was at. I was on Mapel street and that's how shit was back then. Each block had their own thing going on. We had stopped at Harley house where Fatima was at and then we walked up to Hills and Ponder St. "Mr. Marshal" that's my dude and this whole time that's where Shamar was posted up at! Everyone had their own team and Fatima and me was all we had! Shoot again it's enough money out here for everyone. She's my right hand and she was the one that was doing everything because she was from that area and like I said, she didn't mind!! I stayed at the top of the street being nosy, just trying to figure out where his mind was at. But to me it seemed like he wasn't doing too much of nothing. He was up there with a few more niggas. Kool, Shabazz, Sugar Black and Dre and himself. I really didn't too much care about what he had because I had my own thing going on. I really wanted to see how he was moving mainly, I needed to figure out if he was an asset or not. Tired of Fake niggas! Kym did me with that police shit! Wolves in sheep's clothing! That's what I tried to be on the lookout for because it's always hard to tell. Niggas are good at fronting, so I questioned myself if he was worth the wait? I didn't know so I guess I'm going to have to see. I hoped that he wouldn't deceive me but, in my mind, I had to have some of that! But that's the problem now, I was always thinking with the wrong "head" let a nigga tell it. But he was fine to me! Money didn't matter to me. I just needed someone that has my back, front, and side at all times regardless. I wanted what I wanted and at the time I am feeling Shamar a lot! Perfect.

ALL I HAVE

We went out a couple of times getting to know each other better but with both of us being street people, we didn't open up a lot. But, by the third time together we couldn't contain ourselves any longer. We were at the Friendship Inn on Wake Fore Rd. getting it in! And, just as I thought, the meats banging and the head game superb! OMG! He was the total package. Yes, got him! When we were done, he rolled over and went to sleep, and I called me a cab because I had to go. On my way to the hood that's all I could think about was him. I could still feel every stroke he was giving me and there I go again; I think I'm in love!

So, I hopped out of the cab on Mapel St. looking for Fatima. That chick wasn't too hard to find because she lived out there now. She had told me the police had ran up on the block and she had to swallow some. I had no problem with that because that was coming out of her pay and she had started making that a habit lately. She would say that she had to throw this and that, but she was my best friend, so I didn't have no reason to doubt her. So, we stayed up until the sun was coming up and we parted ways. My daughter had started walking and talking and I couldn't make any sense of it but one thing I did notice was she was talking big shit! Shamar was a regular person and Destiny loved him. I'm guessing because he was tall and goofy looking, and I couldn't get rid of him. It seemed like everywhere I went he was there. As the months went by, Fatima and me was going our separate ways. We had our family to take care of and it seemed like we were on two different paths. The losses that she was taking was costly and I must switch things up, especially when it began to come out of my pocket. So, Fatima and Jesse decided to move to Chicago, and I would call her occasionally. The phone charge was $15 to call up there just to check to see how she was doing. I would go to the store and buy one of those calling cards and that's how we communicated. With it only being me and Shamar now. Shamar didn't never do anything after me and him got together. He didn't have to because my money was caked up. His sister had moved back to Vineland New

CHAPTER 7

Jersey, and she needed someone to take over her lease and she allowed us to do that. So, we were set up pretty, living on the North side and hustling on the Southside. The crib was in a gated community with a swimming pool and tennis court so yea, we were living like the white people. I had just turned 18 and I also had a better place for the social workers. So, things were looking brighter. My cousin Candy had her son and she named him Saddyq, but she was still there for me if I needed her. Also, my sister Tonya had a son around the same time Candy had Saddyq and she named him Mykelle. They were 5 months apart. Sometimes I would take Destiny to Carboro Rd. so Candy could watch her and sometimes Shamar would watch Destiny while I would go out. But, on this particular day, Shamar and myself had plans to go out that night because his cousin Jersey was coming down from New Jersey and we was going to show him around and also talk business... See during that time it was a lot of demand, but not enough supply and the streets were out for the taken. So, I had hollered at Candy and we agreed that I would be going to get the baby later that afternoon. "We good, let's go!" His cousin then meets us on the block because I didn't feel comfortable with niggas coming to the house and all, so he pulls up in a cab. He was a short guy with a gold tooth in his mouth. I looked at Shamar and he introduced us. Your name Jersey huh?

After that, I take him to John John's house on the corner of Mapel and Parkwood. I don't know the conversation that him and Shamar had going on, but I was under the impression that he was the man which I come to find out he wasn't. That's why to this day I'm a firm believer that communication is the key because once Jersey got here, Shamar had told me something totally different. I had to tell him that if this all you brought then I can get that off you now and send you on your way! But Jersey wanted the break down money. I didn't know about all that. I did know that them up top cats will take your ass fast, so me I'll tell them quick to slow down because it's all about communication. It was a drought at that time, and he had and undisclosed amount so I knew in that area that would go in no time. "How about this? You a businessman, right"? I told him then I would introduce him to John John who was my dude and since we was in his house, we look out for the house man and I'll help you move it and on the comeback, you let me get it for the same price as what you getting it for. We shook hands and it was on. That product was gone by sunup and that nigga had a smile on his face so big with his one gold tooth. Alright, I done my part, hit me on the comeback. Sure enough 2 days later he was back, and he was a man of his word and it was on n popping from there. But, now here he comes with the extra stuff. Now he on some partner shit. Now that aint my cup of tea and plus for some reason I wasn't too fond of those city slickers. But what I did do was introduce him to a girl that was outside that had become a friend of mine and her name was Monica, Moni for short. He seemed like a cool cat and when my work was gone, I would go and holla at him because he wasn't stepping on my toes and that was Shamar cousin, so what harm could it bring. Well once he started getting in good with the neighborhood, you couldn't tell him nothing. Every time I turned around that's all you heard. Jersey done this; his boys done that. Me and Shamar would be in the house laughing like a MF because we already kind of knew how it was going to play out. Shamar had already given me the scoop about what type of nigga he was. I didn't care though because I was always the type to don't bite the hand that feeds me. I can say that Jersey always gave me the impression that he was thankful that we brought him over that way. Me, I was like Casper because I would slide in and out. When I came through, they knew that I was the water girl. But Jersey that nigga was a smart dude. He brought a couple of niggas down here with him and every one of them was getting paid $700 a week. Now back in the late 90's you could easily get rid of a lot of product. Me alone, I was on some break down type stuff. But picture the profit that was being made during that time. All the trappers that was out during that time feel where I'm coming from. But like I said from the advice of my attorney the amounts cannot be told! Next thing I knew, I see this nigga with

CHAPTER 7

Shirley Temple curls and a manicure. OMG, WTF this nigga got going on? That shit was funny to me! But he dared a nigga to flinch because his goons weren't too far away. So, let a nigga flinch. But he always gave me a lot of respect.

One day we were sitting at home and Shamar's sister called while he was in the shower and I answered. She then asked me why I haven't paid the rent in a couple months, my heart dropped because I knew I had been giving him the money for the rent. So, I told his sister that I'd been giving him the money every month and that I would make sure she gets all the rent that day. I told her not to mention it to Shamar because I needed to see what was going on. So, I went to the office and paid the 2 months he was behind and didn't say a word to him. I had to figure out what really was going on. Also, during this time, he was hustling at a hotel on Wake Fore Rd. at the Friendship Inn. I had been noticing that some of my product would come up missing. Not nothing major, maybe a few grams but now after the call that I got from his sister, I wanted some answers. So, what I did was went and got this girl name Kelly. I got her a room at the Friendship and gave her a ball to find out what Shamar was doing. It didn't take long to figure out. She wouldn't even tell me what was going on because she told me I had to come see for myself. So, I stood to the left side of the door which was the blindside and when he popped the lock, I slid in there. When I walked in, it was 2 females in there and they both had crack stems in their mouths, and he had a blunt in his mouth that had a wooly smell. My nigga was smoking crack and tricking! My whole heart just fell. Now it all added up. All the grams, the rent money, this nigga was smoking my shit up! Damn all that goodness gone to waste. Damn! I went up to the other room and called me a cab and got up out of here. But before I left, I told him I talked to his sister that day and I knew about the rent and now I see that the whole time he was taking from me and now I don't trust him anymore. I then went to the house got what I could and bounced. I got me a hotel room and I cried all night long. How could it be? Hatred filled my heart.

ALL I HAVE

It's one thing to be sneaking around and stealing from me, not paying the rent, but tricking? Now that's a different story. I couldn't even look at him the same anymore. And come to think about it, I should've known because you can tell if a person smoke wooly's or not because it's in their skin. How could I not see that? So many emotions went through my body, but at the same time I loved him!

    I thought to myself. Tina what are you going to do now?

CHAPTER 8

AFTER THE INCIDENT at the Friendship, it had been about a week since I'd heard anything from Shamar. I knew he was straight because I had just paid the rent and I knew he had a couple more months before he would have to go. I had to get away from him. It wasn't just the fact that he was smoking crack because a drug is a drug regardless of how you do it, but it was all the deceitful shit that came with it is what I couldn't take. I couldn't trust him no more! I had to erase him from my memory. About a week later my Mom's friend FeFe needed a roommate at a house she had just rented off Glacian Rd. She was always cool to me and at that time I needed somewhere to go, so I went for it. I gave her my part of the rent and I was good because I wasn't trying to go nowhere near Shamar. I was very upset and done with him and I had the right remedy to get that nigga off my mind. I would move on to the next nigga. Not relationship wise but just for a quickly because niggas couldn't last long once they dip into my cookie jar!

One night I went on a prowl and snatched up this nigga that at one time was hounding me, and the vibe in the atmosphere was right for what I needed done to me for that night. He's a cool cat, kind of chunky and he was doing his little thing. He wasn't no competition with me. I needed something to do, was bored. This would be a temporary engagement. Besides I need someone that was doing more than what I was doing, so it would make me do better. But at that moment to make me feel good about myself, he was the one. His name

ALL I HAVE

Kairi and we always had been cool with each other, to the point that he would speak to me every time he saw me. But he was a jump off because every female had him. Why did I do it? Like I said, timing was everything and he caught me at the right time! That night was the first time we had slept together, and we had chilled and smoked a couple blunts together and brought the sunup on the block but it never went no further. After we did sleep together that night, the next morning in my eyes it was like nothing never happened. But I did make one mistake, I brought him to the house! Now it seemed like I couldn't get rid of the nigga! It wasn't like on no girlfriend boyfriend type thing because it was just a BFF type thing. He did try to hit it but like I told him, it wasn't that type of party! But he was an alright cat to chill with! The couple of months that we were staying on Glacian Rd. we had turned the house into a trap house, and it was booming! People was coming from as far as Wilmington and Asheboro because of a major drought and Jersey was that nigga at the time. When Jersey did come to the house, I would pull him to the side and tell him not to tell Shamar where I was at. But Jersey told me that I needed to go holla at him because he was not doing too good! I had no problem with that because it had been a couple of months since I had seen Shamar and anyways from what I'd been hearing, he was not even hiding the fact that he was smoking wooly's because he was now doing it all in the open! I thought that I did need to reach out to him because I did have love for him, so one night I pulled up on him in front of Jersey n John-Jonh house on Mapel St. He was standing outside and looking a mess. I was in a cab and I told him to hop in. He looked like he was shocked to see me, but he asked me to hop out because he wasn't trying to go anywhere. I told him then that I'll be back because I didn't want anyone in my business. So as the cab was pulling off, he decided to get on in the cab. I took him out to Sandy Forks where the apartment was at that we were staying in, and I got out just to be nosey and to check out how he was living. It seemed like he was going through a lot because the apartment looked a mess. He told me that he missed me, and he was sorry about how things

CHAPTER 8

had ended. He said he didn't have anyone down here, but Jersey and he started fronting on him because of the smoking that he was doing. He said he didn't know what to do, so I told him that he should go back to New Jersey and get his mind together. I had got me a beeper and I told him that I would get him one and that we could always keep in touch. I told him that I still had love for him and that I would also come and visit him soon. He liked that idea. So, I did spend the night with him that night and the next day, we called to find out what time the Greyhound bus was leaving for Vineland N.J. We cleaned the apartment out with some help of a few smokers, hoped in the cab, went to the beeper shop in Downtown Raleigh, got him one, and I took him to the bus station. I gave him a few dollars, bought his ticket, and that was the last time I saw Shamar. I had asked Jersey about him a couple of months later and he told he got up there and tried to rob a bank and got caught. I was hoping he would've changed his ways, but I see not! Life is made of choices!

Business booming as usual. At the time, I was a young girl with a lot of money and really didn't know what to do with it. I never had anyone to tell me how or what to do with the money, so I did what I knew best, I splurged! Bought Coogi dresses, Donna Karen, Gucci, Versace shades, hotel rooms and threw parties. Balling out of control! Didn't even think about buying a vehicle because my problem was finding someone name to put on it. So, taxi cabs it was. I still had social service on my ass, but my daughter didn't want for nothing. She was two years old now and I almost had social services off my back until one day I had stayed out later than my usual time. I don't know why but I didn't let my cousin Candy keep Destiny at my house but instead took her to my Grandma Lynda's house on Carboro Rd. Later the next morning, a fire had happened at the house and the ambulance and fire squad came and Candy, her son and Destiny was the only ones there. Since I was the one who had an open case with social services, they went ahead and took Destiny into Custody. When I went to Carboro Rd. and seen the yellow tape around the house and keep out signs on the doors, I called my grandma's boyfriend's house to see what I had to do to get my child. But that's when she told me that social services intended to keep my daughter. My heart felt like it was ripped straight out my chest! I'm pissed and I had thoughts to find some C4, grenades and assault rifles on some military shit because I wanted to blow social services the fuck up. But my mind told me to hold up because what if my child was in there? Slow down Tina, think! I told myself "okay, I am going to call up there and hopefully they'll let me get my child. So, I called and got the answering machine. I left a message and a million things went through my mind. That night I couldn't sleep at all. It seemed like my world was crashing down. I needed something to keep my mind at ease. So, what I go do? I go and get high! Got me an OZ of loud and a couple grams of powder to try to take the pain away. I went and got me a hotel room and for 2 days, I stayed to myself. On the 3rd day, I called up one of my home boy Poppy to come with me and my dumb ass ended up sleeping with this dude. When I woke up and realized what had occurred, I told him not to never tell a soul and I meant that shit! Poppy and I are the same age and that was my nigga for years, but it was never on no sexual shit between me and him. But I was in a vulnerable state and at the time I needed someone around me I could trust. So, after my 3-day binge I stopped getting high, reality sunk in more. My grandma had talked to the social worker Mrs. Trixey Baldin and she gave me her telephone number and I called. She picked up the phone and she needed to get proof of my income and where I lived at because she needed to do a home visit because I told her I didn't stay there, which I didn't. So, I gave her the address on Decian Rd. but now I'm wondering when I will be able to get my daughter back. When I called, she told me that they usually investigate for 12months after they are satisfied then they close their case. I'm pissed and right then, all I needed to know was Mrs. Trixey's address so I could go blow her shit the fuck up! She didn't know me for real. My baby didn't want for shit! Matter of fact I needed to find out who called them in the first place. So, I was on a mission! I was tired of people fucking with me and mines, so right then I needed guns, a lot of ammo and I needed a

CHAPTER 8

car. My mind was going a 100 mph with thoughts of how I was going to snap on a MF in 2.5 seconds. Not thinking straight I knew I had to go sit down somewhere and think this through, it's too much going on right now and I need to settle down so I goes and chill for a couple days to come up with a game plan.

At the same time, I'm throwing up all over the place. I thought that it might've been because I had stayed up for 3 days getting high off powder. Still throwing up, I figured that I might need to go eat and drink something because it had been a long week. So, after I ate and drank a lot of juices, I threw that up and the first thing that popped up in my head was I know I'm not pregnant. I panicked! Straight to the clinic I went and sure enough I was pregnant again! OMG! It sent me into a deeper depression because I had already had one child in DSS custody and now I'm pregnant again and in my mind, Kairi or Poppy is the baby's father. I couldn't believe it, I truly believed that it couldn't get any worse. I then went home and locked myself in my room for a week. I didn't want to be bothered by no one. It seemed like everything was moving just way too fast. What the fuck I'm going to do now? I have absolutely no one to turn to! I should just end it all here and now!!

CHAPTER 9

EVERYONE CAME BY the house on Glacian Rd. to try to lift my spirits up. Jersey even came by and brought the baby something, but I really didn't want to be bothered. It seemed like the word spread like wildfire. My boy Kairi even stayed there with me. He called himself looking out for me, but I wasn't stupid. The house was booming and so he stayed there to get his shit off. I didn't mess with too many people because I always had been a loner, and females that was definitely a no, no. They start too much drama. At first, I gave the social worker the house on Glacian Rd. address but I knew that wasn't going to work because that was a trap house, so I had to come up with something and fast. And besides, that house was getting off the hook. I didn't even feel comfortable with staying there myself, so I told FeFe that I was leaving and her and Kairi could keep the house because I was out! I made the money; money didn't make me. I wasn't about to stick around waiting on the boys (police) to come. I could set up shop elsewhere because I always kept something up my sleeve. It was this lady I knew whose name was Jackie and she and her husband Julius stayed on St. August Ave. It was a green 3 apartment duplex. 2 Apartments downstairs and 1 upstairs. The one upstairs was Vacant. Jackie had the house on the right and this guy whose name was Barry had the one on the left. Barry also had his son whose name was Big L at his house trapping, and he was a fat funny ass dude. He would sit out on the front porch with his 40 bull in one hand and kept his strap on his lap. Back in 99 that firearm by felon rule didn't apply then, so niggas stayed strapped. I use to always sit back and wonder how

CHAPTER 9

many 40's that dude could drink and how could he comprehend. The crazy shit about that is after a month with me being over there chilling and talking with him, Fatima's cousin Lil Mick shot and killed Big L at Valero's. Lil Mick eventually walked for killing him because it was self-defense. The short time I got to know him, I can say he was a cool dude. It ended up with me over there by myself. St. August Ave. which were 2 blocks up from Mapel St. so I was on the outskirts. My name had always ringed bells because I kept that fire and, once I got settled on Mapel St. all the boys in the family came right behind me. Lamont 9 years old, Wayne 9 years old and David and Chris were 8 years old and those lil niggas was the worst. The police would have to take them to school every day. Smokers also on the block would come and find me to tell me what they were doing. Them was some bad ass little boys and they would terrorize my ass. I would give them $10 apiece and tell them to take their ass to school. But shit, I would see these niggas 4 hours later right back smiling at me. I would ask them what they have done with their money because with $40 they could have done a lot with it and they did. They said they bought some weed, cigarettes and food. Boy, I tell you! These lil niggas got to the point that they collected other lil niggas with them. So, it was them 4 and more and soon it became a football team full of lil niggas. I had to ask them, what am I supposed to do? It's too many of yall. So, I got a room in the rooming house on Flushing St. and that was their home. I couldn't see them outside because these lil niggas wasn't about to be blowing my spot up and besides, no one else cared because if they did, they wouldn't be out there in the first place. I told them to go to school and after school, come and get the $10 apiece and go back to the room, and that's what they did. I was on St. August and they had the rooming house on Flushing St., and I tell you, those boys were off the hook! And before you know it, something had happened to John John and Jersey's spot on Mapel St. It was 3 rooms in the rooming house on Flushing St. I had the front room where the front door was at. One of the other rooms there was vacant, and another guy named Dirty had the back room. So, in time I went and rented the middle room out. I let Lamont and the boys move to the middle room and let John-John get the

ALL I HAVE

front so they could get money. I told them to lookout and pay me $100 a day because that wasn't shit for a spot that was going to guarantee that and a whole lot more. We had a deal. It was Al, John-John, Poppy, and a couple of other people there at the time and I would come over to check on the boys to see what they were doing because they stayed deep in that room. Al and John-John looked out for them by getting them a video game and after that, you couldn't tell them nothing. They had a lil change in their pockets, games and shelter so shoot, they were on cloud 9. Everything was good for a couple of months until one day I happened to pop up on Flushing St. just to be nosey. I really didn't have to come over there, but I had gotten tired of sitting on St. August and wanted to get some fresh air. So, I walked the 4 blocks to Flushing St., and it was packed in there that day. It was like 7 of us in the front room but none of the boys was there. Guns, coke, money, weed, oh we were lit and the next thing we see out the window is the police in jump out suits coming in the yard. Everyone panicked and Poppy started to dive out the window, but his gun fell out of his jacket and he slid back in the window. That's when the police said, "gun fellas!" They then said, "Hey you, back up from the house" So now we got a standoff situation outside and everyone was pissed at this nigga and at the same time, trying to figure out what to do. We had a furnace in the front room that went inside the wall, so I opened the latch and told everybody to drop everything down there, all the dope, money, guns, everything. Al even threw his I.D. in the wall. Why? Who knows! But, now the police on the bull horn asking everyone to come out with their hands up. We were all wondering who was going to take the gun charge, but we eventually went out one by one and they told us to lay on the ground side by side. They asked who's gun it was and because I had no charges, I took the gun charge. The police knew it wasn't a woman who was trying to jump out the window but since I confessed, they charged me with it. They found some weed in the room and charged everyone else with it and took everyone to jail. My bond was only $500 for stolen goods and I hopped out for $75. I went and got my Uncle Rodney so he could help me bust through the wall because the police never looked. So, we got something like a hammer but with a bigger head and he beat and beat and beat on that wall until we got up in there. It was like striking gold in there. Jackpot! Rodney was looking at me like shit, what you giving me? So, I looked out for him, called a cab and threw everything in a pillowcase. Rodney dropped me off on St. August and he went on to his destination. Once I got dropped off, I called the bondsman and got every one of them niggas up out of there and gave Al and John their shit back. Them niggas after that gave me the utmost respect because any fake MF would have bounced. That's not in my DNA so they gave me $3,000 and they took everything else. That was the end of them on Flushing St. Lamont, Eugene, Wayne, and Chris all had other plans because they started hustling. The Money was already coming so why not pick up the pieces? On top of that, they still came and got their $10 apiece from me. These lil niggas was getting on my nerves! But I know one thing, I really wasn't thinking correctly when I took that gun charge. I had just gotten that case with Social Services a couple of months prior and that was going to hurt me a lot. At that moment I was trying to calm everyone down because that situation would have really gotten way out of control if the police would've got their hands on everything. All of us then would've been gone for life but "Thank You God!" When it comes down to the police, you can't freeze up, you must think first and always go off your instincts because time waits for no one. It's a valuable lesson that I've learned after that. The police must have a search warrant for every room in a rooming house. If Poppy wouldn't have tried to jump out that window and dropped that gun, they were never coming in that room because they only had a search warrant for the boys' room, the middle room. So, people if you got to do what you got to do, do your dirt in one room and have the other room as a safe room. But in the safe room, don't do no business there and if or when they come, they only are able to go in the room you conduct business in and not the safe room.

Now I'm sitting pretty money wise but on the other hand I am pregnant and it's kicking my ass. I had an agreement with Jackie and Julius. I'd use Barry's house next door to work out of and I paid him $100 a day and I also paid Jackie and Julius. Man, the morning pregnancy sickness I had was terrible, I didn't even want to get up at times, but I had to go get that check. So, one day I decided to go check Jersey out because it had been a while since I last seen him. For some reason he had dropped off the face of the earth, so I called him up and he told me to come see him on Ranson, behind Food Mart on Caleigh Blvd. I went and checked him out but when I got over there, I had seen this cat that caught my eye. "MMM! Where is he going?" I was saying to myself. Then I see Jersey pop out the back with his linen suit and slacks. Okay they looking spiffy tonight but never mind Jersey, who is that other cat he with? Brother was looking fine to me. His head was kind of big but that was a small thing compared to his overall appearance. He had a young Lawrence Fishburn look and he moved like he was so confident with himself. Then I saw the two ladies they were going out with. Okay I see y'all. I copped a little something then I left. So now I'm on a mission because I needed to know who this cat was that was with Jersey. But I knew exactly who to ask, ReRe! Okay, so I went to St. August, got my work together, weighed everything out in grams because I only bought an ounce just to see what he was working with. But when I went, I saw something that I wanted and what I want I tends to get. So, once I got me straight, it was now time to do the DNA! ReRe wasn't hard to find because she was standing out on the block. I be bugging sometimes because I knew how Jersey was handling ReRe. That nigga thought that he was a pimp which he was but fuck all that, I still asked ReRe who that guy Jersey went out with tonight! She said, "oh you are talking about", and before she got the name out, she stopped and asked, "went out?", I said "yeah and who was the guy with him?" She said something that I couldn't make out because she was too upset. She was then on a mission to find out what club they went to. Why, who knows because all Jersey was going to do was beat her the fuck up. That nigga was something different. At first, he was cool. Well let me rephrase that, he'd never done anything to me. It was just his attitude towards women that through him off to me, but one thing I can say about him he was a smooth criminal. So, I went

CHAPTER 9

ahead and let ReRe vent a while until she found her a cab and I hopped in with her. Somehow, she knew exactly which club he was going to because we pulled up and told the cab to put us on waiting time. We paid and she went one way and I went the other. The next thing I see is Jersey giving ReRe a 2 piece in the club and she dropped dead to the floor. I saw people scattering and then I saw Jersey leave out the front door. While ReRe was trying to get up off the floor I was saying to myself, if I would've known all this was going to happen I wouldn't have never said anything. I know next time, so we hopped in the cab and she let me out on St. August and she went on to her destination. After all of that, I still didn't get to see who I really wanted to see, and I still didn't know his name. Boy that ReRe, she was something else! So, I was still on my mission to try to figure out who this mystery man was. I knew then that I wasn't about to go through ReRe anymore because after everything that went on that night at the club, they were all boo'd up like nothing never happened the next day. After what I went through with Kym, I lost a lot of respect for niggas that treated women that way.

I had this nigga whose name was Unc that was throwing me the work for a stupid number, $600 a oz. He kept that heat. No one on that side of town could touch what I had, and I was solo. I always ran by myself because the more people you put in your business the worse off you were. You can't tell on yourself. I would send a smoker to Criss St. to see if the mystery man was over there, but he was barely there. I tried to find out who he was dealing with and I did and come to find out it was a girl whose name was Tina also. She stayed on Criss St. Okay that was a plus because we had the same name and so I would ride through there to see if he would be outside, but I could never catch him. I did catch up with him one time when my boy Chuck took me over there. Because niggas didn't know me, they charged me $200 more than what I was getting them for, but I just had to see him. It was my chance to see him up close because that brother was fine to me.

ALL I HAVE

He had on a Polo cap, Polo shirt to match and shorts with some shell toe Adidas that set it all off. All I could say was, "what's up?" I couldn't get nothing else out of my mouth. Besides they had a house full of people over there and also, I thought that it was his girl house. So, I just got my shit and left. I asked Chuck what was his name and he finally told me "Chico"! That name to me was the sweetest name I'd ever heard. It was like I was infatuated with this man and we'd never spoken before. OMG! Something was wrong here because to me that wasn't healthy. But once I got his name, I couldn't get it off my mind. With a name now I was one step closer to achieving my goal. But after that night that was the last time, I'd laid my eyes on him, it was like he dropped off the face of the earth. I had heard a few stories that the police had hit the house over on Criss St. and that's the same house I had went with Chuck, but I didn't hear if they took anybody or not. ReRe disappeared also so I figured Chico was gone and I didn't even have enough time to get to know him. But life went on. By this time, I was 2 months pregnant and things wasn't going too good with my Social Service case because of the gun charge I had recently got. I was put on probation for that and at the same time the Social Service lady was trying to figure out where I was working at. I told her I'm cleaning houses at night because it seemed like this bitch wasn't trying to let up. One day my social worker came to the house and I then look to the left and see one of my smokers ducking trying to hide from Mrs. Trixey. I thought that he was hiding from a car going down the street or something but, Naw it was her ass! I didn't find that out until a little later down the line, but it's a small world! And this bitch had the nerve to be all on me. She needed to check her household first. If I only knew that then, I would've had leverage on her ass. Her husband was smoking more rocks than a lil bit!! But now the world going to know, and this is facts I'm stating. But things weren't going right with Destiny my daughter situation and it had almost been a year. I hated this fuckin legal system! So, I went into a deep depression and mind you, I'm pregnant again but this time I didn't have the strength to get up. All I did was sleep and my Uncle Rodney would come chill with

CHAPTER 9

me. Tamara, Jackie and Julius were there and money was being made but I just wasn't working. Kairi would sometimes come through and smoke a blunt or 2 with me and getting on my damn nerves when he kept asking me was I pregnant by him. I would tell that nigga no! But a nigga going to be a nigga. Poppy would ask me the same thing and I would tell him no also and to just get out of my face because I didn't want to look at a nigga. To me I didn't need no nigga because I had mines financially. The police had picked up my brothers and cousins and took them to a group home. I looked at it like, now they could get to school and try to get something going right in their life because at that moment, I had my own stuff going on to be bothered with anyone else. The spot was booming, and Jersey would send a smoker to the house to buy what I had, and he tried to cook his like what I had, but he couldn't. I respected him for showing me respect, when he didn't have to but when the smoker would tell me who sent them it would be funny to me! Me and Unc had a good thing going on and to my knowledge I was the only one he was dealing with because he didn't need anyone else. The house was booming to the point that I couldn't stay there anymore so I went and got me a hotel room The Studio Plus on Wake Tow Dr. They had just built those hotel rooms there so by my girl Dee working at the front desk, she hooked me up with the Suite on the first floor. It was nice and for $125 a night it was a small thing to a giant. At 18 years old at the time, I still didn't have any guidance so all I knew to do was make money, spend that shit and make it right back up. When it came down to clothes and shoes, when I stepped out, believe me, all eyes are on me! Females stayed hating but it didn't make me no difference because I was used to it. It got to the point that I couldn't even keep enough coke over there because Unc would come over and sit with me and that shit would fly out the door so quick. I was loving that, and I was not even selling any weight. On the bust down and it was flying straight like that!

CHAPTER 10

HERE COME KAIRI. It seemed like everywhere I went this nigga would pop up! But that was my nigga. He was down to earth and he wasn't a troublemaker. One day he asked me could he and his homeboy come over and work at nighttime. I didn't have no problem with that because I did a lot of Bingo also and by 7pm I would go and play Bingo anyways. I told him yeah but he had to explain to his people that you all would have to use the back door and I was going to use the front door, and as long as you paid the house people, it didn't make me no difference. We shook on it. He then told me he would see me the next day at the same time. Instead of me going to Bingo that night I sat around just to make sure everything went as planned. I didn't know the guy he had with him, so I wanted to make sure it wasn't any misunderstandings. I suddenly heard a knock at the back door. I kind of figured it was Kairi, but I was busy in the front room with a few of my people. In the back it was the kitchen then beside the kitchen it was the bedroom and then the living room, bathroom and front door. Kairi came through and spoke but the other guy stayed in the back. I really wasn't paying any attention to who was in the back as long as we knew it wasn't the police but, Barry was on the front porch so we could see everything that was going through the backyard. So, I'm making my money in the front as agreed and I don't know what Kairi had told this guy, but he popped an attitude of trying to figure out what I was doing there. Once I really laid my eyes on this dude, my heart dropped, OMG! It was CHICO! He was asking why I

CHAPTER 10

was there, and Julius was like she the one that's been here man, calm down. Chico got crunk real quick and now I'm looking at Kairi like why you didn't holla at him before you all got here, then it wouldn't be any miscommunications. Kairi said he thought that I wasn't going to be there then, but he would holla at him now. I told him that I thought that now would be a good time because he a lil hostile for what reason? I wasn't feeling Chico's attitude because he made me feel uncomfortable around him. I was pregnant so that could've had something to do with it. But what I did was closed the door in Jackie's room so they couldn't look and see everything that was going on with me. Plus, I wasn't worried about them taking my clients because my shit was set in stone. No one had what I had period! But I did tell Unc that from now on I wasn't going to meet him over there because it was too much going on money wise and Unc was an asset like lights and water, so I needed him safe and sound. I would see him before I came out or when I went in. A few days had gone by and Kairi and Chico had their routine going smoothly. They worked the back and would take turns going to the block and bringing the money back to the house. I had Julius tell me on the low "Alabama" liked me. He called Chico Alabama because that's where both of them were from so Julius and Chico became close because of that. That was music to my ears because I was feeling Chico way before he could ever imagine. So, what I did was made sure I was fresh every day because he caught me off guard when he first got there. But once I realized who he was, I knew that was my opportunity. He's on my court now and I wasn't going to let him slip away this time! It just seemed like every time I was around him, I would get stuck. I wasn't the shy type but for some reason I would get butterflies in my stomach and would get on that shy shit. I didn't know what was going on with me. If Kairi was around, I would be my normal self, rolling blunts and laughing but as soon as he would leave, I would go in the living room. I couldn't be around Chico for some reason. Maybe it's because I didn't know him like I knew Kairi. I don't know, but one thing I did know, I didn't want him to slip through my fingers like he did before. As a matter of fact, where did he go? It didn't matter because all that mattered was that he was here now. But how was I going to get the ball rolling? On the other hand, should I even try; I thought to myself because he seemed like he had some issues. It was something up with this nigga. The more I was around him I told myself to hold up Tina, let's get to know this one first or at least try! But things had worked out smooth in the house once we got on one accord. They had their peoples going to the back and I had mines going through the front and I would sit in the kitchen with them, smoke blunts, and I would also cook my crab legs. My pregnancy for some reason had me craving crab legs so yes, I cooked those. For a while I had stopped going to Bingo so I would just chill and enjoy their company. I remember one night after we sat and smoked blunt after blunt, we had gotten so high the whole house had fallen asleep. Niggas and babies were everywhere in a one-bedroom house. All a sudden, someone woke me up by calling my name. I was asleep on the couch and I knew where I was at but the voice I couldn't catch. Once I adjusted my eyes because it was dark and the music was playing on the radio, I heard him say "Tina" again and that's when I caught that country accent. It was Chico. He was asking me if I was awake and I told him "yeah, what's up?" I then sat up on the sofa and he came and sat beside me. Everyone was knocked out because all you heard was snoring everywhere. Jackie and Julius was in their room on the bed, Kairi was laying on the floor in between their room and in the living room, my Uncle Rodney was laying behind the front door in the living room and Tamara and her baby Pepsi was laying in front of the radio in between the front door and the bathroom door. We were deep in there that night but we were comfortable at the same time. I had some weed left over and he did also, so I took my weed out and rolled a blunt. He matched a blunt with me and he got right to the point. He asked me was I seeing anybody. He kind of shocked me when he asked me that because I didn't see that coming. I was hoping but not that soon. So, I told him no and then he asked me about me and Kairi. I told him that was just a one-time thing, nothing more because he was just good people. Chico

CHAPTER 10

said he wanted to see what my answer was going to be because he had already asked Kairi the same question and he gave him the same answer. So, then he asked me what I was looking for in a man. He messed me up with that question because I'd never thought about it. I paused for a few minutes to really register what was going on because it seemed to me like he was going to ask me out. I couldn't believe that the whole time, he was feeling me also. WOW! It was a good feeling because now I'm coming to the realization that I'm the girl that all the niggas dream of! I'm the Janet Jackson! I wouldn't have never thought of myself as one of the popular or pretty girls because to this day I don't. But the attention others give me makes me think that it's possible. When I answered his question, I gave him the first thing that came to mind. "The only thing I'm looking for in a guy is for him to keep it 100% with me, that's the bottom line." His response was then "I got you" and after that, we kissed, and it was the best kiss I'd ever had in my life. It was like a dream come true and that kiss lead to him up inside of me. It was like fireworks and after we got it in, we wind down on the couch. A slow song came on the radio. It said that they kissed at 3:36 in the morning and when both of us looked over at the clock it was the exact same time as the radio! We looked at each other amazed and laughed about it, put our clothes on and he fell asleep between my legs on the couch. When I woke up the next morning he was gone. No number or nothing. So, I caught me a cab and went to my hotel room. I had bad morning sickness and I didn't even feel like going back out the next day. I stayed in, but I did keep a cell phone and I told Julius once Chico got over there to give him my number to call me. He did call and I told him to come see me after he got off that night. I didn't feel like working none that day although I knew that I would be missing money but all money isn't good money. But my body felt like I needed the rest. I didn't see Chico until 3am when he comes knocking on the hotel door. We slept the night away! The next day I asked him about the girl named Tina from Criss St. Who he was dealing with and he had told me that he wasn't messing with her anymore because her sister had taken $800

ALL I HAVE

from him and Tina allowed her to do it. I left that conversation alone. But after that night that we first got together we was inseparable. We would be out late nights together trapping and the house would be so packed that we would dip to Mapel St. go through the cut to get to Dennis house, knock on his backdoor, rent a room out in his house and we would have sex there. OMG! And the way he would kiss my cookies umm!! Amazing! Nose wide open! It's over for me. OMG! Every time we would have sex, we would always make love to each other. I fell in love with him at first sight and Chico had me wrapped around his finger and there's no need to front about that. But I use to always wonder was the feeling mutual? As much as we were making love, you would think so but he had a weird way of showing it. It might've been because of the age difference. I was 18 and he was 23. But one thing I could tell, he loved the cookies and the meats was good also, so I had patience! Things started to get hectic on St. August St. After a while with Kairi and Chico being Jersey homeboy, here comes Jersey smiling in my face with that one gold tooth, talking about "Tina! We need to talk!" Oh boy, here we go! Okay "Jersey, what's up with you?" I kind of figured what he had wanted but I wanted to hear him say it. I'd already made up in my mind that whatever agreement we made, Jackie and Julius house would be off limits. But what I did have was another spot for them right on the corner at Daphne and Marvin's house. I told him that he could have his people meet them there and that Bobby also had a room at the rooming house across the street so they could chill there with everything and have the workers at Marvin and Daphne house. It was Perfect! And that's how he played it. I would pull up on the block and would catch his partner who name is Money. He was posted at the rooming house playing the porch and Jersey would be right across at the other house while me and Kairi would be at Jackie house. They really weren't messing with my money because they were the heavy hitters. I always dealt with the smokers. But once Jersey came around, I didn't see Chico as much. I asked myself, was he too ashamed because I was younger than him? Or was it something else? I really didn't let it get to me as much, but I would get to the bottom of it eventually. He did come to the hotel and stayed the night with me, but he never brought no clothes, so I used to ask myself where was he staying then? He had a lot of secrets with him. He was a very mysterious person, but I never pressed him. I knew he would come around during his own time. Some nights at the hotel I would see Jersey come and holla at him and every time he would leave out. I would see his pretty smile and it would make me feel good inside to see him smile. Chico also had one gold tooth in his mouth in the same place Jersey had his. There I go again in love and pregnant with someone else's child! But it didn't bother him one bit. The work they were getting couldn't touch the grade of work that I was getting so when I would purchase something, Kairi would ask me to snatch him up something also. I'd charge him the same Jersey was charging him and I'd keep the rest. Nothing personal just business! After that, Kairi wanted to cop from my people directly but I would never tell anyone who I was getting my work from.

One day, I was sitting outside in the car with Unc coping my shit from him and the next thing I know I see Chico and Jersey pull up behind us and parked the car in the parking spot. I looked in the side mirrors hoping they can't see me, but they looked dead at the car like they knew who the nigga was. I'm not sure if Unc recognized them or not because he was too busy rolling the blunt, but I was on their ass because I didn't want them to know who I was sitting in the car with. As I continued looking out the side mirrors, Chico and Jersey went ahead through the side door of the hotel, but I see both of them looking out the second story stairs hallway window and Chico eyes locked right with mines. The look on his face told me that it was time to go see what's on his mind. So, I went ahead and wrapped it up and headed to the hotel room. As soon as I got in the room, I was hit with third degree questions, so I showed him the work. I never knew what they were working with but I only had some light shit and that wasn't shit! I wouldn't never get no more than I could make disappear because I didn't like holding on to a lot of work. I liked my shit to be gone in that day and that's about how long that took on the bust down. So now he had seen what's going on and plus he already knew the quality, so I was kind of nervous to see how this was going to play out. I got ready to go out but before I went out Chico stopped me while I was heading to the door. He asked me could I get them some, so I called him up and got them what they needed. It shocked them how quick he came to bring it to me. So, the transaction was made and they were satisfied. So, I leave and head to the block. I didn't put the tax on him because that was my nigga. I wanted to see him come up and that's exactly what he did eventually. Then one day I was looking for him and I couldn't find him. I called his phone got no answer. I called his people and got no answer. Something said call the hotel room, so I called and no answer there either. I called a few more times and finally someone picked up the phone but hung it back up. I know this MF was still there because someone picked up. I then called a cab and went straight to the hotel room. I couldn't wait to get up the stairs. We were on the 3rd floor and I didn't even want to wait on the elevator so I went straight for the steps. I knew that the nigga was in there so then I began banging and saying "Chico, you gonna let me in?" Finally, the door opened and quickly I was snatched in and one of them put his hands over my mouth. Okay, now y'all got me fucked up! I look behind the room door and I see another nigga I didn't even know. WTF y'all doing in this hotel room and why this shit looking like this? Then I see guns, OMG! It's too much going on so one of them takes me to where the bed was, and I see someone wrapped in duct tape from head to toe. I saw the guns but when I saw duct tape, boiling hot water and salt, I wanted to say something but the look on their faces they meant business and then I see Kairi. He told me to be quiet. Boy when you think you know a nigga; you are often proven wrong. So, I didn't say one word. He walked me over to the window and I saw ReRe and a dark-skinned lady parked at the hotel next door. I'm still dumb founded as to why? And who is this person duct taped? When I looked back with confusion on my face, one of the guys

CHAPTER 10

proceeds to take the tape off slowly, starting at the top of his head. He wouldn't take it off his eyes but when I saw the bald head and complexion, I knew instantly who it was. UNC! Damn my nigga! The whole time that nigga was using me to get access to my connect. All kinds of feelings had gone through my head. Hatred, fake, phony ass niggas. They played me! How could they do that to me? I was really feeling him, and he played me like that! What happened to keeping it 100%? All that shit went out the door. I was getting lightheaded and I had to figure out what I should do. At the moment there was nothing I could do with 3 big niggas with guns, so I put a brave face on and watched Unc get poked with a knife, salt poured in his wounds, hit with boiling hot water while his mouth was duct taped so he couldn't scream. His hands and feet were taped so he couldn't go anywhere but this nigga Unc tried to jump out the window headfirst anyways. There wasn't enough impact because his legs were taped so he was trapped. My heart was aching for him because that was my boy. I couldn't help but beat myself up about how I'd allowed my privacy to be invaded like that. I should've known better and the one I was close with I couldn't believe how he out of all people allowed this to happen. While Unc was being tortured, and one of the guys was on the telephone getting instructions from someone on the telephone as to where to bring the money and product to. They had let Unc rest for a while and then Kairi kicked him, then said if he's dead she must die too. In my mind I'm trying to figure out where Chico and Jersey come in at because these niggas wouldn't even have access to my room unless Chico gave them the key. Hatred towards Chico came over me I said to myself, if I make it out in one piece, I will never speak to neither one of them. I looked at Kairi like you really going to play it like this? Damn homie, I thought we was cool? Then suddenly Kairi said no wait a second, let me make a call first to see what we are going to do with her. After he hangs up the phone Kairi then say we can't touch a hair on her head, we must take her with us. So, I'm guessing that was the phone conversation he needed to hear because we left the hotel right after that. We all left in one car and we went across the street to another hotel and picked up ReRe. But who was the other lady? I kind of figured it to be Unc's wife because who else would have brought everything they wanted? So, after picking ReRe up, they then we went right up the block to the Homeland Suites on Wake Fore Rd. I'm looking at ReRe and she's looking dumb founded. I'm like Bitch I know you know what's going on but y'all got it! Just let me go and yall niggas don't never have to worry about me anymore. "Fuck all yall" I said to myself. I wasn't gonna say that shit out loud after what I'd just seen. These niggas were crazy as fuck!

We finally got to the other hotel room and another guy was there waiting. Just like the other cats in my hotel room, I didn't know who these guys were. They had this shit all planned out and if I wouldn't have never suspected something was wrong when whoever pick up the phone and hung up, I would've never got caught up in this shit. If I would've never met this nigga! Matter fact where is Chico because I haven't seen him yet? Then it's a knock on the door and sure enough it's Chico and Jersey walking in. They always say looks can be deceiving! He was a wolf in sheep's clothing! I knew this nigga was behind this but in the back of my mind I was hoping he wasn't. He wasn't there at the time but shit what difference does it make. One of the other cats locked the door behind Chico n Jersey with ReRe and me frozen on the couch in the living room part of the hotel room waiting to see what was going to happen next. I see them all in the kitchen counting everything and splitting up everything. As they are splitting everything up and everyone is about to leave, one of the guys pull the strap out on another guy and patted him down and took the gun off him and took his half. WTF! These niggas are ruthless and then he told him to get the fuck out. After that Chico, Jersey, ReRe and myself we all got in the car and bounced. I had no idea where we were heading but I just wanted to go home. I had a banging ass headache and I done saw enough for the year. I was done at that very moment. I was ready to retire and go get a job. These MF's done just robbed my connect, robbed one another

CHAPTER 10

and it's no telling what they about to do with me. We were driving for a while and we finally stop at a gas station. ReRe then gets in the driver seat and the whole time these niggas were riding listening to Mary J Blige "My life" now these hard ass niggas was singing Mary and knew every song from beginning to end!

CHAPTER 11

Be careful what you ask for!

I DIDN'T SAY a word the whole time we were riding on Highway 20, going towards ATL. We ended up in Birmingham, Alabama. Me and Chico had argued before we left. And when we got there Chico took all my things. I had no phone, no money, no nothing. Jersey did the same with ReRe. They then took us to a house in the boonies where it seemed like people were guarding us to the point that we couldn't go outside, and they left us there for almost a week. It was the worst feeling of my life where I would pray "LORD PLEASE GET ME BACK HOME JESUS!" And where is my shit? He had taken my clothes, money, all my shit. At the time, I hated this dude and I never wanted to see this nigga every again! When they finally came to see us, they said that we were finally leaving to go back home and I was so ready. We're in Alabama with crocodiles and alligators, fuck all that, let's go! When we got back to NC, I couldn't get out the car fast enough. And it wasn't no need to say nothing to me period! I was out! I hops out and I parted ways with ReRe, and I went straight to St. August St. I asked Jackie and Julius had they seen Kairi and they said it had been a while since they last saw him. Karma is a bitch, just make sure that bitch is beautiful! In my mind, I'm thinking like I'm not never going to see Chico or Jersey again. Well check this shit out Chico and Jersey come popping up on St. August St. and instead of them coming to Jackie house, they went to Marvin's house. I just stayed in the house

CHAPTER 11

and cried because I couldn't believe this nigga. I loved Chico so how could he do that to me? I dried my face off and I went up to Marvin's house because I wanted answers. "Okay, so where my shit at?" He had it the whole time and was waiting on me to come and say something to him. He gave me my shit back and I got out of the picture. As soon as I leave St. August street walking towards Mapel St. I see these lil niggas go into Hills St. store. I walk up to see what's going on because it was my cousins and a couple more lil niggas was robbing the place and they had no one to lookout. I couldn't just leave them in the blind, so I stayed out on the corner to make sure they were straight and once they ran out, I bounced. These Niggas crazy! It stayed lit out there! I walked off from the store and went around the corner to find ReRe. I couldn't find her, so I walk back to Marvin's house, but Chico was gone. A couple minutes later Chico came busting through the door blanking on me because someone said I had something to do with the store getting robbed. He then left again, slamming the door behind him. With Chico, I experienced just about everything for the first time. The years before him I'd never had an orgasm (or a nut as the guys would say), but with him just kissing his lips would make me melt. I would get out the shower and he would have the baby oil sitting on the dresser waiting for me and I would just lay on my stomach and close my eyes. Just knowing what was about to happen I would melt automatically and once the baby oil hit my back and his hands followed, I would want to just flip over and jump right on him and just do all the work. Yes, the chemistry we had together was "sacred". Damn, hold up, I lost myself for a minute! But during that moment and time all that sacred shit was out the door! I couldn't believe he just came at me sideways like we didn't just leave Alabama. And now I must worry about how Unc was feeling about the situation. Matter fact how did he end up at my hotel room in the first place? Shit real out there!

A few days had past and I haven't heard anything from Chico, Kairi none of them niggas so I'm guessing these cats done got missing,

ALL I HAVE

thank God so With these niggas gone, it's now time to face reality and try to move on with my life. As much as I wanted to rewind back time and wish that I'd never met Chico in the first place, I couldn't. My connect was gone also, so I had to do some serious thinking. ReRe would come around sit and smoke a couple blunts with me on St. August Ave. and all she would do is sit around and talk about Jersey. At first I had thought she had something to do with the set up but after seeing how Jersey was mistreating her n also holding her against her will then I knew she was in the blind too so I let my guard down when it came to her. I was tired of hearing her talk about them because what was done was done. I'm almost five months pregnant and I'd gotten nothing accomplished. I told ReRe, "Let's get this money!"

So, after Jersey and Chico had left, me and ReRe formed a good relationship. We were the go getters out here. No one didn't bother us at all because they didn't know where Jersey or Chico was at. Them niggas had the streets on lock! Niggas was with that gun play for real. People would ask where Chico and Jersey were at but we would always say they out here somewhere. A couple months had gone by and things were looking up for me now. I had met some Cuban cats that had that fish scale. Their prices were cheap and during that time coke prices had went up drastically. So that was love and I had met them from one of my smokers that would come see me. She had her peoples in Burlington, N.C. and she was telling me what type of niggas they were. But at times she would get tired of the drive and ReRe would try to get me to turn her on to my people but this time I told not a soul. I would sell ReRe hers but I rock solo when it comes down to my business! You live and you learn! Plus, she had a son by Jersey, so I most definitely wasn't trusting that. Man, every time I thought about them niggas, I would get heated. When Chico had first left out the house after the argument, I thought I was going to see him later on, but a week went by with no contact at all. I had got feelings for him fast. Love at first sight for sure. Two more weeks went by and still nothing. Not even a call. A part of me wanted him back so badly but

CHAPTER 11

my gut was saying let him go! I was so confused. With him heavy on my mind while sitting on the porch on Ponder St. playing solitary and a lady came by and she said "I bet you don't even know what game you play" I said "why? What's up?" she said "you are playing against the devil. You can make a bet and if you win the two out of three, your wish will come true but if you lose, the devil can have your soul!" Because I knew that I was a good player in the game, my dumb ass bet him! I then said if I win, I want you to bring Chico back to me and if I lose you got it. I wouldn't advise no one to even play when it's pertaining to your soul because it's one of the dumbest things you could ever do. But "Thank God for his grace", I won. But the shit really didn't faze me because it was only a game. After that, I never saw her again. During the first month of him leaving, I was missing him but after time had went by, I saw what his true motive was. He wasn't a real nigga after all. Damn, they all played me! Fuck'em all!!! I finally got Chico off my mind and he had become a distant memory. I'm 7 months pregnant and I must think about my kids and bettering myself to be thinking about any niggas right now. Besides Thanksgiving around the corner it's time to get ready for this drought that comes around during this time of year so it's time to stack this paper. And on top of that I can't wait to see what my grandma Lynda is cooking for the holidays. By this time Jackie and Julius had left St. August St and had moved to the West side off Gormen St. near Eastern Blvd. I'd known way too many people to be left out, so now I'm on Flushing St. at a lady whose name was Valarie house. Me and ReRe stuck together and we paid her $50 a piece to hustle from her house. We wouldn't pay $100 a day especially if they smoked crack, and I been knowing Valarie since I was 8 so she didn't have no problem. It's a typical day out on the block. The block was flooded with the police today, more than the norm. I would usually pay someone to check the perimeter but for some reason I decided to walk to the store myself to see what I could find out. I'm glad I went this day because while I'm walking a car pulls up beside me and roll down the window and tells me to get in. When he pulls the hood off his head, I knew right then who it

ALL I HAVE

was, Unc! My heart jumped out my body. I was hesitant of getting in the car, but he said, he knew that I didn't have anything to do with what happened. I felt a 1,000lbs lighter but still on guard. So, I gets in the car and I tell him to pull in the store parking lot. I also let him know that the niggas had left right after that incident to let him feel more comfortable. He said that he'd heard when I came knocking on the hotel room door and what they said when they finally let me in. So, I asked Unc what made him come there and that's when he told me that he was dealing with Kairi before me but he had beat him out of some money and that's why he stopped dealing with him. He went on to say that Kairi had called him and said that he wanted to cop something from him and pay him some of the money that he owed. So Unc took that as a good look. And once Kairi told Unc that they could meet at my room he felt even better. But when he got there, he knew he was in trouble and once he heard me banging and talking shit outside the door, that's when he knew that I had not a clue what was going on. Thank God! I had told him that I'd been worried all that time that he'd thought I had something to do with it but now I knew that I was good! But what I didn't understand was why would you come after the nigga beat you before? Unc's reply was "Greed"! Get you every time! Unc further said that he'd been looking for me after the incident happened to let me know that he knew that I wasn't involved and to get up with him and that's when he gave me his number. He then let me out at the store, and I went on about my business. I was able to finally exhale because that was a huge relief off my shoulders. I told no one of the conversation that we had.

Thanksgiving came around and as usual my grandma Lynda threw down. Your traditional Thanksgiving with the regular deserts. ReRe had even came and enjoyed the holidays with us. But while we were there, ReRe phone began ringing. Her eyes lit up like she'd saw a ghost and went to the bathroom and took the phone call. I really wasn't paying her no attention. At almost 9 months pregnant, food was the only thing on my mind. So, she comes back but this time it was a

CHAPTER 11

whole different expression on her face. She asked me to go with her to the back yard because she needed to holla at me about something. When we get back there, she told me that Chico and Jersey had a shootout in New Jersey and Jersey's car was shot up and Jersey was in the hospital. OMG! That was the last thing I expected. "WOW! Is he going to be O.K.?", I asked. ReRe said she didn't know but they were going to get back in touch with her once they heard anything else. "Is Chico Okay?" I asked. She said they didn't say if Chico got hit or not, but they did say that Jersey had got hit. I reasoned that if it wasn't one thing, it was another. I never wished no harm to come to anyone because I wished people the best. I then told her to keep me informed. It had been almost 5 months since I'd talked to Chico and so I really didn't care for him like I used to. I'm good with erasing a person from my memory and after how he just up and left me like that, I didn't care for him anymore. But, ReRe had just had a son by Jersey and I could see it all on her face that the news really hurt her to the core. She took her plate and left. Me, it was still food there, so I didn't go nowhere no time soon. Besides we stayed at the same hotel together, so she'd keep me informed! Ok, well Jersey didn't get shot but his car was a total loss. She said that it was bullet holes all through his shit! Whoever they pissed off tried to make sure them niggas didn't make it out alive. God was with them boys! I told myself that I hoped they would take heed and go sit their asses down somewhere! But it wasn't my problem. Chico left me to fend for myself, so I was doing just fine. I didn't have any kids by him, so I wish him the best. I also didn't care to hear anything else about them either. ReRe on the other hand was different. I didn't know what type of hold Jersey had on her but if that nigga had told her to jump off the Eiffel Tower she would've. I think she loved that nigga more than life itself. He was all she would talk about the whole time we would be together. I started to feel sorry for her. To me them niggas left us dead and stinking. I would tell ReRe that I didn't want to hear nothing else about them niggas, and fuck them real talk, but she wasn't trying to hear that.

ALL I HAVE

December came and since my birthday is on 12-31 I was hoping that the baby would come anytime now so I could bring in the New Year strong. ReRe was still screaming down my ear about Jersey and saying that Jersey want to come back to Raleigh but he's not going to come back unless I talk to Chico. WOW! This dude had a nerve. I didn't want to talk to Chico because that nigga not one time thought about calling checking up on me. Nothing! So why would I want to talk to him. It had been too much time lapsed so now, I'm alright! But she begged me and with her talking about them wanting to come back after all this time, I didn't mind seeing him because I had a lot of questions that I needed answers to. So, after all the crying that ReRe had done I told her to call them! So ReRe made the call and she put me on the phone and Jersey then put Chico on the phone.

CHAPTER 12

NOW I GOT a Kool-Aid smile on because I couldn't wait to see what his response was going to be once, I popped this question. "What happened with you keeping it 100%?" It took him a while to respond to my question, but he tried and I just stopped him and said, "I'll holla at you when I see you", and left it at that. It was up to them on how they wanted to play it. Well not all the way left up to them because that's if they really wanted to come or not, I did my part. But sure enough, they came a couple of days afterwards, and when I laid my eyes on him, it was like all the feelings that I had towards him came rushing back. Me and ReRe was staying at the Days Motel off South Anders because everyone else was at New Burn and Capitol Blvd. I guess they wanted to be incognito. At first, I had to find out what was on his mind and why he played me like he did. All I asked him to do was keep it 100% and he couldn't even do that. But for some reason I couldn't even do that. I couldn't even get the words to come out of my mouth to ask him those simple questions. I had been trapping all day and I was due any moment, so I just went to lay down and went to sleep. It felt kind of strange with being in the same room with this man. I did make sure I got a double bedroom because I really wasn't sure how this was going to play out. I wasn't a stupid bitch; I knew he was fucking someone while he was gone and the only reason why he was here was because of my friend ReRe. She loved that nigga Jersey. That nigga couldn't do nothing wrong in her eyes, despite all the ass whippings that nigga would give her! It seemed that she loved him even more every time. But just for her to be happy, I obliged. Besides it was a win-win situation because ALABAMA was a fine man himself! "So, what's the plan peoples because I know y'all got something up your sleeves?" I asked them the next morning. We talked for a while came up with a plan that worked for all of us and we came up with the idea of putting our money together and splitting the profits. No one knew that they were here but us and we were told that if we had any problems just pick up the phone. I didn't mind $2,500 a piece out of $10,000. That was a pretty penny coming back on the bust down and it wouldn't even take that long. So, I had no problem with that, let's do this! I'm guessing Jersey had some peoples here already lined up for us to get the work from because I knew I wasn't going to never trust niggas again! So, my Dominican connect was put on hold. J-Cole said, "Fool me one-time shame on you, fool me twice can't put the blame on you!" But it seemed like they were on some different shit. I think that last incident fucked them up to the point they were content with chilling in the hotel, smoking weed and watching T.V. They didn't have to do nothing. Yeah, they had it made. So, me and ReRe got to work.

I would always tell ReRe about her attitude towards the smokers, about how they didn't have to come and spend their money with her because they had a lot more people they could go to. I remembered Jersey saying "you all not in competition", but in my mind I was saying, if my shit gets gone first, I'm out bottom line. Don't knock the hustle and I would say something to Chico about Jersey slick ass comments but that was his boy, so I left it alone. He was his boy, not mine!

Christmas finally came and it was a good Christmas. Everyone was getting along. Jersey and Chico had went shopping without us even knowing. I felt kind of bad because I didn't get him anything, but he wasn't sweating it. I guess they was thankful they had someone that had their backs. If the police weren't looking for them, trust and believe it was some niggas out looking for them. I remember Chico handing me a few bags and when I looked in them, a big Kool-Aid

CHAPTER 12

smile came across my face. He had got me a pair of construction Timberlands, a gray sweat suit with a fleece bubble vest to go over it. The sweat suit had a hood to go with it so I loved it. I didn't have anything to give him, but he was good regardless. Then ReRe came over and showed me what Jersey got her for Christmas and it was a pair of diamond earrings. You couldn't tell her nothing! I felt some kind of way at first because diamonds are a girl's best friend. But they did have kids together, so it was cool. Well back to work as usual....

3 Weeks later Jan 8, 2000, I'm in the hospital and my contractions were coming back to back. The baby was coming, and they told me that they didn't have time to give me an epidural I had to get ready to push. With no one there with me but the nurses, they kept telling me to breath in and out, push and on the last push the nurses said Tina give me a big one, Push!!! When the baby came out crying, I was scared because I didn't want Social Services to get in my shit. It was another girl and I named her Brianna, but Damn I wanted a boy. It's cool though as long as that's done and over with. I remember saying, "I don't want to go through this shit again". ReRe had to tell Chico where I was because I gave ReRe everything once my water broke. Then Chico and Jersey came to check on me and congratulated me on the little one. Jersey left out the room and that's when Chico told me that Jersey was trying to make a run so he was going to send our money with him so we can get ours way cheaper. Lately I hadn't been feeling Jerseys aura because he'd been talking slick, but Chico had been knowing him way longer than I had, so whose side was he going to take? His nigga from childhood or a female he barely knew? I told Chico to give him his half but don't give him mines. "Chico, did you hear what I said?" I asked. His reply was "yeah Tina I hear you." I didn't like the way he said it, so I figured that I had to get home to my shit and fast. So, I asked the nurse, "How long am I going to be here?" Her response was that "you got here yesterday so you will be getting released tomorrow" Good! Later on, that night, I called Chico and asked him was everything okay? "Yea, everything good" he said. "So,

what are you doing?" I replied, "playing the game" he responded. "Okay, Chico so where Jersey at?" "He's gone". "So, you gave him the money?" He tried to explain but I knew right then and there that something in my "know it", let the older people say it, that we'd just took a major loss. $10,000 loss. I told Chico that that nigga had better come back with our shit! Bottom line.

I was released from the hospital and went back to the hotel room. They had decided to move from the Days Motel and moved to the Lodge Suites on Capitol Blvd. It was a brand-new hotel and it was equipped with kitchen and all. "Perfect". So, we got a double because I just had Brianna Desire Lynda Cantrelle Gilchrist. Yes, some of everybody had a part of her name just like my first daughters name. She had her own bed and Chico and me on the other. Chico had paid the room for a week so I could afford to take a couple days off work. I also had gone and got the money I gave ReRe before I went to the hospital, so we were good until Jersey got back. So, we waited. Chico was helpful when it came to Brianna even though that wasn't his child. I can say he was there for me. I appreciated that a lot because that alone showed me it was another side to him that I didn't mind knowing. I guessed it would be further on down the road in our relationship because technically speaking, he just had gotten to the point of coming home at night. Why didn't he? I didn't know because he didn't have to do nothing but have my back. I could tell that it wasn't going to last long because he didn't seem like that type of guy to be a leach. He was just like me in a sense, a go getter. He would always seem like he was in deep thought. I would sometimes just look at him and he would have a mysterious look on his face. I would ask him at times on what he was thinking about, he would say nothing, but I took it as he didn't want to trust me at this moment with his deepest thoughts. So, in time I would walk away because I didn't want to disturb him. But one thing I did know it had been almost a couple of weeks and Jersey hadn't come back with that bread yet and I could see it all on Chico's face. Karma! I told that nigga not to give that

CHAPTER 12

dude our money and he did it anyways. I asked him what was going on with Jersey, and Chico looked at me in disbelief and he said that his phone was off. That's all I needed to hear. I got up with what little bit I had. One monkey doesn't stop no show. We had to survive, and I knew in my heart Chico needed time to be alone. That was his best friend and that nigga had robbed us blind. Damn, it's getting realer and realer! ReRe was looking dumb founded next door at her hotel room and Chico knew that she had some money, so he extorted her ass and took most of her shit from her. Not all of it because he knew Jersey didn't give a fuck about ReRe for real. She probably was in the blind on this one, but Chico swore up and down Jersey wouldn't never just take his shit. All I knew was $10,000 of ours was gone, and I was getting tired of niggas for real. Another week went by and still nothing and every time I would go back to the hotel, I would see Chico sitting there in the chair looking confused and in disbelief. I would try to cheer him up because I knew deep inside his heart was ripped out because they'd known each other for 15 years and Jersey was the reason why Chico was in North Carolina in the first place. In my mind, I was waiting for him to leave to go back to Alabama any second because what was the use of him staying? He really didn't know me like that, so all I could do was make sure he was comfortable until he decided to make his move. I provided food and weed because he didn't drink, "Thank God." He had a video game and shelter and I kept my distance. But I felt his pain because when he left me it was kind of how I felt but I know he's touched harder. He didn't come out of the hotel for almost 2 months, but I wasn't rushing him because I was hoping that he wouldn't leave me. So, I tried my best to let him know that I got him. There was a 5-year age gap but with a little help I knew I could make it work. And that's what I showed him with my actions because I wasn't the talking type. My actions always speak louder than words. And as time went by, he noticed that. My thing was that we only needed each other and no one else and all I require always from him was just keep it 100% with me and I'd do the same in return. With that, we started all over again. Chico

ALL I HAVE

started to loosen up some because he would call Worm who used to hang around him and Jersey and Worm would come and pick him up. I always kept my money at the hotel, so if he needed anything it was there already and when leaving he would come and tell me everything that was going on with him and what kind of moves he was trying to make. Whatever I could do to help, I did because money wasn't a problem and while him and Worm got close, Worm invited him to a house over off Shepherds St. It was a rooming house that Worm was getting a little money out of.

Worm, Tang his baby's Mother and their 2 kids was renting out a room there and he allowed Chico to come over there and get his money up. My thing was good because it gave him a little hope and that also let me know that he wasn't going anywhere. I then sat back to see how this would ride out!

It's been a long time since I've seen a house do straight money on a bust down on a Friday night got you over 10bands but that's what kind of numbers Shepherds St. was doing when Chico started going over there. That house was booming so hard that that shit made the newspaper! It was in the perfect location, right at State campus. Shit Fuck Mapel! I was proud of that because now he was doing his own thing and I was doing mines. But I was still battling with these Social Services people and now that I'd had Brianna with an open case still, they were all on me about her. I tried my best to duck and dodge them MFS, but it seemed like everywhere I went, they were there. I also never went and resolved that gun charge that I caught a while back so them bitches was on me then about that. I was like fuck them crackers, they going to have to catch me all because I didn't have a job. While these MFS was all on my ass, my baby didn't have to want for shit. I wished that they'd all just die! I've learned that life is made up of choices and that was the worst choice I could've ever made because one they did find me, they ended up taking Brianna from me also. She was 10 months old, so both of my kids were gone off one phone call. The pain I felt was indescribable! A person can only take

CHAPTER 12

but so much and it seemed like I was getting hit back to back, boom, boom, boom! It seemed as if it wasn't one thing it was another. I just felt like dying. Both of my girls were gone, and the Social worker had told me that if I'd go ahead and sign Brianna over, then they would make sure that they both got adopted together. She had also wanted me to sign my parental rights over which I didn't, so I had to get ready for a court date to have a hearing for that. Okay, not a problem because at least I'd be able to know where they were. If I would have only communicated with them white people used their resources, my outcome would have been different. I was thinking that they were against me, but they were doing their job and was basically trying to help me, but I was so stubborn I didn't realize that.

During this time, me and Chico had gotten us a room in a rooming house off Brook Ave. to save money. It was 4 blocks from Shepherds St. and it was a nice room. The overall rooming house was very nice and clean, you couldn't even tell it was a rooming house. It was also in the cut and no one would ever suspect that we were staying there. When I broke the news to Chico about what had happened to Briana it was like he felt my pain because he made things feel a little better because I had someone to lean on. I didn't have that Mother or Father support system. My Aunts and Uncles was out in the streets also. Since I was the oldest of May's kids, I had to cope the best way possible and to keep my mind off reality, I hustled harder and started using Percocet. I had picked the habit up from Chico. It was his drug of choice, so I didn't see no harm in that. To me it was better than messing with the nose candy and besides, it wasn't lady like to me keep messing with your nose. So, I would turn the nose candy off and on as I wished, Thank God! At first, I was the only one who done powder but during this time it seemed like everyone and their Mama was sniffing nose candy. MFS was going crazy! They couldn't handle it, so I had to fall back because people were making doing nose candy a bad thing. See me I was a believer that it wasn't what you did but how you did it because people might suspect all they want, but you

97

could never tell if I was on it or not. That's the beauty about being a loner because you weren't supposed to tell on yourself. But Percocet I liked that high more. Back then there were 5's. You didn't find the 10's and 15's like you do now, so I would take 3 or 4 at a time and I was good for a while. Get me an orange juice and you couldn't tell me nothing. I was popping them shits all day just to cope with reality because what happened with my kids was killing me on the inside. And how Chico was beginning to act towards me didn't make my situation no better.

CHAPTER 13

Always make the money, don't let the money make you!

IT SEEMED LIKE once Chico started making the money, he began to change. He didn't need me as he once did, once I saw how he was moving towards me. He was doing his thing I am not going to front. He had got him a nice Camaro, went and threw rims on it, and got a flip flop paint job. I'm guessing it was a down south thing. Who's name the car was in, I didn't know but all I knew was that I was always in the passenger seat majority of the time. During the time he had bought his car, things was turning out good in our favor. Chico had run into this guy name Money who was one of Jerseys and his people and he was the nigga that could lay his hands on them bricks for the low! So, once he started dealing with him, it seemed like shit was on a fast track. That's when things started to get really complicated because that's when Chico started to figure out what he really wants in life because it was starting to show. Me, I felt like I had always been the same person. People that knew me would tell you that Tina changed for the better as I made the money because that's what I did. It's the very reason why he was with me because I'm going to rock with you no matter what and through thick-n-thin. But why front on me when the money started rolling in? It made me wonder if it was because I didn't have the right credentials needed to move to the next level. Niggas needed more huh. I loved this man to the moon and back so in my eyes he couldn't do no wrong. I believed every word that came out of his mouth because with time he showed me that his word was good. Some nights when he didn't come home, I would wonder where he was and he would tell me if I'd ask where he was, he was going to tell me I knew that. But I wouldn't ask because I didn't want to know. I had gone through a lot with Chico because he was a handsome man and all the ladies wanted to be on his arm and the ones that couldn't be on his arm would wish that they could. He was a go getter and if he made up his mind that he wanted something, he always went and got it by any means. Now don't get me wrong, I was a dime piece also Thank God. So, when we stepped out it was like Jay-Z and Beyoncé in the hood! We would pull up and people would literally come to the car before we could even get out! Yes, trend setters and with me by his side, I knew I couldn't be slacking period! Money wasn't a thing and cars, oh we had them. Yes, the good life. And once his partner Money came into the picture, things really turned up. We had finally moved off Brook Ave. and we got us a 2-bedroom apartment in Cary N.C. I liked it, it had a living room, dining room and a place that I set my computer up in. I loved it because it was our first place together, besides the rooming house. We were young and it was a lot going on with us at the time and Chico didn't have anyone up here that he could trust. We had the product and it was plentiful so now we needed a team. That's when he decided to call his cousins in Alabama to see if any of them wanted to come and join him. But it was coming our way. The cars, clothes, material things don't phase me as much, so I kept me a safe in the closet in the office room. It seemed like once we got the apartment in Cary, I started to see less and less of Chico. In the back of my mind, I knew he was cheating on me, and I thought that I knew with who! So, one night, I went through his phone and jotted down some numbers that would call him and this one number stood out. So, I called it and a female answered. "Who dis?" I asked her. "Tera" she replied. "Ok, why are you calling Chico?" I guess she put it together because she hung the phone up. Chico came to me about it and that's when

CHAPTER 13

he told me that she was his baby Mother. It was always one thing or another with this dude. So now you got a baby Mother? And then on this particular night he didn't come home. So, I drove to Vanderbell St. because that's a spot we had off Hillboro St. He wasn't there. Then I drove in our Ford Probe around looking for his Camaro and it was not in sight. I then go and pick up this guy and I take him to the phone booth to dial Tera's telephone number. I tell the guy to tell whoever that answer the phone that he's D.J. I picked D.J. because he was a guy that worked for Chico so I knew he would answer for him. I then told him to tell whoever to put Chico on the phone because it was an emergency and he did as he was told. It was like 2am and he passed me the phone and I hear Chico say Hello. I liked to jump through the phone! I was pissed! I was getting tired of him playing me because this wasn't the first time this had happened, and from the looks of it, it wasn't going to be the last. After I cussed his ass out, I hung up the phone. In my mind, I was like ok Chico since you want to play these type games, then 2 can play! I was the one out there risking my life with the police and if any nigga that came sideways if they choose. Where was these bitches at when you were broke, down and out? Now all a sudden, they pop up. I didn't see this bitch out there grinding. All she had to do was fuck and suck his dick. Yo this nigga was truly getting on my fuckin nerves. I couldn't wait until I laid my eyes on him. It was about 2 hours later when I saw him walk through the door and this nigga had blood everywhere. My immediate thought was "What's going on Chico?" He called me in the living room, and he asked me "Did D.J. make that phone call to Tera house?" I asked him "why did he ask me that" and he said "Tina, just answer the question." I told him he would come to the phone for D.J. and that's why I used him. He told me that he'd pistol whipped D.J. and hoped that he was alright. He couldn't believe that I would've done something like that. My thing was why would you automatically go and jump on D.J. anyways without knowing the facts in the first place. So now D.J in I.C.U and he didn't even have a clue why. I didn't even say anything to him that night. I went into the other room and went to

ALL I HAVE

sleep thinking about how much he made me sick! After that night, it seemed like things was getting more hectic in our relationship. I guess his head was getting too big and he didn't need me anymore and I was getting tired of this nigga playing me like I was a nothing ass bitch. Nigga you forgot huh. But it's all good because I was going to sit back on his ass. Then he began to put his hands on me! Enough was enough! I even had a smoker come tell me that Chico took her in the basement on Vanderbell and she had the nerve to tell me that it was good! Now any other time I would of knocked this bitch the fuck out but I know what type of nigga I was dealing with so I believed her in a sense but I also told her to describe the place for me just so I could confirm her story and she did. Right then, I knew she wasn't lying. So, I went and confronted this nigga on the block and didn't give a fuck who heard it. In front of everybody I said to him, now you are fucking crack heads. The girl was about 22, with green eyes, black and she was cute, but she couldn't touch this. But he gave the bitch an 8 ball (3.5gz) and I could've got me a pocketbook with that pimpin. So, check what this nigga does. He jumps in the car and just so happens the girl was right around the corner. I ran to the corner to try to catch up with him, He then parks the car in the middle of the street, hops out and he beat the shit out of that girl badly for telling the truth that he was with her the night before. Enough was enough so I run down the street to get him off her. I didn't even tell him her name but from the looks of things she was telling the truth because he went right to her. He tells me to get in the car which I did, and we went home.

CHAPTER 14

"Chico, I'm about to leave"

I WAS GETTING tired of him handling me. I wasn't a bad looking person and I could do better. With all the arguing that's been going on lately, I began packing my stuff up to leave and he goes in the closet in the office and grabs my safe. WOW! I asked him, "Can I get my money?" His answer was "No" Then there's more arguing. Tired, I then calmly said "Chico just give me my safe so I can go." Now he's not letting me go nowhere. Then he begins checking my pants pockets. Now we are fighting. But a female doesn't have any wins over a nigga. I'm 140lbs soak and wet so he just strong armed me and took all my shit. My dope, and all my money. All because I wanted to leave. I'm the one going through the bullshit! I'd done nothing to deserve that treatment from him. But this nigga had really lost his mind. So, as we fought blow for blow, I couldn't keep up and said, "fuck it" and just went in the bedroom and closed the door. I couldn't believe he put his hands on me for nothing and robbed me of $9,000 and my work. I'm tired thinking to myself, I don't know this nigga at all. I heard when he crunk up his car and left the house, so I goes in the living room and was hoping that he left something there for me, but no, he took everything, even the phones. I couldn't even call me a ride if I wanted to and the nearest store was a 30-minute walk from where we stayed. I was hurting physically and mentally in disbelief because how could he do me like this? I don't even know him

ALL I HAVE

anymore. Where was the Chico I first fell in love with? And the sad thing about this situation is that I never got my shit back. But after all of that, I still took him back every time. Believe me, that was one of the many incidents we had with each other. He had turned into a mad man and it seemed like after the very first time he put his hands on me, it just got easier every time. I loved him so much and after every time he would put his hands on me, he would come crying telling me how sorry he was. He would bring flowers and candy, but he would turn around and do it again. It could just be something I said that he didn't like that would trigger it. It got to the point that I was on pins and needles around him. We broke up a few times before, but the longest time was about a week and during that time, I found out I was pregnant and I told not a soul, but Tracy, and associate of mine. She knew how crazy he had gotten, and I already had 2 kids that I didn't have so having a baby by Chico during this time, I refuse to do it. So, I snuck off and terminated the pregnancy on my own. I couldn't do it! It had gotten to the point that I was scared to leave him at times. But at times I didn't want to. I loved this man to death! Things won't always bad because we had some good times. I remember driving to Alabama to go to a club called Platinum and his Mother Pam didn't like me at all. I guess she took me as a gold digger not knowing I made my own paper. But on this day, I took his younger sister Knee-Knee with me to the mall and bought us 2 Coogi dresses that cost me $2,000 for those dresses. While we were there some guys in a store had a lot of cameras and people around them, but it was like they had their eyes in our direction. Chico wasn't far behind and I really didn't have time for the drama! I had my hair put in braids already and the Coogi dress I bought was tan and brown and had no sleeves with the back out. It came down to my ankles and I had tan boots on under it. I already had a coke bottle shape, so it was fitting me perfect. His Mother Pam laid eyes on the price tags of them dresses and she told Chico to take them back. Knee-Knee said Mama she got her own money, that's not Chico money. That messed her up! You couldn't tell us nothing that night. Chico had just copped a J30 Infiniti and put

CHAPTER 14

18-inch assassins on it and he had a greenish blue flip flop paint job with cream leather inside. It was beautiful but after my safe had got taken, all a sudden, the car popped up! It wasn't a coincidence because I already knew what it was but that night, I knew I was the shit and couldn't nobody tell me otherwise. Knee-Knee was about 16 or 17 years old at the time, but she was in the building with her Coogi dress on also. I had my hair in Janet Jackson braids, and it was pinned up. I was showing off my curves and everything went perfectly. I didn't want to be all up on Chico that night because he has with his people which were his homeboy from Birmingham AL and his homeboy's wife's and a few others. I always felt insecure when it came down to it and by Chico being 5 years older than me, I felt out of place in a way, but I didn't show it. I kept my head up high because that night I was looking like a million bucks. We up in VIP and to keep all the drama down, I made sure I was in his eyesight. I would check on him to see how his aura was at times, and he was just laid-back chilling. He was really feeling the atmosphere, but I did see him a couple of times cutting his eyes over at me, like "yea, I see you shorty" in that southern slang accent! But during this time, I glanced over at him and when I turned around to see what was behind me because I could feel someone like right up on me, two guys approached me. They were two good looking brothers, but they didn't look better than my baby. I suddenly got nervous because when I looked back everyone that was with Chico was staring so I was nervous because I didn't want Chico to make a scene in that club. Then I looked at Knee-Knee and she had her hands covered over her mouth like she was in shock but I didn't understand why, It was like she saw a ghost or something and I looked back at Chico and he did not budge. It was like he was cool with what was going on. So, I continued to talk to them because they were asking me a lot of questions. I told them I was there with my man and I did thank them for their interest, and I walked off. Once I had got to the table, Knee-Knee said, "Chico I bet you she didn't even know who she was talking to." Which I didn't and that's when Chico said it was 8ball and MJG!!!! At the time I didn't know who they were until I got back to Raleigh and that's when I started paying attention to their music. It made a lot of sense why Chico let me rock. After that it seemed like nothing could stop us. Things was moving in such a fast pace. They say time flies when you're having fun and fly it did. We were back and forth to Alabama and Atlanta. One time we ran across Goodie Mob at Eddie's in Atlanta when we rode there out of the blue one day just to get our teeth done. When we pulled up, Goodie Mob was getting inside their limo that was parked outside the shop. Eddie was about to close but that night I learned a valuable lesson and to this very day I live by this motto ... "Money talks and bullshit walks", because Eddie opened those doors up and made it happen. He scraped up some diamonds and worked it out. Mel, Chico's cousin had drove. He got tops and bottoms in his and Chico got permanent tops and bottoms with 4 big diamonds and to this day 3 of the diamonds are still in his mouth but one of them fell out. I got two on the right side with two little diamonds in mines, but my diamonds fell out eventually. Where I have no clue! In my stomach probably! We were always arguing and fighting over the simplest things where it could have been over something that I said that he didn't like or the way I looked at him. Timing was a key factor also. But that still didn't give him the right to put his hands on me neither, but I was so gone that I would've endured anything he put me through. It was like I was under a spell that I wanted so desperately to get out of because of all the abuse that I endured, but at the same time I loved him so much. I would've taken a bullet for him. Hands down. The black Bonnie and Clyde and we were untouchable. Like Pastor Troy would say "We Ready!" But damn Pastor, you should've left Master P alone! You would've gone a long way! My bad homie, I drifted off for a minute. Anyways we were doing big-big things and Chico felt like he needed some help because we had a lot going on out there. Me alone was getting rid of a lot of product in a day and I would only be out from 12pm until 7pm, "Bingo Time". Yes, money basically grew on trees, and everyone wanted to be on the team but as time went by, people started showing their true colors. I had to cut a lot of people

CHAPTER 14

off because for one, Chico was a crazy ass nigga that didn't like no one and a lot of people that I thought I knew, started to act funny, and began hating on me. I didn't see it because I'd never been the type to be stuck up because during my childhood, I was bullied a lot, so I always gave people a chance. Yea, we had it going on from the outside looking in but shit isn't always what it seems. Well Maybe! We were always deep because Chico had brought his cousins from Alabama up here to help him control the traffic although Chico was a one-man army. He didn't need no one really and the only one he trusted was me when it came down to it. But I guess he wanted some of his kin folks here that he could really do some damage. And once them big 6ft 250lbs plus Alabama boys got here, they took over quick. Since they were fresh meat in the city, these females didn't know how to act and sitting back watching how all of this played out... The shit was funny to me. They weren't no bad looking fellas but of course none of them couldn't touch my baby of course! They played their position also. They were fucking all of them females and everyone tried to have conversation and I paid none of them no attention. I had no time for basic bitches because this wasn't a game and we was doing way too much to be playing around. Just come spend your change and keep it hot and no new friends. During this time ReRe had left and went to where Jersey was at and she would call occasionally, to check in with me. I was still feeling some type of way because that nigga didn't even show his face. Coward, but Jersey knew what type of nigga Chico was and he knew to stay away because Chico wasn't an average nigga. So, by him staying away, Jersey most definitely played his position because I was hearing that the nigga had ReRe and a few more females going state to state, pimping those hoes out. He would set up dates for the girls and niggas with money and he would come in and rob the niggas. He was going from Florida, New York, Chicago, that nigga was lame for that because how could you go from being that nigga to resorting to that? "Karma", and I'm a firm believer because when ReRe did come back to see me, she looked like one, with her Platinum wig, short dresses and her pumps. Damn,

ALL I HAVE

I felt sorry for her. She didn't stay long but when she was around, Chico kept his strap close by. He couldn't wait to see that nigga. He had a stick especially for that nigga, one of those big guns with a scope, infrared beam, banana clip and kick stand. He showed me how it worked one day, and boy was Jersey in trouble. While sitting on top of a house from long distance, that scope could zoom on anybody, so it wasn't no messing with that nigga! He called that his Jersey gun! And he taught me how to shoot just in case anything popped off and if he needed me. Chico knew I had his back so why did he treat me the way he did? That's the million-dollar question.

Things was running smooth once them Bama boys got up here. I had a house ready for each of them and they posted up and got to that bag. But Chico kept his cousin Courtney away from all that and he used him for his credentials because he was a brick mason by trade. So, he came and started working but I'm guessing Chico wanted to go legal. I saw that he was trying to figure a way to get out. But it was something holding him back. Like one or maybe 3 things that I could think of. He had the money, power and respect. I can admit that I was enjoying the gifts, popularity and all the perks that was coming with being the "IT" girl. I was the only female with a group of niggas, and we were turned up. But it really didn't mean anything to me because I was just doing my job and playing my position. Was basically just being me. But at the same time, I'd wished for a simpler life. We had a lot to worry about. Police, especially haters and making the money on time to meet the connect. I would worry about Chico a lot because I knew what type of nigga he was. But the crazy thing is, he was all about getting his money. Chico wasn't really a troublemaker but it seemed like everything would come at him. Why? Because he had the looks, his swag was on point and the money wasn't a problem so niggas would be jealous of him and because he also had a dime piece on his side, and she was a rider. Out here in this world you have to always be on point so Chico didn't never look for trouble but he wasn't the type of nigga that would back down neither because if you came

CHAPTER 14

his way, I hoped you was a stand up nigga because if not you were on borrowed time. But I think things between Chico and myself went downhill shortly after Jersey had ran off and it was quick. As I'm writing this down, I'm filled with so many emotions because I was young, and I tried so hard to make sure he was comfortable. To let him know I had his back, but everything I did seemed to fall on deaf ears. I was still in my teens, 19 to be exact and I loved this man so much. But all the cheating he was doing and all the fighting we was going through, I knew it in my heart that we weren't going to make it too far. I tried to make sure that he was safe with me going out handling everything but when he did come out, I'd find myself on high speed chases with the police with me on the passenger side. One time while on a chase, he had the gun on his lap, and I reached on his lap and takes the gun as he tried to lose the cops. He did and for a split second we jump out the J30 and hit the woods and something tells me to throw the gun up in the air as hard as I could, and I did. A bunch of police soon with dogs came and as we hid in a barn, next thing we know we hear the dogs barking. "Damn Tina, here they come!" Chico said. With guns drawn, the police detain us. They asked us, "Why did y'all run?" Chico's response was because I thought I had a warrant. So, they searched and had us out there about an hour or more and they found nothing. They eventually charged us both with fleeing to elude and we bonded out that night. The next day we went back, and I showed Chico exactly where I threw the gun up at and Thanks to God, it was hanging on a tree limb. He grabbed it and we left. But, that's not even the half and although I would've jumped in front of a bullet for that nigga, he still couldn't see that! And if he did, he never showed me any signs that he did. Well material wise he did but to me, things was deeper than that. I made my own money so I could buy my own things. I wanted loyalty, respect. What happened to that? When I asked him to keep it 100%, huh? Even though he didn't never lie to me about anything, in my eyes it was deeper than that also. I was getting really stressed out because I was deeply in love with a man that couldn't or wasn't even satisfied with one woman. I was the one that

ALL I HAVE

was risking my freedom and life out here with him but was too young and naive to see that every fight that we had was a warning sign. But I didn't care, I loved me some Chico. Things had got so out of control that niggas were moving so much work a night, re-up was like we are going on a shopping spree. As in walking in the mall and going to a certain spot, pick up the Victoria's Secret bag and walk right out. Up under that lingerie what you think going on? Game meant to be sold not told. But the whole time it wasn't a thang to me! Our team had to eat so we did what had to be done! Southeast Raleigh on lockdown.

CHAPTER 15

Worser and Worser!

NOT THINKING ABOUT the bet, I made while playing solitary, I was trying to figure out why was all of this happening to me. I couldn't see what I was doing wrong for this man to treat me the way he did. One minute we are making love and everything is cool and with one word I said wrong, we were fighting. One day Chico and I was sitting and talking, and he said to me that he wanted to try something with me, but it would be there the next day. He also told me that everyone back in his hometown of Birmingham was talking about it. I said cool and the last thing he said about it was he'd call me when it got there. Boy I tell you! So, the next day comes and while on the block, he calls me and tells me to come to the house. I worked on a schedule because it was like a job to me, but I took off early because I wanted to see what this was all about. So, I gets to the house and went and took a shower because that's what I did from being outside all day and because anything could pop off at any time if you know what I mean! So, I hops out the shower and on the kitchen table I see a big freezer Ziplock bag full of color pills, about 1,000 of them, maybe more and mind you this was the year 2000. "Okay, what's this Chico?" I asked. "Ecstasy pills!" Now we already on Scobey snacks because pills were our drug of choice but when he took two out and gave me one, he told me that he wanted me to try it first. We eventually agreed to do it at the same time. While in the bedroom both of us gets a glass of water out the bathroom and sit on the bed and on 3 we took a double stack pill at the same time. Then we sat back on the bed and we waited. It took no more than 15 minutes max when we both look at each other and Chico said "Tina, you feel that." I turn his way and while my hands were feeling hot and sweaty, I tell him "yea". I then started touching him because the feeling I was feeling that day was unimaginable. It was like my whole body was electric and it was the best feeling I had ever felt in my whole life. And, because I was with the right person at that very moment, we made love all night long from 6pm until sunrise. After that we slept for two whole days. When we woke up two days later, we had missed mad money! It was a wonderful feeling and after that night with me, no one couldn't tell me nothing. 1,000 pills were gone in two days! After that we had them by the thousands. First ones to ever bring them to North Carolina to my knowledge. People was popping them things like they were candy. People walking around like zombies. When you saw anybody that had orange juice outside, you already knew what type of time they were on, yea they are rolling! And me, I never spent a dime. Since we had them, I'd kept the shake and it was what it was. I knew you had to stay hydrated because that why I never took a trip to the E.R. but during this time I was so stressed out worried about who Chico was sleeping with or worried about what kind of attitude he was going to be in once I seen him because while I was out, I did my own thing and he did his own. Some nights I didn't even see him and just because I didn't feel like arguing, left it alone. During this pill popping era, I dropped from a size 10 to a 0-1. Yes, 120lbs and yea you couldn't tell me nothing. I knew I was a dime piece because I'd never been the size which was skinny that men preferred on television. Also, during this time I had gotten on probation for that gun charge. A possession of stolen goods that they dropped down and a coke charge from a few years earlier that had finally caught up with me. So, during this time in my life, I was going through a lot of changes and I would talk to God on the regular. I was young so I didn't know exactly how to look for warning signs, but I would always say "Prayer answers all things and to have

CHAPTER 15

faith that God will do it and it's done". So, I would ask and wait to see what happened. "As small as a grain of salt", I would say because I knew that I had that much faith. But later on, I found out that it had to line up with his will! With me going to see my probation officer, popping Ecstasy, and smoking weed, young and dealing with Chico, I was going to have a breakdown. Let alone the police! At first, I was 165lbs with a butt, hips, I had a coke bottle shape, but after losing 45lbs, Chico didn't even want to touch me. He even told me one time that I looked nasty. Enough! I found myself on my knees and I prayed. "Lord, please let Chico fall in love with Tera so he would leave me and never come back to me because I'm tired of the fussing, fighting, and insults. He will do better without me." While on probation and when I would go and see the probation officer, my urine stayed dirty with opiates, weed, coke (because of handling it, I'd long stopped sniffing), ecstasy, but instead of my probation officer sending me to jail, she violated me into drug court! Yes! But I'm really going through a lot. I was going through a vulnerable time in my life where I was feeling like I wasn't wanted because niggas tend to forget where they came from and chose to let the money make them. I was so tired of the cheating, the fighting, and the name calling but at the same time I was in love with this man, deeply. Exhaled! LORD PLEASE HELP ME!

We would argue, Chico and myself and right after, he would cry every time and tell me how much he loved me and that he wouldn't do it again. And every time I would look at him crying also and feel sorry for him not knowing why? But I would always forgive him, and we would make love. Things were bad! Now looking back on that situation, how could I allow myself to take that kind of abuse? At the same time, it only made me stronger. Facts!! But popping Ecstasy, Percocet's, lust, fighting, making money was a recipe for disaster! Nevertheless, during that time, I didn't care as long as I was with Chico. I didn't know what this man had over me but whatever he had done to me that would hurt me, I didn't love him no less! I used to ask myself, "was it the way he would make love to me? Was it the

ALL I HAVE

way that he kissed me? Was it the attention that we got when we were together? Or was it the cars, clothes or the money? What was it?" But those things didn't really matter to me. We could've been broke living in a shelter, and I would've still loved him the same! And Chico knew that also and that's why he was acting selfish and doing whatever he wanted to do. He didn't care about my feelings at all, and that was the sad part about it. My heart would ache with every beat that I was with this man because at that point anything could've happened, and I didn't want to see anything happen to him or anyone on the team as well as my own safety. During this time, I found myself talking to the lord even more. I was so confused and lost. I'd never been in a relationship like this. To the point of truly loving a man like I loved Chico. So, all of this was new to me but, I knew that things were moving way too fast and the physical abuse and the cheating made matters that much worse. Chico had gotten to the point that he couldn't even give me a weekend to not cheat on me. In drug court, I had to go to the day reporting center from 9am - 5pm Monday - Friday and had to take drug tests Monday, Wednesday, and Friday. I also had court every other Friday so I couldn't do shit. I had to leave everything to Chico because I had violated of course from smoking weed and Ecstasy. This was in Sept of 2000 and whenever I got a dirty urine or didn't complete required N.A. meeting they would give me a weekend or two in jail. I'll admit that I never went to N.A. meetings. I would pay my Aunt Nita to go to the meetings for me or would pay anyone because all they had to do was get the paper signed by the teacher and that's it. So one time when I'd gotten home from doing a weekend, I'd got out that Sunday and while Chico and myself was chilling on Mapel St. at one of the houses we had, as we was walking up the street, a female kept calling Chico's name. So, I turned around and she started walking towards us while steady calling his name. I gets Chico's attention and I say to him "I know you hear this girl calling you" and he looked at me like Tina leave me alone. So, the girl blurts out "you won't acting like that when you were eating my pussy

CHAPTER 15

Saturday night!" My heart stops, here we go again! Saturday night, I was doing my weekend!

I knew for a fact that bitch wasn't lying because she could've said any day other than a day that I was doing my weekend! I didn't even get time to say nothing to him because that nigga turned around so quick it seemed like in 0.3 seconds, he was on her ass beating the shit out of that girl! I didn't even have to touch her. That was the beauty of it all because I never got my hands dirty pertaining to fighting a female. Why? Because I never fought fair! I saw her hair weave flying one way, tooth going the other and he just hit her with a two piece. She tried to defend herself, but she was hopeless! After he finished, I cussed his ass out. Now of course we got to arguing and once we got home, we were fighting. "LORD I'm tired of this man!" I prayed while scared at the same time because I didn't think that I could just leave Chico like that. He wouldn't let me go, but on the other hand, I don't think I tried hard enough. It had gotten to the point after the incident with the girl, that in my heart I didn't want to be with him no more. Enough was enough. I found myself anxious to go to the day reporting center (DRC) is what they called it. It was the only time I felt I was safe from 9pm - 5pm and after that, the days I had to go to N.A. meetings, I would go on my own just to stay away from him I was getting to the point that I didn't care anymore. I'm guessing the Ecstasy played a major role in the escalated treatment because it seemed like the violence progressed once we started taking Ecstasy together. It was then that I began praying to God for a way out. I would never wish any hard on him, but I just wanted out! I went to DRC with bruises on me and the director would ask me what happened and I wouldn't ever talk about it because I was the one who had to go home, and plus I would've never brought the police to my business because I hated the police. So, I made it my business to stay away from him and when I got home, I didn't even call to check on him. I didn't care. Sometimes I didn't even go straight home because I would go to Tang house in Hershey Park who was Worms baby Mother. She stayed 30 minutes walking distance from the DRC. I would chill with her for a while and

ALL I HAVE

I would end up walking home which was 45 minutes from her house. I'd catch a cab or walk just to avoid him and was glad sometimes he wasn't around. Besides, while I was going to the DRC I had met this guy and he was a cool dude and I would conversate with him while I was there. As the months went by, I started confiding in him because he would always listen to me, give me advice and a shoulder to lean on. He never came on to me period and besides he didn't look better than Chico. If I wanted sex, I could just fuck Chico so sex was nowhere in the equation. But I did need someone to talk to that could give me some feedback from a man's point of view. They were the same age and since I thought that I was a good judge of character, I felt like he fit the bill, so we had become good friends. This was in January of 2001.

CHAPTER 16

I'M STILL GOING through the DRC program trying to get a GED or trade but couldn't seem to stop smoking weed and popping Ecstasy, I'm still doing the weekends and I'm still going through the same shit with Chico. Fighting, arguing, making love, getting tired. Chico started looking very unattractive. But on Valentine's Day 2001, as I'm leaving from DRC his cousin Courtney came to give me a ride home. I gets to the house and I get out of the car and heads upstairs because I'm tired. I take my clothes off and shoes and I lay down! Next thing I know Chico comes in and tells me to go with him. I didn't feel like going because I had a bad headache and didn't feel good, but he wouldn't let up, so I get up. We were walking towards the front door; he tells me to close my eyes. At that point I wasn't really interested in Valentine's Day. Didn't care for the day at all but I close my eyes and he takes my hand and we walk on the porch. He then tells me to open them and when I opened my eyes, I saw a brand-new drop top, candy apple red 2000 Eclipse Spyder with black bow wrapped around it. He then hands me the keys and says, "Happy Valentine's Day!" It put a smile on my face, and I was thankful, but I also knew that Tera had something to do with the car. But it was the thought that count, so I was excited, and I jumped in the passenger side and he got in the driver's side and we drove off. While we were riding he told me that the car was mine, but he didn't want no one else driving the car and not to drive it in the hood. So, the next day, I drive the car to school and the director asked me whose car it was, and I told her

ALL I HAVE

that it was my Valentine's Day present. My director was a cool black woman and she was very understanding. She also knew of Chico and knew that something wasn't right with him, but I never said anything bad about him to an outsider. When I got out of class that day, I went to my grandma Lynda's house on Carboro Rd. and showed the car off and my mother May asked could she drive it. I told her "Sure, just come to the DRC tomorrow and you got it." and after that I left my grandma's house and rode around for a while although I didn't go to the hood, a few hours later I went home. I was loving my drop top. You couldn't tell me nothing, and boy was I feeling myself! The next day I get up for school although I'm tired and not feeling well I couldn't miss any days out of school unless I had a doctor's note. So, I go to school. When I get there, my mother May and her boyfriend Alamo are outside in the parking lot ready to use the car. I'm running late so I give her the keys and told her to come back by 4:30 and she left. So, after school let out, my mother May is outside on time and I leave and go home. I pull in and went upstairs and as soon as I opened the door, here this nigga goes with all the bullshit! He just so happened to bump into them near Hershey Park and people had told him that they were all in the hood and everywhere else. "Okay, it was my car and I let my Mama drive" I told him, but why did I say that? The next thing I knew we were fighting hard and that was it for me. I was like fuck him and that fucking car and I bounced. I called me a cab and I went to Hershey park where Tang was staying at and asked her could I stay at her house for a while. I didn't want to go back to my apartment so staying in the kids' room was perfect because there I could save money and DRC was walking distance from her house. I didn't want nothing, the cars, money, nothing. Tang had a 3-bedroom apartment and she had an extra room, so she let me stay. I didn't want no one knowing where I was at and I didn't come out the house because I needed to get my mental right, so I wanted to be alone. All I did was cry, slept, went to school, and shortly after I went to Tangs house, I started throwing up. I wasn't smoking weed or popping pills, so I was trying to figure out why I was throwing up? OMG! I went

CHAPTER 16

flying to the drugstore and got a pregnancy test and didn't tell anyone what was going on with me. I went upstairs in Tang's bathroom and took the test and sure enough it was positive. I started crying so hard that Tang came upstairs to see what was wrong with me. I told her to come in and I asked her to please not to say anything. I begged her and I showed her the test. She was happy for me, but I wasn't. I had aborted a baby before this one and I didn't want Chico to find out about this one because I just wanted to be over him. If Chico had found out it was no telling how this was going to go, so Tang gave me her word that she wouldn't tell him. Then Chico's cousin Courtney came to her house being nosey I thought, but I soon found out that Tang's word was no good because it seemed like right after I told her, laid down and dozed off good from crying, I wake up with Chico standing over me. When I saw him, I started crying! He then sat down beside me and asked me what was going on with me and I showed him the test, I cried more and more because I couldn't believe that Tang had opened her mouth anyways. I knew right then and there that I couldn't trust her! Chico then asked me why I was crying, and I told him that I didn't want to have any more babies. I didn't even have the first two so that's why I didn't want to have any more children. And plus, I was trying to get away from Chico. But there I was pregnant! Now I had to figure out how I was going to play it. I was still upset from the fight that we just had a couple of days prior but then I saw why I'd been so tired and not feeling well. I really didn't feel like being bothered at that moment and Chico got the picture, so he left out the room. I didn't move because my feelings were hurt even more because Tang had opened her mouth. I cried so much that day that I couldn't even cry no more. I had run out of tears! A couple hours went by and I stayed upstairs in Tang apartment because I didn't want to be bothered but once I got up and went in the boys room to look out their window, Chico was sitting out there in the Infiniti. I couldn't understand why he was still here, so I go downstairs, and I speak to his cousin Courtney and he tells me Congratulations. I say, "Thank You", and while Tang sat there smiling and everybody else all except me, I goes outside wondering what was on his mind. I walk to the car door and asked him what we going to do? He tells me to get in the car and I like an asshole I do, and he pulls off. I set myself up for that one. I asked him to take me back to Tang's apartment because I did not want to go back to our apartment. Period! But of course, that fell on deaf ears because he kept driving. He said that all he wanted to do was talk and then he said that he would take me back. At that point, I had no choice but to sit back and chill and listen to whatever he needed to say so he could take me back to Tang house. We then pull up at the apartment and he tells me to get out. I walk up the stairs with him, but I knew I made a big mistake.

He told me to relax. We went in the living room, sat down and he started telling me that him and Jersey had run into each other. I listened but I really didn't care to hear it because at that point I just wanted to get away from him. He felt my vibe, so I cut him off. "Chico, where is my car? Oh, so your bitch got it huh?" Because I know me, there we go arguing. I'm now demanding to go back and then he corners me in the back room, but I was able to make my way out the back room into the kitchen. Once in the kitchen I don't know what was said but suddenly all I felt was his fist in my face and in the midst of us fighting, I'm taking blow for blow, slamming and breaking shit, I'm like Chico why are you doing this and I'm pregnant!" and once I said that, I guess something clicked in his head and he stopped right then. He then got up and went in the room and as usual cried. Then out of nowhere I heard a knock at the door and then I heard another knock but this time louder, then I heard someone say "Police, Police, open the door". I asked Chico what he wanted me to do. He looked worried so I told him to give me the gun and I would open the front door with it hoping that they would lock me up because I was willing to do anything at this point just to get away from him for a while. But, of course, he said no. Boom, Boom, Boom! "Ma'am, police opened the door. We're not leaving until you open the door." As quick as I could, I washed my face, throw a shirt on and I open the

CHAPTER 16

door. The police said that they got a call from a neighbor saying that it was a domestic dispute. They asked if I was alright and I told them "yes". The officer whispered "Ma'am, can you talk to us?" I said "yes" but then he said, "just wink and eye and we will help you ma'am." I told the officers that I was alright and Thank You for coming to check on me and told the officers to have a goodnight. The officers then left. They sat outside for a while. I couldn't go anywhere with no funds, no phone, no transportation so I went into the other room to lay down and went to sleep. After the incident, I concluded that I was out here alone. I felt that no one cared about me but me except for the God and Jesus, but human wise, no one. I kind of always had that mentality because that's why I didn't depend on a nigga, but at times someone will always need someone and at that moment in life, I needed Chico because the court shit had me occupied. I was pregnant, I had DRC from 9am - 5pm, N.A. classes 3 times a week and drug court, I truly broke down and prayed, "Lord I need your help!" I truly poured my heart out, because I was tired of being in that relationship. All I could do was try but I was 20 years old, so what else could I do? But I did conclude to just keep my mouth shut about anything. My opinions I would keep to myself and if he left and stayed out all night or even days, so what because eventually he was going to leave. I had given up and I didn't want Chico anymore. But I was still very deeply in love with that man but the way he treated me made me feel like I was a burden to him. I would've rather seen him happy without me. I just believed he kept me around because I was a money maker. An asset! So that's something that he doesn't want to let go and now I'm pregnant. OMG! Could it get any worse? I wanted to get an abortion because I wasn't feeling the pregnancy at all. And I knew Chico was not going to give me the money to get an abortion! I would've done it on my own but couldn't make no moves with all that shit over my head. I was going to have to thug it out, so I stayed to myself. I bothered Chico whenever I needed a ride to DRC, my meetings, court and that was all. I kept my distance and prayed, and it seemed like once I let Chico take over, things were getting worse and worse. We suddenly had to leave the apartment and moved to a hotel room for a while, going from place to place. He took all of our furniture, the Valentine's present he got me was gone, so I chopped everything up as a loss the "The Lord didn't like the arrogant and wicked. The wrath that comes from the Lord is real" and I never thought about that until this very moment. Amazing because things was really going downhill for him. Most of his cousins had left and went back to Alabama and after we moved back into the same rooming house we first moved in on Brook Ave. things had turned around for the better. By this time I'm 5-6 months pregnant and it looked like I was having the baby. I also gained 50lbs making me 170lbs now so I blew up quick. I'd been going to my doctor's appointments and when the doctor did the ultrasound, they showed me how it's legs was wide open and with a little pecker showing, it was determined that it was A BOY!

CHAPTER 17

ON A MISSION!

AROUND THIS TIME, I'd been noticing a change with Chico. He wasn't the same as he once was. I had got swollen quick and my stomach was so big it seemed like I was having twins. But I'd already been in drug court 8 months, so I had only 4 more months to go! My goal was to finish drug court because if I did, I would graduate right before I had him. So, I was on a mission! But, during the time we had moved back to where we had started, I was starting to like Chico again. It might've been because he was going broke! I mean, he could've sold a car or jewelry to get back on but since I was showing a lot more indicating that it wasn't just us anymore, we had a child coming, we needed to tighten up because I couldn't take another one being lost to the system! I refuse to let that happen. I really didn't know what was going on in Chico's head but after the police incident we only had one more incident after that but this time I was fighting his ass back. Something like that of Ike and Tina in the back of that limo! And yes, I was showing, and I think that baby saved me on that fight because it could've been worse. But, after that there were no more arguments or fights and he always stayed home, and also, he was working! Yes, Chico got a job painting houses! Now shop wasn't completely closed but Chico was trying to find a way out. I started to like Chico again more and more, but I didn't let my guard down! Chico would also go back and forth to Alabama because that's where he eventually wanted to move to. That's where he took the furniture from the apartment, the 64 Impala, and the J30. It was whatever to me because he was gone, and I knew he was in Alabama and plus we were not arguing. But this nigga was always full of surprises! Okay people how about when this dude was going back and forth to Alabama, I found out that this nigga had a bitch he had done moved down there. Her name was Josephine and when I found out about it when I was 7 months pregnant, on 9/11/01. For some strange reason my cookies weren't feeling right, so I made an appointment. While in the waiting area is when I saw the airplanes crashing into the Twin Towers! I was like "Oh, shit!" and the doctors were all watching it then. This was after I peed in a cup to get my cookies checked and when the results came back, they called me and told me that I had Trichomonas! Yes, this nigga was fucking a dirty, nasty ass bitch raw and she burned him, and he brought that shit to me. I couldn't wait to get home and show him that bullshit. The first thing I asked him was who he'd been fucking? He lied and said no one but when I reminded him that he was going to always keep it 100% with me, I could see it on his face. Poor thing! It was a look like how she knew but he maintained his innocence until I pulled out the paperwork and showed him what he brought to me. I even told him that they said that stuff could cause the baby to be blind and when I showed that to him, that's when he broke down and told me what happened. WOW! So, I gave him the paper to go to the clinic and get his dick right and made that nigga call that nasty hoe so she could get her pussy cleaned! "You know what, I'm good you can go back to her" I told him. But I made him feel low because he jeopardized our child because he couldn't keep his dick in his pants. Sorry ass! Oh, and I was on strike!

I had just two more months to go until my due date. A son was something that I'd always wanted, and I wasn't trying to do anything to jeopardize that! Also, my probation officer gave me an ultimatum to either go to prison or get my GED. I was working on that at the DRC and when the officer told me that, I asked her was that a trick question? It only took one month for me to accomplish that! By October 2001, it was mine! But during this pregnancy things was different. I stayed clean and sober, no morning sickness hardly and I gained a lot of weight opposed to my first two. It might've been because they were females. My favorite food was crab legs and popcorn and I also achieved my GED. I also listened to a lot of music with him. And Chico and I fought only twice in 9 months! And I finally graduated from drug court! Thank You God! I personally never thought that I could do it! There were times I told Miss Fisher my probation officer to go ahead and violate me, but the lord gave her to me because he knew she had a good heart. Thanks Pam! I didn't know what God's plan was with me and Chico, but I could really tell the change in him since I got pregnant. It seemed like he was getting in position to play the Dad role because after that last incident when he was thinking with the wrong head, yea Josephine, He didn't leave my sight unless he went to work! He looked like a changed man! And he was showing me he appreciated me finally! He would sit and put his hands on my stomach and as big as the baby was when he moved, you could practically see it. You didn't even have to feel it. It was nice! But, as soon as I got off papers, guess what? I went back to work. It was a minor setback for a major comeback indeed, so I hooked up with Mrs. Easter and Bull and that's where I went back to. I would pay Easter $100 a day to be at her house and I would also be at Mr. Joe's house that stayed next door to Mrs. Easter. So, if a friend of mine pulled up, I would tell them to stand on Mr. Joe porch and I would be on Easter porch and pass it over. We screened in Easter porch so that we could see out of, but no one could see in. It was a nice set up. At first no one could stand Easter because she was the police! She had a big mouth and stayed in other people's business. But I always had a way with people and even the toughest people I could break. I was all over the place from Mrs. Clara, Mrs. Gwen, Easter, Mr. Ben, and all the other older people on Mapel St. They all were tough cookies until I came with that smile and my aura. Hooked them and of course money talked, and bullshit walked! Known Fact! So, I was back and now 8 months pregnant so I could pop any day. But I was getting it! Chico couldn't handle his morning sickness because he had more of that than me. He loved pizza and slept a lot, but I was enjoying seeing this side of him. He was growing up and talked about God a lot more! It finally seemed like I was about to get what I'd always wanted, a family! Chico was content with working and me, it didn't make a difference who was out on the block just as long as the bread came to the same house. Niggas I grew up around wasn't ready for Chico. Most of those so called "Gangstas" wasn't on that type of time. They would talk the talk but couldn't walk the walk. One thing I did know, don't make no enemies out here because the streets of Raleigh N.C. will get your ass out of here. These niggas in Raleigh has always been fake. "Some" was real, but very few so I was glad Chico had come to that conclusion, I had it! So, when I was out trapping I had not a worry in the world because niggas knew that if they see me, Chico wasn't too far away! It was a perfect arrangement.

On 11/08/01, I'm at Al and Mrs. Gwen's house chilling on the porch listening to Juveniles 400 degrees album and all a sudden, my water broke and them contractions was hitting me. Boom! Boom! I pleaded for them to call the ambulance, but Al went and took me in his car. He was flying down New Burn Ave and I told Al to call Chico and tell him to come to the hospital. When I get there, they hurry and take me straight to the back and fortunately I'm taking these contractions like a champ! But they were crucial so they got me back there and started the epidural process and once I got back not too far behind me was Chico and I was shocked to see my mom May come. With Chico there right beside me and May sitting beside me, I was tripping because Chico was looking all nervous like he was the one who was gonna push the baby out! So, I got the epidural and things are a lot better now. Thank God! Shortly after that, my contractions were getting closer and closer together and the doctor came in and asked "okay, are you ready to push?" May left out the room and Chico came and stood beside me and held my hand. I pushed with each

CHAPTER 17

contraction the doctor is telling me to push but the baby was too big. He wasn't trying to come out, so the doctor said that she needed some help pushing because he was a big baby. Two nurses came and they each got on both sides of me and put their hands on my stomach and when I pushed, they pushed down on my stomach so he could come out. So, we all pushed, and the head came out. They kept telling me to push and to keep pushing and then boom, there he goes! But something was wrong. The nurses then came and grabbed him and started sucking stuff out his mouth and nose. He was covered up with green stuff, so they rushed him out. I asked the doctor what was going on and what I discovered was all that stuff on the baby was dookie. The sack had broken and when he used the bathroom it was all in his eyes, nose, and mouth. So, they rushed him to suck all that stuff out of him and washed him off. The doctor told me that he would be okay, but I was being sarcastic when I said, "so Doc, you are telling me that our son came out full of shit?" The doctor laughed and said "yes!" That was funny to me, but while they were cleaning me up, they were weighing the after birth. They told me the sack he was in weighed 22lbs. They were shocked! But it didn't take them long to clean him off and let me hold him. He was funny looking because he looked like a white Chinese baby! Chico was looking at me crazy! OMG! There we go with the bullshit! I asked him, why was he looking at me the way he was and Chico said, "because the baby look white". In my mind I'm thinking, I just had him, duh! Don't start nothing man! So, I let Chico hold him and his eyes was big because our son was so huge. The nurse picked him up and put him on the weigh scale. He was 10 lbs. 13 oz.! Everyone in the room was amazed. It was a smooth pregnancy no laceration nothing and the doctors or the nurses couldn't believe that. But yes, we did it! They then took the baby out; Chico went out and they cleaned me up and took me in another room. When Chico came back in, he looked like the happiest man on earth when they brought the baby back in. The doctor came back in and asked me could they place my placenta in the Wake Medical Records as the heaviest placenta in Wake Medical

ALL I HAVE

History. Sure, shit I felt special because out the gate my son came out making history! And on top of that, I looked like I had two babies in one! So, I signed the papers, it was truly an honor! "Thank you, God, for a healthy baby boy!" on 11/09/01 my son came into this world. The nurse asked what is his name and Chico looked at me like what are we are going to name him and I said "Rodrequise Lavell Calhoun Jr." and that made Chico year. A baby boy named after him, and you couldn't tell him nothing and me neither because now I had two Chico's! Little Chico and Big Chico. Double the trouble!

One month later.......

I got in a car accident a month prior to me giving birth and I had to spend the night at Rex Hospital because I was in the front seat of a cab and a lady came behind the cab and hit us in the back. I went straight to the hospital. My stomach had got bruised from the seat belt and the hospital was afraid for the baby and just for one night in the hospital they gave me $6,000 about 6 weeks later! When I got home with lil Cheek, Chico did not let him stay with no one period. He didn't let no one hold him, he was very protective of him, but I was thinking it was because of what happened to my first two kids. Chico was with me through what I was going through, and he use to go with me to the Social Service building to visit them. Which is why I trying my best to erase from my memory. When a child gets taken away from a parent it hurts and with me being young with no support system at all, it's hard and I eventually tried to cope the best I could. But that whole ordeal played a part on why Chico was overprotective of him. Lil Cheeks color was coming in and he was a handsome lil fella! Big Chico would go shopping for him and I didn't have to do nothing. When they would come to the block to come through, they would have the exact same outfits on, same hats, shirts, pants, socks and shoes. The only thing they would have different was the underwear and if he could have worked that out, I believe he would have. I would be sitting on Mrs. Easter porch and there they go walking

CHAPTER 17

up. Chico didn't stay long out there because he had the baby and Easter wasn't too fond of Chico because of the fighting we use to do. She always felt funny towards Chico. But things were different. Chico would come and then he went back home. He had stopped working for a while because I needed to work, and he stayed home with lil Chico. Yes, Big Chico took the Mother position and I did me. I was truly feeling the family thing! One day I'm sitting on Easter's porch and someone in a cab pulls up. When I looked, Kairi got out the car! Okay, what do this nigga want? I thought. I had run into him a few times but now I was wondering what's on his mind. He told me that he got some work that he was trying to get off and if I would let him rock, he would let me get the work for the same price he was getting it for. Okay, I then started listening. Every trap since back in the day I had Kairi there. After that Unc situation we had talked and he had apologized about how things had gone but I wasn't the type to hold grudges I learned to pray on it and the Lord will handle it accordingly So, I looked at him as a friend and he getting Ounces for the low and that was right up my alley because right then I was paying just about double the cost he charged. I then told him to let me holla at Chico and I needed to holla at Easter and Joe. I also told him that he'd have to pay Easter $100 also a day. "Cool", he said, and he gave me a couple of grapes so I could find out what he was working with. I gave out a few samples and it's what I was needing! So, I talk to Easter and she was with $200 a day! Joe, I had him so now I had to holla at my baby Chico. When I got home that night, I talked to Chico and let him know the proposition Kairi came to me with and asked him would that be fine with him. I loved my Chico so I wouldn't have done anything to jeopardize my family and I let big Chico know that and because he knew I loved him and he trusted me, he was cool with it. But he said if he got uncomfortable with the situation, he was going to let me know and then Kairi would have to go. My reply was, "Ok, Bet!"

CHAPTER 18

CHICO HAD BEEN very content with our arrangement like I said earlier he took over my role. I looked at it as him being a real man. He loved his son. Every time I would see Chico, he would have a glow on his face and lil Cheek was right there in his arm. Chico had bought something like a book bag that goes on the stomach where the lil one would be on his chest. So, things were looking even more promising on top of me finally getting my insurance check. It was $6,000 so that came in handy but when I got the money, Chico had wanted to put it with what he had to go get right in Alabama. But I didn't want to do that, so we got to arguing about that. Me trying not to let the argument escalate, I leave with lil Chico to let Big Chico cool off not thinking that I left my money in the pocketbook in the closet. I then leave and come back 30 minutes later, and Chico was gone. When that nigga didn't answer his phone that's when I noticed that my money was missing. I remember thinking "Damn, that nigga got me again!" His cars were in Alabama so where was he going? Okay, I got his ass! I then called the bus station and asked "What time did the bus leave going to Birmingham Alabama?" and the operator told me that the bus had just left an hour ago and the next one would be the next morning! Damn that nigga get on my damn nerves! I had to get to Alabama quick, so I called the train station and the next train for Birmingham departed at 10am. I told myself, "Think Tina!" Although I had never ridden on a plane before I especially wasn't trying to get on one after that 9/11/01 shit had just happened 3 months earlier, I

CHAPTER 18

was like forget that, time was ticking. He'd been on the bus for 5 hours now and it was an express bus so he would be there by 10pm. I thought that if I caught the plane, I would beat him there, so I had a trick for his ass. I then called the airport, booked me a flight to Birmingham Alabama and me and lil Chico was in the air. OMG! That was a crazy experience! I prayed so hard but Thank God because he got us to Birmingham safe and sound. Lil Chico had won everyone over on the plane hearts because all they kept saying was, he a big boy! And he giggled all the way. Lil Cheek was a good baby! We landed at the airport in Alabama and although I only took a diaper bag with him and some changes of clothes for lil cheek, I didn't take anything for me because I could buy something once I got there. I hopped in a cab at the airport and went straight to Chico's mother's house. I paid for the cab and knocked on the door and when Big Chico opened the door, his eyes were like golf balls. It was as if he'd seen a ghost! But all he did was laughed. Both of us did actually and he reached in his pocket and gave me all my money! Chico said he had just got there, and he was wondering how I had found out that he was going to Alabama. I had been with him too long, so I felt it. He then took the baby from me and went and showed him to his mother, but Ms. Pam Chico mom is something special. I don't know what it was, but she loved her some lil Chico. But you really had no choice because he was a pretty fat baby! So, we went to sleep and woke up the next morning went to his Grandma Margie's house. I love Ms. Margie! She is a down to earth woman; she is a cool older lady to me. If she has anything bad to say about me, she never showed me any signs that she didn't like me because she never came at me sideways! I also knew why Chico was so eager to show lil Cheek to Ms. Margie. He wanted her opinion about lil Cheek! When we pulled up in her apartment complex, he got out with lil Chico and I'm right behind him. Margie was sitting in a chair in the kitchen as she always had done, and Chico handed lil Chico to her. She looked at him, lifted his neck and started kissing on it and she said "Now, that's my baby!" She was so happy and big Chico went in the back room and brought a picture out and showed it to me. For a moment, I'm just looking at the picture because it was red. I knew it was lil Chico in that picture, but I asked big Chico how did he get a picture of lil Cheek that looked red like that. He told me that it was him when he was a baby! That was amazing to me because they looked just like twins in that picture! After that, I could rest easy because that very moment Chico knew who lil Chico father was. But Big Chico always had a guilty conscious, so suspicion would have always been in the back of his mind if his grandma didn't approve. Chico once told me that when he brought Tera down there and showed Margie Tera's baby, she told Chico that wasn't his baby. But, lil Cheek! She would not let him go. It was like looking at Big Chico all over again! We had a good time in Alabama those couple of days I was down there. He introduced me to his pops and Chico looked like his pops but his pops were darker than him. We went to a few cookouts and the girl that burnt Chico wanted me to come to her house for dinner! Okay, really? I declined. Margie had lil Chico and I think the size of him really got her because he was two babies in one. Huge! After a while I was ready to get back to N.C. because I needed to work but Chico was getting tired of N.C. and he was trying to find a place in Alabama, so he stayed. I would've rather him stayed also to get peace of mind. Before I left, we went and hollered at one of his people in Alabama and got right. Him and the baby stayed. I hopped on the bus and headed back to Raleigh. All Chico did when he was in Raleigh since I had the baby was stayed in the house anyway. It seemed like something had really been on his mind, but I couldn't never get him to open up to me. The past 2.5 years I'd been knowing Chico, I never opened to him either. There was never no personal communication between us. I always wanted to ask what was on his mind but was too afraid to ask! When I got back to Raleigh with the special batch, I was itching to let one of my friends tell me how it was. We had let someone down there try it but my friends' word on that issue was what I went by. I couldn't do nothing but Thank God when I made it back to Raleigh safely so now it was crunch time. I went to put my stuff up, got myself situated and

CHAPTER 18

headed to the block. Before I left, I went ahead and got everything situated with Kairi, Joe, and Easter. He had been working the whole time I was gone but he wasn't no competition. I already had the spot booming, so he just wanted to eat. One day he didn't even come out, so that was even better for me. I had called ahead of time and let him know I'll be out shortly, but I guess he just wanted to let me rock! It was enough money for everybody to eat and besides, I'm not a greedy individual when it comes down to my people's, but I am an antisocial person and my circle is very small. But, on this particular day, I stayed out late. Both houses were rocking and what I brought back from Alabama was some drop so basically, I locked the block down. But, while up in the spot about 9pm or 10pm I hear a knock on the door. I ask Bull to get the door because it was only him and myself there. All I remember was sitting in the recliner watching T.V. and when Bull opened the door 4 people with mask come in the house. Bull went running out the front door hollering "call the police!" LOL! I was trying to check out the features to see if I recognize any of them and automatically, I knew who they were! They walked right by me heading to the back. I said "D, Kairi not here" and he said "Naw Sis, I got to check, I don't want you anyways." So, they went and checked and walked right out. D, Bro, Head, but the fourth one I couldn't make out. So, you know that was the talk of the town the next day. I heard "Tina got robbed last night", but it didn't make me no difference because I knew what happened and they knew also so I left it alone. But, when Kairi came out the next day I did let him know that some niggas came to rob the house the night before and they were looking for him specifically. So, after that he always came with the strap on him. I had done a few things that I'm not proud of and by the Grace of God I had nothing to worry about. I'd hoped and prayed to God that Kairi didn't think that I would've done anything to hurt him. Kairi and my relationship is a true friendship in my eyes, when me and Chico would argue, I would go to his house off of Spring Forest Rd. and would sleep on his floor because he didn't have any furniture so if I wanted anything to happen to him, I hoped he knew that I could've easily took it to his domain! Chico had kept his clothes at Kairi's house before Chico and myself hooked up so I hope he wasn't thinking that way or he could've been because his home boy had just gotten killed a few weeks earlier in a robbery at a hotel. So Kairi could've been feeling some kind of way because of that. Why I say that is because when I went out there, I felt the tension. It was so thick; you could slice it with a knife. I had to tell him that Chico wasn't in the state and that he and our son was in Alabama and he wasn't coming back. I could see the relief on his face after I said that and while he was sitting on the porch, Bro's baby Mother, June walked up and came and sat with us on the porch. She said that she knew who had come to rob him the other night and Kairi was like who and she said "Bro, and D". I already knew that, but it wasn't my position to say anything because the niggas that came was my people's also. Shit was deep out here man. Survival of the fittest! And she offered up that because June was my people also. She was only trying to lookout for me because she had known me longer than Bro although Bro was her baby's father. I think I would've kept my mouth shut because in that situation there's no sides! With that type of information, Kairi was on a mission and now everyday he came out, he took his strap to Al's house which was two doors over from Easter. Mind you that this is the set up that I had previously, but money talks and bullshit walks and that's how I told him to play it because at the same time it was benefitting me too. But, deep inside I knew I had nothing to worry about.

    A month had passed, and I was missing the two most important men in my life so when I talked to Chico he told me that he was coming to N.C. to visit for a while and was heading back to Alabama. I couldn't wait to see them so when they arrived, both of them looking like Siamese twins joined by the chest. Kisses, kisses and more kisses were everywhere on my fat baby's because Big Chico had gained some weight also eating all that good country cooking! Same hat, down to the shoes, it was too much! It was a dream come true! We decided to stay at the Lodge Hotel on Capitol Blvd because Chico

CHAPTER 18

was trying to get us situated in Alabama. With him being 26 years old and I being 21, I guess he wanted to settle down, so I was going to support him regardless because I was truly in love with this man! When we got ourselves situated at the hotel, he breaks it down to me, that he asked his mother to help him get an apartment in Birmingham and she wasn't willing to help him. The money wasn't an issue, the credentials was the problem because neither one of us had a job, but I told Chico just to be patient because "The Lord was going to work it out." I asked him how long was he going to stay up here this time, and he told me that one of his homeboys had just got killed and he wanted to go back for his funeral in 5 days max and of course he was taking lil Cheek. I was cool with that. I only had a little more work left that would take a couple of days, so I chilled there with the fellas for 3 days enjoying every bit of it. All we bought lil Cheek was a swing and we sat him in front of SpongeBob, and he was good all day long unless he needed his diaper changed or food. He was truly a good baby. So, after them 3 days was up, I was ready to go back to work so I could finish up and head back with the boys to Alabama!

April 2002....

I head over to Mapel St. to get ready for work and Ms. Easter pulled me over to the side. She told me that Kairi came to her and Joe and said he would pay them double what I was paying them to keep me from coming over there. This nigga was bugging the fuck out. How is he going to bite the hand that feed him? When he walked through Easter's door, the first thing I said to him was "dude, I brought you here, what you thought Easter wasn't going to let me know?" He was sitting there like whatever man, so I ended up telling him "A, yo you got to go!" He was like he wasn't going nowhere! So, I go on to say, "You about to get the fuck out of here." Easter then told him "Yea, you're gonna have to go because I'm not with all the arguing". Kairi then goes next door but now I'm thinking to myself "I know this nigga don't think I'm solo?" Right then my phone rings and it's Chico and he tells me that I'd took his jacket with his money and lil Cheek needed diapers and milk. My response was "Ok, come and get it". I wasn't going to put Chico in-between what was going on because I know I can handle it. I then walked over to Mr. Joe's house next door because I was trying to see if he came at Joe the same way he had come at Easter. Mr. Joe was an alcoholic and, in a wheelchair, so all he did was drink wine and sit at the window. And Joe admitted that Kairi had already paid him for that day so I then told Joe that this would be the last day dude was going to be there! I couldn't figure out where all of this was coming from but the nigga really got me to thinking that he really was a grimy ass nigga after all because how could he? The phone rings several minutes later and it's Chico again telling me that he's caught a cab over there to get the money from me. I was like "Okay, good because I needed the money off me anyways". Until then I was hoping that I could talk some sense into Kairi's head without getting too out of control. The phone then rings again "What's up Chico?" I asked. "You got some weed?" he asked. I answered by saying "I was about to get Easter to take me to Quarrel St. to cop some, you want me to snatch you some?", "yea". So, I go ask Easter could she take me to snatch up some weed from Evon house and Easter said "yes". I called Chico back and asked him how long he was going to be. He said he was pulling up, so we waited until he got there. Chico arrive and I looked at Joe's house and Kairi looks dumb founded. I didn't put people in my business and besides Chico didn't have a clue what was going on with this situation. Why because Kairi wasn't a threat here pimpin. But if you can't stand the heat stay out the kitchen. I guess this nigga thought Chico was out the picture. So, when Chico pulled up, I paid the cab fare and asked him where was lil Cheek. He said that a friend of ours had him. Surprised, I said "Ok, here is the money and you can wait here, or you can go get the milk and come back." I then leave to go get the weed. Now from the time I leave from Mapel St. to Quarrel St. which was a 20-minute max drive, I cops the weed and we pulled back up on Ponder St. We were about to make a right on Mapel St. when we saw that the police had Easter's house taped

CHAPTER 18

off. OMG! I jumped out the car with it still rolling and Easter jumps out. I immediately saw that it was Kairi laying on the porch with Keosha standing over him. Once, I saw that, I panicked. "Where's Chico?" There was only one place he could be. I went straight to my cousin's house in May view. When I get there, I blurt out "Yo, what the fuck happened?" Chico just sat there silent! He had on his face a look of defeat and worry. My response was "WTF!!! Why man?" He then told me calmly that the nigga Worm came over to give him a ride back to the hotel and saw Kairi and confronted him and when he went to slap him with the gun, the barrel of the gun hit the coffee table and he shot him by mistake. He also said that he thought it had something to do with robbing Kudah. Kudah was Worms other baby mother. So, it made sense because a couple years back, Kudah and Worm was staying on Ranson St. and Kudah, Kudah's mom Theresa, and Kudah's sister Pink was there the night Kairi robbed them barefaced. Prior to Kairi being shot, I didn't know any of this and I guessed it slipped Chico's mind also. I then received another phone call and it's my mom May telling me that she was at the hospital with Kairi and I said "okay", and to keep me posted. She calls back 15 minutes later and she said, "He's gone!" The news coverage said:

Karim Emanuel had got shot and killed 112 Mapel ST. and the authorities are looking for two suspects. A 26-year-old Rodrequise Calhoun, and a 23-year-old Deshawn Bennet. Anyone that has any information, contact Wake homicide.

The phone rings again but this time it's my grandma Lynda telling me that the police had the house surrounded and was now inside the house and wanted to make sure that I was safe. They also wanted to talk to me, and I told her to tell them that I was safe, and I was coming to the precinct. I turned to Chico and told him what was said "Just tell the truth Tina! Go ahead down there and see what's going on." My response was "Chico we can leave now and go to Mexico, Let's go now" But Chico was like "Tina, I have to think. I should've left when

ALL I HAVE

I said I was. "Just go Tina." So, I called a cab from the Harris Teeter which was 5 minutes away and they dropped me off walking distance from the police station. I then walk in the precinct.

When I walked in, I gave them my name and told them that the police had come to my grandmother's house looking for me. The officer knew exactly what I was talking about because his demeanor told it all. So, a black lady comes downstairs and escorts me up on the elevator. She introduces herself by saying "Hi, I'm detective Bullock and I'm the officer in charge of the case." We shook hands and she continue to escort me. The first person I see is Worm! They had caught him in a cab. WOW! Me and the detective left right in time because I hear Mrs. Easter's mouth in the next room. They made sure I had seen and heard all of that and then they took me to the interrogation room. They pulled out the tape recorder and told me that I wasn't under arrest and that they just wanted to ask me a few questions. The first question was, "what was I doing at Easter's house on Mapel St.?" In my mind all I hear is Chico telling me to tell the truth "That's my trap house!" I said. Her next question was what was Karim (Kairi) doing there? I then told her "well he asked me could he come and trap with me and he was going to pay the price we paid Easter $100 a day" Her next question was "So who are you to Karim?" "He's just a friend, nothing more." I answered. "Well people telling my officers that you all tried to rob Kairi" she replied. Right then I had to break the shit down to her by saying "look, I knew where Kairi lived so if robbery was the motive, I would've taken it to his house! Why would we do that on Mapel St. in broad daylight with all those informants out there?" She then says "Ok, then Gilchrist, what was Chico doing there?" I told her the truth by saying "He came to get some money to go get diapers and milk and was waiting for me to bring him back some weed to smoke." "Gilchrist did you know that Rodrequise had killed before?" she asked me. My heart dropped. OMG!! My response was "No, I didn't know that." She continued by saying "yes, he did 3.5 years as a juvenile. We can also link him to over a dozen crime

CHAPTER 18

scenes, but we don't have the evidence." Frustrated out of mind and because I wasn't going to snitch on Worm, I blurted out "I killed Kairi, I did it." Thinking back, that had to have been the dumbest shit ever but I loved Chico that much" Yea, I know someone reading this may be talking shit, but you'll soon find out that love will make you do some crazy things. The officers then look at each other and they walked out the room. 30 minutes - an hour later Detective Bullock came back in and says "Gilchrist, we know you didn't do it. Easter alibied you and the officer that was on the scene corroborated her story, so we know you didn't do it." I immediately started crying because I just knew that they were going to take my love away! So, I went on "Bullock, I'm telling y'all I did it, I shot Kairi, it was me." Her response was "Gilchrist you are free to go and if you talk to Rodrequise tell him it's in his best interest to turn himself in. Another thing, do you know where he is?" Scared, my response was "He caught a bus to Atlanta, he's gone." So, I left the substation walking and once I thought I was safe, I called a cab, got off up the street from where Chico was at and walked the rest of the way. When I got back to the house where Chico and the baby was at, Big Chico was still awake, but the baby was asleep. I then told him everything they said, and I told the officers the truth of why he was there. I told him that they had Worm already and Easter was there. I also told him that they thought that he was in Alabama so we could go away from here and let them catch us. I was ready because we had a little change. We could leave the work there and we could bounce, but for some crazy reason he wasn't feeling that. This nigga looked like he was at peace! Shit! I was ready to fuckin go! Chico then said that his son "Worm" was going to tell them the truth as to what happened, so he wasn't going to be gone long. He also said that running was going to make him look guilty when he didn't do anything. WTF! I wasn't trying to hear that shit because I knew Worm was a Bitch! Before I went to the precinct, I had called Worm and he had already said that it was an accident confirming what Chico said happened but I was like "look Chico, fuck all that, let's go!" I began crying because I didn't want the love of my life to go nowhere. I didn't realize how deeply I was in love with him until I prayed "God Please Help Us!" While still crying I asked him, "Chico what are you going to do?" His reply was "I'm going to enjoy my son and you and I'm going to turn myself in tomorrow!" Right then my heart was snatched right out of my chest! I begged him please don't do this to me, I love you, we need you here Chico, and I remember staying up all night. But that night he didn't touch me, didn't kiss me, nothing. He just sat quietly like he was at peace with the whole situation. When we got up the next day and sat and talked Chico said he felt something was going to happen for months, but he didn't expect this. He said "Tina, I don't want to take you and my son on the run because God knows I didn't do this crime and I believe Worm got my back. He also thought that turning himself in would be the best look in that situation. He then told me to not let anything happen to our son and if I needed anything to call his grandmother Ms. Margie because she had me. He then gave me her number. So, we called a cab from May view and went to Polar Dr. to May house. The cab stopped and he got out of the cab with me, gave lil Cheek a kiss and me a hug and kiss and he got back in the cab. I told him one more time, we can go Chico, but he looked like he had given it all to God! And like that, he was gone......

News coverage: Both suspects in the shooting death of Karim Emanuel are in custody at the Wake Detention Center without bond....

CHAPTER 19

My King is GONE!

THERE WERE TIMES that I cried so uncontrollably that I couldn't stand looking at my own child. When I would look at him, I'd think about his father, I'd get angry at the world and ask God, "Why me?" What had I done to get that kind of treatment? Why couldn't I ever have happiness? Why did you have to take him from me Lord? All my life I'd been mistreated. No one liked me and although we had our ups and downs, Lord he was changing. God, this wasn't his fault. Please Lord do something! I have faith in you Lord, don't let them take my love away! …. The feeling that I felt once they locked away my love was emptiness, hatred, coldness, a fuck the world mentality. Anybody could've got it, and what was the worst part of it was because I knew for a fact, he didn't do it. I'd talked to Worm myself and he'd told me the whole story. Then my phone ring, it said that I had a collect call from the Wake Jail. It was Chico! I immediately said "Hey my love" as I wiped the tears from my face. He went on to tell me that "they had charged him with first degree murder", and my response was "I told you about that dude in the first place Chico, that nigga wasn't built like that". All he had to do was remain silent. He then stated that he couldn't get a bond. My heart stopped listening to his voice on the phone. I had to mute the phone so he couldn't hear me cry. I then regretted not telling them what Worm had done when Detective Bullock interrogated me. He must have sensed it because he just went ahead and let me go. I completely lost it! So many emotions went through my mind, because I had endured a lot of pain getting Chico to the point he was. He began appreciating life and he was becoming the man that I was looking for. He was showing me that he loved me and his son. OMG! I was praying the pain hurts God and to take the pain away and lil Cheek would start crying as if he knew what was going on too. But I knew that in the mental state I was in, it wouldn't allow me to care for myself let alone care for my son, so I had to think! Big Chico didn't call me for a few days, and I was wondering why because I wanted to hear his voice at least but I had to try to understand his situation. I was letting Big Chico know that I was in a deep depression and that I couldn't eat, didn't care about my life and I was tired of trying to hold my head up just to always get let down. I was tired of getting mistreated, I was never happy because all my life I'd never had anyone that loved me, let alone like me and right then I had no one to talk to, because no one cared, I even told him that. I felt like killing myself! Chico began telling me to hold it together for his son because lil Cheek needed me and if I didn't hold it together Social Service was going to take him like they took the girls. But, at that point I didn't even care about life so I told him "how could I care about anything else Chico? You there for a crime that you didn't commit." It would've been different if he had done it, but I know for a fact that he didn't do it. Chico could tell that I was in trouble, so he gave me his grandmother Ms. Margie's phone number again and he told me to take lil Cheek to Alabama. So, I called Margie and she already knew what was going on. I remember not being able to stop crying when I was on the phone with her, and Margie told me to bring her baby to her and that's exactly what I did. I had a friend (smoker) of mines car and I hit I95 to 20 West straight to Alabama. I got there in 6 hours max, gave Margie all his stuff, gave her some money and turned back around. 14 hours round trip! I had to get my mind right or at least try because all of it caught me off guard, so I had to evaluate what was going on. I needed time to think. Now check this, the time that I was gone, I was getting messages from my Mom May and ReRe

CHAPTER 19

telling me what was going on out there after all of this happened because I hadn't been out there behind all of this. It was too much for me to handle. Kairi was a friend of mine in my mind, Chico was my sons' father and Worm was Tang's baby father. I had no problem with no one in that circle. So, my mom May tells me not to come over that way because Kairi's people was riding around looking for me because they were saying that I'd set him up. So now I had some Jamaicans riding around looking to kill me on Mapel St. For the life of me, I couldn't understand where these people were getting their information from because like I said, anyone that messed with Kairi knew that he stayed off Spring Forest Rd. Even Chico knew that so if they wanted to get him, what better place to go? So, I was like "fuck these people!" and besides I was good because I could afford to stay in hibernation for a while. So, I made sure Chico had bread, and I chilled. But, with Easter and Joe house booming after all of that popped off, guess who was at Easter house trapping? My mom May, and ReRe! Yes, my mom and so-called friend! These people were scandalous! It gave me the impression that they could've been shooting me the bullshit the whole time so they could go plant seeds in Easter's ear. But what these traders didn't know was, I'm a bonafide hustler and I made the money, money didn't make me!

A few months go by, and I'm all over the place. I'm not at one location because I couldn't trust no one but God. But God is also the only one I'm fearing. Before Chico left, he taught me how to shoot so I always kept the strap on me. Known fact! So, I never left home without it and I got to that bread. I needed $25,000 to get an attorney to represent Chico so I first prayed about it, "Lord, can you help me get this money for Chico's attorney in Jesus name I pray, Amen" … I also had to figure out where my next trap was going to be. It didn't make no difference to me; I just wasn't feeling Mapel St. like that because it was too many snakes over there for me. These people were screaming they hustlers, or real niggas but every last one of them folded under pressure. I could name every one of them fake ass wannabees names

ALL I HAVE

that were out there and I bet each one of them are on someone's motion of discovery. So, fuck'em all because they're not worth my ink unless they're relevant to my testimony. But I did end up meeting two cats from Partin St. that would call me to get some work by the name of Carlos and Raymond. Now they weren't getting much about 7gs or less, but I knew what house they were in on Freemon St. Carlos was a former basketball player at State College during 2000-2001 but he got into trouble and they kicked him out of school. He was from Mobile Alabama and he was a down to earth dude. Chico had been locked up about 8 months, so I was nowhere near trying to fuck with no one. I was just trying to get situated so my friends could come to me instead of me meeting them and the house that Carlos had was the perfect house for me. So, I hollered at him and he was cool with it. "Let's get it!"

Back on Partin St. my reputation alone was going to bring the money because the smokers knew that I was A1. So, my worry wasn't the smokers, it was the haters on the streets. Like I said, I always kept a strap and me not personally knowing Carlos like that, I didn't know how he was moving so I asked him did he have a strap. He said yes and he even had a gun permit. Ok now we were cooking in grease! Two was most definitely better than one so it was perfect. After the first week of me being back on Partin St. that spot was booming! But that first week I did hear stories about Carlos letting smokers take his work, him tricking with this smoker and that smoker and he also had been robbed a couple times. I asked him about it, and he didn't front, he kept t100 and he told the truth. Ok, he had gotten robbed a couple times, but hold up! I kind of figured something was off about this cat but damn man, come on! He had no respect out here! Okay, I had to think! I had been around for a while and I knew a lot of these cats out there, so one day while I'm on the porch sitting with Carlos, I heard a chick outside across the street popping off at the mouth. After a second or two I then right nicely got up and I got my 38 special rubber grip, no hammer, 6 shot revolver! All I had to do

CHAPTER 19

was pull the trigger and what I'd been hearing about this bitch was that she was the police. Her name was Kimmy and she had dreads in her hair. She had used to mess with Carlos, but I didn't care about that. I was trying to get that check! But this bitch was talking out the side of her neck, so I walked up on her to check this bitch but then she goes over and got this other chick whose name was Demesha. I had already heard about Demesha because people had told me that she had them hands that it was all good because I never made a move without my little friend! So, both of them walks up on me, but with my love gone, I drew the gun down on them bitches, and WTF y'all think them bitches did? Backed the fuck back and left. But Damesha came back by herself and she walked up on the porch and I went to see what she wanted but I had one arm in the house with my hand on the trigger and the other out the door. I asked her, "What's up?" and her response was, "Hey sis, they did pay me to come and get at you, but I like you. I can respect your gangsta but look, watch out for Kim because she was talking about some police shit." I then shook Damesha's hand and she walked off. After Damesha left, I took my strap to Fred's house who stayed two doors over, but Carlos had his two straps so we were good in the house. I remember getting on the couch and falling asleep and suddenly I heard BOOM, BOOM, BOOM, POLICE! SEARCH WARRANT and then the door flew open! Damn! And right then I jumped right up ran to the right-side window that was open and dove out of it and started to hit the cut! But then I saw officer Benefield and he told me to "Get on the ground!" When he apprehended me, he told me that in all his years of working he'd never saw a female move as fast as I did "But cuff her!" I had to think quick but luckily, I had nothing on me, Thank God! So, I was good! I ended up telling officer Benefield "I'd thought that someone was coming in to rob Carlos and that's why I jumped out like I did. I was asleep on the couch." Then one of the officers said "yea, he just made a report last week of someone coming in the house robbing him and taking his guns." Saved by the police! But officer Benefield went on to say, "Well we got a call saying that you Gilchrist pointed a gun at some people earlier." In my head I'm like "That snitching ass bitch!" But I was quick on my toes Thank God! I explained, "look, it was a girl named Kimmy that Carlos was messing with and she doesn't like me being here with him. She's just jealous that's all officer." The officer then said, "Well she described the gun to us and we got a warrant to search and we know Carlos has a permit, so Carlos bring your guns out and step to the side so we can search." "Thank You God!" I'd got it out in the nick of time. They searched up and down and found no other guns or nothing else. They then left the house! That snitching ass bitch! But next time I knew what to do with that bitch if I saw her again, I was going to get Damesha to whip her ass! Right after that I told Carlos we had to relocate ASAP! So, we went across the street to some apartments across from Gunter School on Delvie St. It was a smoker's house that was only temporary until the house cooled down after that incident that took place on Partin St. But how about the night that we was there, I was in the back room sitting on the toilet when I heard a loud BOOM, then a bullet came flying right past my head while I was bending over pulling my pants up. Then I heard someone say, "Come out with your hands up now!" So, I came out with my hands up and it's Cous, Booboo son. I hurry up and put my hands down. He then says "Tina, I didn't come for you now." But I was like "Damn Cous!" I couldn't do anything because that was Cous, so he got low and left and I said after that night, I can't be around this cat. These people had no respect for dude at all and I demanded respect! So, I got my strap from the couch and I left. Plan B!

It had been almost a year since my love had gotten taken away, and my mental state isn't getting any better. The only reason why I hadn't pulled the trigger on myself was because I believed that God would forgive you for anything except self-murder! Thank God, I didn't want to go to hell! So as the days turned into months it was getting harder and harder for me to cope. I would go downtown and go stand where Chico's window was at and stand there until he would pop up in the window on the 10th floor. I would go to the top of the

CHAPTER 19

parking deck and he would do signs in the window or write to each other on paper posters or we would just stand and look at each other through the window. On the fourth of July one year, I took fireworks down and lit them up for him. But, not only every holiday I would go just about every day. We didn't talk on the phone much because the phone calls were too expensive so after that first year, I took it even harder when the state of N.C. tried to use Chico's past juvenile conviction to give him the death penalty! That's when I lost it, now they were trying to kill my sons' father. I would pray all the time, "Jesus what have I done? Lord he was a changed man Lord, why? Why are you allowing this to happen to us?" Hatred filled my heart instantly and I was beginning to believe in suicide because if they were going to kill him, then I was leaving too. Point blank! I hated my life because everything I loved was taken away from me and God allowed it to happen. I would pray "God what have I done to you lord to get this treatment? Lord, I love you but why don't you love me? Answer me now Lord! Because I need some answers now! You are the Alpha and the Omega so I need your help now!" I would often cry myself to sleep to wake up hoping it was all a dream, but when I would turn and look beside me, I would be all alone. I hated my life! While in a state of deep depression, all I could do was try and figure out what I'd done for the Lord to allow the devil to bring such pain on me. All I had ever done was try my best to respect others, treat people how I want to be treated and try my best to stay away from trouble. It's exactly why I kept my circle small. At one point I thought that the Lord was finally going to answer my prayers because I had the man of my dreams who was beginning to love and appreciate me for me. I finally had the son that I'd always wanted so things was starting to look brighter! I was starting to feel happy. I finally had a family of my own but to only have it taken away from me 5 months after I had my son! Oh, my heart ached so badly! I didn't want to live, but if I committed suicide I was going to burn in hell for eternity! So, I continued to pray, "Oh

Lord God, please bring my love back to me, I'd do anything!"

CHAPTER 20

2 YEARS LATER......

    During these past couple years, I'd been trying to get the money up for the lawyer but for some reason every time I tried it was always something that hindered me from accomplishing my goal. It had been a drought for a while so that was one of the main reasons and my mental health wasn't right neither behind all of this. I had been moving kind of reckless because of everything that had been going on in my life. When my baby father got took away and a friend that I thought was mines life got snatched away, it was a lot to handle. I started feeling cold towards God! Thinking that God didn't even like me. But, at the same time wondering why me? In a 3 year time period my daughter's had got taken away, my love, my heart got snatched away from me so all I had was my son, and at that time he was in Alabama because I was scared to death to bring him to N.C. because if I lost my son, I was most definitely going to kill myself, known fact! I couldn't take that! I had gotten to the point that I didn't even want to think about the situation anymore. Back then I never once talked about this to anyone, but it was eating me up inside. But I had no one I could trust, and I was scared to talk to God. During those two years, I had done a lot of thinking as to why these events had occurred in my life and I finally came up with the conclusion. I came up with it when I'd been seeing a bunch of guys who wore a lot of beads around their necks. One day I overheard an old coon talking about the meaning

CHAPTER 20

of the beads and he also said that it was a form of voodoo! He also said that once you use voodoo, black magic or anything that's in that category, that's against God, then you better be aware of the consequences that comes behind it. So, I asked the old coon what he meant by consequences that comes because I thought that it was supposed to help not harm. He said that it did help for the moment but nothing in this world was for free! He also said that, whatever you ask for and God didn't allow you to have it or it's not from him, it will come back to haunt you! And that's when everything came back to me. The day that I sat on that porch playing solitaire with the devil and I won, and my wish was granted and now look! It was all my fault! I was willing to bet my soul for this man, young and dumb! The thing is that I didn't really believe in voodoo, so all of this had to had been a coincidence, but I decided that I needed to help him get out of that place! So, I started going to the law library downtown Raleigh and every time I went there, I would ask the woman up front questions and she would help me out a lot. While I was going, I learned a lot about the law in general and especially the drug laws. I needed to find that loophole! Worms trial was coming up in a couple weeks and they decided to try him first because they already got a statement from him. But my baby Chico had been going through hell! He had went before a judge at a hearing one year after he got locked up and they wanted to give him the death penalty because of his juvenile record in Alabama and because they said that robbery was the motive, that constituted first degree murder. But that was a lie because when they were saying that Kairi's pants were pulled down and his pockets ran through "Charles" Fatima cousin went in Kairi's pockets to take the drugs and the gun off of him so the police wouldn't find it. And, "Kosha" turned him over and pulled his pants down to see where exactly he was bleeding. The guy got hit below the waist. Common sense would tell anyone that wasn't intentional! I knew what happened and like I told Chico, just "Have faith the size of a mustard seed" because he was coming home, and because the state of N.C. went into Chico's Alabama juvenile records illegally, the judge ruled that they couldn't use his juvenile record against him because it happened in Alabama and in Alabama you are considered a juvenile until the age of 18, so the death penalty was off the table! Thank God! By the time Worm's murder trial came up, Worm and Chico had been communicating. Tang and I would make visits at the same time that allowed both of them to conversate together during the visit. They were even together in the same pod for about a month until they found out about it and moved Worm. The whole situation hurt but what hurt most was Worm because Chico showed that man nothing, but love and he turned on him at the drop of a dime! They even offered Worm 5 years if he'd get on the stand and lie but God knew Chico was innocent. I also heard that Chico had gotten saved in there also. He was preaching to people at the time. But, the Lord said be careful for what you ask for, so after all the fighting we had went though and all the times he did me wrong, I would pray to God and ask him to "please let Chico fall in love with someone else so he could leave me alone." because I was tired of getting mistreated, but the Lord knew that wasn't going to happen so he took over the situation and what we were going through I believe was the end result!

I wanted my love back! I didn't want this to happen to him so I prayed, "Lord I'm sorry for whatever I've done to get this kind of treatment from you, but Lord please listen to me because Lord you know my heart. I love you Lord so please have mercy on me!" Also because Worm wouldn't take the plea of 5 years to lie on Chico but instead got on the stand in his own trial and admitted that he lied about everything on October of 2003, Easter and an unreliable witness for the state whose name is Al gets on the stand and in less than two hours Worm was found guilty of first degree murder which meant life in prison without parole! So, when all he had to do was keep his mouth closed or told the truth, they used his own statement and testimony against Chico against himself. All that fronting and Big Boy talk,

Now look! COWARD!

CHAPTER 20

Now with Worms confession, I just knew that we had a chance because they'd convicted Worm of the shooting, so Chico was coming out strong! Johnny Galvins was Chico's attorney and I had been leaving things on his answering machine as time went on. I would call Chico's grandma to tell her to tell Chico to call me, but he never would. I had gotten in trouble with the law during this time on some petty drug offenses, nothing serious but I had got put back on probation because I was still smoking weed and popping perks so I couldn't keep my urine clean. I just didn't want to think about life. I got tired of being stressed so I needed something to take the pain away. My suspended sentence was 6-8 months if I violated probation, so I wasn't trying to give those crackers that. But, I am not going to front, once they found Worm guilty deep down inside, I didn't know which way they were going to go with Chico. So, when I did get a chance to talk to him, I tried to hold my composure because I realized that he was trying to do the same. He just knew he was coming home and that's how I wanted to keep it. It took almost two years until Chico finally had his day in court and I tried my best to hold things up but mentally I was a mess. I ended up going to ATC (alcohol treatment center) did a psych evaluation. They ended up checking me in to a two-week program. After they convicted Worm it was like hope was lost. I felt myself doing something that I would regret and my probation officer said that I had to get help, or she was going to lock me up so, ATC was the next best thing. I had to wake up at 8am to go to classes that stopped at 5pm. I had also talked to a psychiatrist and just told her everything that was going on with me and why my life had made a turn for the worst. I felt like no one loved me, not even God because how could God love me and allow me to go through this pain? I was a strong minded individual, but a person can only take but so much! I remember telling the Dr. please help me! I also told the doctor about my whole life up to that point and within the two weeks I was there, she was the only one I talked to. When the Dr. evaluated me, she told me that I was a Schizophrenic and a Manic Depressant. She also told me to try to forget the past and try to move forward because for me to get better, I had to move on. But I didn't want to because I still wanted Chico. After the 14 days was up at ATC, I got the certificate and went to my probation officer and she took me off papers. Right after that I started on my healing process. I tried my best to try to cope without thinking about him, but I also said that he could be home as soon as he went to court. So, I had faith in my Lord Jesus because he could do it!

When the day of Chico's trial came up, the state of N.C. called me as their witness, so I got on the stand. The state went on to ask me about a statement that I made in Deshawn (Worm) trial where I told them about the fights and the arguments Chico, and I had. Even George Highs, Worm's attorney said to say anything that could help him so I did but on some slick shit the D.A. called me up on the stand during Chico's trial and asked me did I make that statement in Deshawn's trial. I realized then that I had been setup. So, I plead the 5th amendment! While I was sitting on the stand Lee-Lee, Kairi's homeboy, stood up and said, "She needs to go to jail with them." Police ass Niggas! I then told the court that the statement I made was a lie. But, once I said that, the judge dismissed the jury and it was a big mess going on because I told them I lied under oath. I was told to step down and I went and sat back down. After everyone's arguments the jury was dismissed again, and we got ready to walk out and the police put me in handcuffs and said, "you're under arrest for perjury!" This police ass nigga Lee-Lee got up clapping.

Now, I'm in jail with a $200,000 bond on a perjury charge, can't get out and had no one to help me get out. But once Chico got out, I knew that he would make something happen. So, I get dressed out and they took me upstairs in the blue pod at Wake Jail. A couple of people knew who I was, and I asked the guard did she know Chico and she knew exactly what I was talking about because the news had been covering it. At 9pm that night, the guard came in and said "Guilty of 1st degree murder. Natural life in prison." My heart exploded! God knew that I wasn't going to be able to take that verdict on the outside, because if I had been out on the streets that night, I would have killed Easter and Al Them lying ass Muthafuckas! I had so much hatred in my heart, I think I would have shot everything moving and probably turned the gun on myself. Them two was the only two witnesses they had on Chico and my statement from Worm's trial but I perjured myself so they couldn't use that. I cried for days and plotted because as soon as I hit the door, somebody had to die since he was gone. Bottom line! Once again, I am completely alone. No one sent me one cent, no one sent me not one letter or even tried to see how I was doing. No one cared about me. I had absolutely no one. I didn't want to eat; all I did was sit in my cell and read the bible. I needed answers because I wanted to know why the Lord was allowing these things to happen to me. Everyone else had a father, a mother and they also had their baby fathers around. Some even had the love of their lives. I soon found myself in prayer again. "Lord, I love you. I always have loved you. You are the only one I've ever had to talk to but now it seems like it's been a mistake talking to you because it's not helping me out none Lord. It seems that it's going in the opposite direction." I was in jail and had no one to call, so I'm up day and night reading, trying to find some answers as to why I was getting treated like this. I began questioning myself with crazy questions like "Am I a bad person on the inside? Am I the devil? What is it?" But I believe in Jesus and I knew in my heart I love the Lord. But one thing I did know was that I had to come up with something because I wasn't going to get out of this mess unless I did. I had been in that situation before and the Lord came through, so I kept reading through the Bible to try to get closure on the situation that I'd gotten myself into. I thought he said just have faith as small as a grain of sand and it would be done? What happened to that? I knew that God could do anything in this world so why not let my love out? I was constantly reading the Bible and nothing else, humbling myself so I could try to seek the Lord in order to hear the answers to my questions, but I wasn't hearing anything. Maybe it was because my head was all cloudy! I prayed, "Lord, help me out here!" A couple of months had gone by since Chico's

ALL I HAVE

guilty verdict had come, and I was sitting in jail and no one showed no love. At this moment I realized that I absolutely had no one except God. I'd knew that but dang not one coin. Worry triggered worship, "ok Lord I surrender." I was going to stay away from people like Easter and Al and I was going to let him handle them both. Vengeance was his because that might have been why Chico was where he was now even though the crime didn't go nowhere near what the D.A. said. They didn't care about the truth as long as they could do what they wanted. I also guessed God wanted it that way because Chico wasn't no saint either. He did mistreat me, but I would never wish his circumstances upon anyone. So, I was going to be careful what I asked for and was going to forget about what Al and Easter did. As a matter of fact, I was going to stay away from them and try to get my life back on track. I also had to come to the realization that I was going to always be a misfortunate person. I was just gonna have to try my best to be thankful. There was really not much you could do with a natural life verdict. All I could do was be a Mother to my son and try my best to keep my head up. I had to remember to stay to myself because people out there in the streets were not who they claimed to be. They swear up and down they gangsta, but they couldn't take the heat. So, I was going to continue talking to God, but I was going to be careful what I asked for. I was going to try not to ask God for nothing because I couldn't take anymore disappointments. I didn't think I deserved this kind of treatment. No father, no mother, children gone and the love of my life gone forever, I didn't know what I had done to get this treatment but I prayed, "Lord Jesus, I'm sorry for whatever I've done for you to do this but, Lord please forgive me because I'm a sinner living in the flesh and I know not what I say or do in Jesus name Amen."

5 months later....

"Ms. Gilchrist get ready for court." I was told finally! When I went to court the same D.A. Jeff Crowder was there for my court case, and a black man whose name was Mr. Turner was my court appointed

CHAPTER 20

attorney. Mr. Turner told me that the D.A. was offering me a one-year unsupervised probation plea but he also said I could beat the charge because I plead the 5th amendment. At that point I was just ready to go so I took the guilty plea of perjury. So, while the D.A. was speaking, he had a smile on his face and finally said, "If it wasn't for Tina Gilchrist's testimony, Rodrequise probably would have walked" and smiled. WOW! I hate these people with a passion, and I wanted to shoot him right then. I even seen me pulling out and POW! But I had to snap back into reality. The judge went ahead and took the plea and I looked up to the ceiling and Thanked God! I was on my way out!

CHAPTER 21

2004

I'M BACK ON the scene and my mom May, ReRe, my brothers Lamont, David, and others were all at Easter's house. Mapel St. was packed from Parkwood Ave. to Booker St. I really wasn't feeling none of them MFS because none of them cared enough to put $1.00 on my books. But they are hustling out of a spot that I made!! But it was all good because fake shit I don't like so I played the outskirts and it didn't take me that long to find me a spot on Jones St. It was the same rooming house we had years ago, and Bobby and a guy named Reggie was there and since it had two rooms available, I went ahead and copped both rooms. Of course, it didn't take long for me to bounce back on my feet. I had to get my pockets right so I could go get my son. When I called Ms. Margie to see if she had talked to Chico, she told me she did, and I would leave her a number and I told her to tell him to call me but he never did. With me feeling like my love was gone for the rest of my life, in order for me to cope I had to erase every memory of him, the good and the bad. I was so upset with Chico because I use to always tell him that he was going to reap what he sowed. I made myself believe that Chico didn't really care about no one's feelings but himself because if he did, he would have been there with me. So the only way I could get him off my mind was to think about the bad times we had together which was more than the good times and I turned that love into hatred and erased him from my memory little by

CHAPTER 21

little. I tended to always beat myself up to get over the problem, but one day my phone rung and on the other end was the love of my life. I was so happy to hear from him because it had been two years, maybe less since the verdict came in. When he told me that he wanted to see the baby and that he was at Dash Correctional I made the appointment for the following week. My money was right by then and I had been sending money orders down to Alabama every 3 months I would go get them and cash them in and start all over again. During this time, Tang and her 3 kids got a 3-bedroom house in Worthdale. It was nice and in a quiet area and since she wasn't working, she was my babysitter. Our arrangement worked out because she would watch lil Chico when I picked him up and I would pay her and pay half of the bills. Perfect! So, I caught the bus to Alabama and picked up my lil Chico! When going to see Chico Sr. I caught a Greyhound bus to Nash County N.C. and from the bus station I caught a cab to the prison. When I got out of the cab and walked to the visitation area with lil Chico the officer said that I wasn't even on the visiting list, but Thank God they had sympathy for me because they went ahead and let me visit him anyways. Once me and lil Chico got in, we was told to sit at a table in the visitation room and while waiting for Chico I looked at the right and it was Mike Peters, the producer that was convicted of killing his wife, sitting at one of the tables. I then looked to the left of us, and it was Ray Carthy the baseball player that hired someone to kill his baby mother. I asked Chico once he came out if that was Peters and Carthy just in case I thought I was tripping, and he confirmed it. Oh shit! I thought, this shit real! Yes, Dash Correctional Inst. pull up the records! Then my baby smiled from ear to ear. I stood up with lil Cheek in my arms and I gave him the biggest, sloppiest hug and kiss ever! He was so happy to see lil Chico because the last time he had seen him he was 5 months old and now he was two years old. He couldn't stop grinning. The visit was two hours long and I enjoyed every bit of it. I also asked about getting the Infiniti and he told me he was going to tell Tera to switch the title over to my name. I had to get my license for that but that was a small thing. He just told me to stay focused and keep my head up because he was coming home soon. I remember saying "Okay my love, see you soon!" when I left, I called me a cab and headed back to the Greyhound bus station and back to Raleigh N.C. I hated I had to leave him there because I couldn't help but think to myself "if only there was something that I could do!" But at that point, it was out of my hands because I felt that I wasn't one of those blessed people that God favored. It seemed like I could never have something good going for myself. Everything that pertained to me wasn't good. Why? I had no clue. On the way home I talked to God and I said "Lord, every time something good comes in my life it always gets taken from me. Lord, please don't let anything happen to my son because if something did happen to him, I'm not going to be able to bare the pain. And Lord, since I don't have my first two kids, I'm Ok with what I have so please Lord hear my prayer. If you allow me to get pregnant and have a baby, please let that man be the one you choose for me to live and be happy with. Please Lord hear my prayer because I'm tired of hurting. In Jesus name I pray, Amen."

After that trip, Big Chico became a distant memory. It was hard to think about him because he is still to this day the love of my life and it hurt me so bad to think about him. I slowly began praying asking God to help me to move on with my life. Deep down inside I believe that God could do anything in this world, but you also reap what you sow. So, I had to move forward for lil Chico, and I was going to need God's strength to do so. And I took it day by day. "Thank you, Lord, for everything you have done for me!" As time passed by, people began to forget about what had happened out there. Well if they hadn't, they just didn't bring it up to me. But nothing had really changed out there. I was always by myself and I would come out about 7am because my motto was the early bird catches the worm. So, I came out early with that fire and all day they would come to me. You see, out there on Mapel St. they would come out at nighttime mostly because they couldn't compete with me and what I didn't get, May (my mom), ReRe, my brother's (Lamont and David) would. Basically, we

CHAPTER 21

had Mapel St. on lock from Booker St. to Ponder St. and then Ponder St. to Parkwood Ave. It was some other people down there, but it was still enough money out there for everyone although my family was the deepest. It was my mom May, two brothers, my mom's boyfriend Alamo, my Uncle Rodney, my Aunt Nita, whoever Nita's boyfriend was at the time and ReRe who was messing with my brother Lamont, China was messing with my brother David, my cousins Wayne and Chris who was my Aunt Nita two children! I was the first to go on Mapel St. and that brought the whole family over there. I remember May telling me a few years earlier that she was coming to get Mapel St. but I told her to be careful what you ask for and right after that, the incident happened with Big Chico. Then she moved right in at Ms. Easter's house. Reptiles in the grass, keeping it cute!!! It still didn't stop me none. I posted up at the people you least expected houses. It was something about me that made the older people out there respect me because over the years I would give out change here and there and I would always respect my elders because that was what I was taught to do in church. Anyone that saw me knew that I was a loner and wasn't about the drama so I would go ask them could I pay them $100 a day to be at their house with the promise that I wouldn't have no one in their yard as I sat on their porch, and they had no problem with me at all because of how I moved. My people would pull up and I'd walk to the car, serve them and that was that. I had two people watching the corners when no one else was out, where one was on Booker and one was on Ponder. If they saw one time (police) they would holla and give me enough time to dip in the house. Perfect! Like I said, it was me out there for a while on my own then my brothers and cousins who were like my sons showed up. My cousin Chris who was a high-ranking blood gang member was off the hook. Chris and his brother Wayne were Nita's sons and they were both menaces. Both was on cocaine powder and drinking at a young age. Wayne was now 18 and Chris was now 17 give or take, and they would be on the block snatching smokers money, beating up older people and selling them dummies. My Aunt Nita couldn't do anything with them.

ALL I HAVE

They had been out at a young age with my two brothers and the only one they would listen to was me. I would go talk to Chris and tell him "You got to stop disrespecting your Moms and these older people out here like that because you don't need enemies on the streets because they will get you out of here. You have to respect your elders, or your life is going to get cut short." They would listen for the moment and calm down but them boys was ruthless! They would be right back at it the next day. Family members would call me when they were getting out of control and I would tell them that they were bugging and they needed to chill, but it fell on deaf ears. Their family also talked to them, but I was the mother figure to them. They only respected me which I didn't blame them because with their mom Nita was smoking crack, I was all they had out there! But it was always only for a short period of time because those niggas stayed locked up! They were never on the streets for long so with all of us out there on Mapel St. we had a lot of haters.

When it came to females, they'd always hated on me. Why, I haven't a clue. Had to have been because I was a loaner and I just didn't mess with them. I made my paper and kept it moving. People was probably a little intimidated by me because they'd hear stories about a lot of things that had went down in the hood and they knew that I wasn't with all that talking shit because my gun was loud and I will let that thing fly if need be! So, if you weren't about that life then they needed to stay away from me because I stayed ready! But, that's one of the reasons I choose to stay solo because I wouldn't tell on myself. If you came my way, we do have a stand your ground law in N.C., so they needed to think twice. But, keeping it 100%, God gets all the credit for everything to do with respect I got out there on the streets. So, I got what I put in and I also moved in silence. With me being back out there alone with lil Cheek at home with Tang I knew I needed someone out there to have my back. It had been going on 3 years since Chico had left so I want to see what was going on out there. I really didn't like Raleigh niggas because most of them niggas

CHAPTER 21

were soft and fake, so it wasn't no one out there at the moment that was on my level. I had let this nigga Tommy eat the cookies a couple times, but he wasn't built like nothing neither. He also had messed with my cousin which I wasn't even thinking about at that time and also this other girl that's supposed to be a high-ranking blood whose name was "Tink" but she was locked up for something. She also was the furthest thing on my mind but one thing I did know about Tommy, that nigga had some banging ass head but that came a dime a dozen. I remember when Chico extorted him and Thaxton at the laundry mat and these niggas was shook. Thaxton had gone behind the washer machines taking out all the dope and the money. That shit was funny to me! But I didn't know all of that was going to pop off but with Chico you had to stay on your guard, and that's one of the main reasons why things didn't make it that far between me and Tommy. At the time I really didn't want no older nigga for some strange reason. But I did want to see if I could take a younger nigga and train him into what I wanted him to be. So, once I made up my mind, I got on the prowl.

After a couple of months I finally got to talk to my love on the phone and I asked him about the vehicle and he told me that he had talked to Tera and she was going to switch the title of the car into my name. So now after all these years I would finally get to meet the lady that gave me so many problems. My girl Tasha was friends with her and at first Tasha told me that Tera wasn't trying to give me the vehicle. Tasha had known Tera for a while and Tasha, and I had known each other for years so Tasha knew who was the one that really bought that car. But Tera finally gave in and although I thought that it was messed up, I had to go through Tera for that, Tasha went with me out to her house and she gave me the title notarized. When I saw her, I really thought that she was a pretty lady and she seemed like she was cool people. Chico had been gone for a while, so I didn't hold nothing against her. It was Chico I had a problem with, but I now had the car so that's the bottom line. I had to get a truck and head to Birmingham Alabama because that's where it was. And that's exactly what I did!

ALL I HAVE

I got a smoker's Suburban put the Infiniti on the hitch, and I drove round trip with Tasha, myself and Chico's youngest sister Knee-Knee back from Birmingham. I was whipping the hell out of that Suburban that when we pulled in to get gas one of the guys that was driving an 18-wheeler asked who was driving and I told him I was. He said, "If you can whip that, you need to drive trucks!" I smiled and said, "that sounds like a good idea" and the next thing I know we were on 40 West almost home. "Thank You God!"

You couldn't tell me nothing! Chico had the J30 decked out with 18inch chrome assassins, peanut butter seats, flip flop paint job and the system on fleek. But, two of the low-profile tires were flat. They cost me $200 per tire. It hurt but I was good. You think niggas was hating before! They not going to know what to do. Once I got the car and everything straight, I was ready to go. I was living comfortably, I had home straight, had me something to ride and my pockets was right. I had to really figure out how I was about to play it. Anyone that knew me knew I was about that check, so niggas out there was intimidated by me. I would have to be the one to make a move, and that's how I wanted it. I didn't want a nigga that made the move on me because the one's that wasn't intimidated of me was the ones that I knew I was going to have problems with. Anyone that hollered at me I turned down. I was tired of my feelings getting hurt. So, one day my brother Lamont had brought this guy whose name was "B" around, he was 18 years old. I didn't know what it was about this dude, but it might have been his cute face because once I saw him, I said, "Okay, I got me one!" He was in Raleigh East apartments and he was doing his little thing, he had a lil car, so he had potential. I learned from the best, so I said, let me see how this is going to work out. But at the same time guarding my heart. So slowly but surely, we began chilling out together. He would come over to the block and one thing lead to another that he never left. I started messing with B in early 2004, but towards the end of 2004 I had found out that he loved the nose candy. I looked at it like everybody got flaws and had went through

CHAPTER 21

the same thing with an older nigga that was out there. One thing I did know was that I wouldn't have felt comfortable with a working nigga. Or maybe if I would have tried then he could have helped me out legally but at the time, I wasn't looking that far ahead. I lived just for the moment, but it might have made a difference if I had someone that would have took the time out to try to put some knowledge in my head. My mom was even out on the block with me, so I had a hustler mentality. My thing was that if I'm gonna be out there getting that paper, I knew that niggas do hate and if shit pop off, I was going to need someone who had my back. It was like playing chess but the difference in my eyes was I was the King and I was looking for my Queen. On the block I knew that those niggas out there money wasn't as long as mine because their clients were nowhere near as long as mines. I had the main thing that others were afraid to use but I always did and that's talk to God through Jesus. I'd talk to them about everything! I'd smoke a blunt, and I'd just talk to God. Now I see why in the Rastafarian religion, smoking weed is a way of life because if you smoke a blunt of loud and then talk to him, then you'll feel me if you fear God. But, anyways, the niggas out there wasn't on my level, so I tried to make things work with B. I didn't know what I was thinking when trying to rock the cradle, but I know I'll never do it again! He was a cool dude and he had ambition, but he was weak when it came down to the nose candy. I believed that niggas that's weak minded and not use to nothing, when they get a lil attention they can't handle it. The reason I say that is because I noticed that since he was now dating me, he was now getting recognition. I always thought I was moving in silence but the whole time I was standing out like a sore thumb. So, after he had been with me for a while, he started getting his money up because he really didn't have to do anything. I already had things set up for him. All he had to do was help me run the spot and listen. When I came out it was just like a job where I came to work and then I went home. I did no drugs besides weed at the trap, but niggas had to learn the hard way. I can give him one thing, he listened to everything I told him. We would sit bottles up on the fence and with no problem I was knocking them bottles down, with a BB gun because practice makes perfect. I could tell that negro loved me but why wouldn't he? He had it good, and lil Chico was also growing fond of him. He liked lil Chico also but after the first year that me and B were together, his nose candy habit started to get worse and he was beginning to become annoying to me. I was beginning to have second thoughts about our relationship around late 2005.

I moved out of the apartment I had off Carthage Dr. that was right across from Carthage Middle School because too many people knew where I stayed, and I wasn't feeling comfortable. Also, during this time, the Lord sent me an angel whose name was Ebony that was keeping lil Chico for me, after the fall out that Tang and I had. Ebony and her Mom Ms. Karen needed somewhere to stay, and I was looking also so we got a 3-bedroom apartment and we split the rent 3 ways. It was a nice arrangement because they both worked at a daycare and got Chico into it and I paid it every week. The Lord knows how much a person can handle and "I would like to Thank God for sending them in my life at the right moment. He worked it out for me "Thank You." Ebony and Ms. Karen loved lil Chico like he was their own. Lil Chico even called Ms. Karen Grandma. Also, during this time, I wasn't feeling B like that anymore, I didn't know how to break it off with him because he was young, and I really never had to do anything like that before. So, what I tried to do was break it off slowly. Once I left Carthage Dr. I told B that he had to go back home because I wasn't getting another place anytime soon. And besides his people had money. They owned a cab service that picked up school kids and houses. So, his Mom had bread so that nigga was straight. When B and I was going through our problems, everyone around me was going through their own problems. My whole family just about was out there on the block and if they weren't on Mapel St. then they were locked the fuck up. Sad situation but I loved them anyways. My Aunt Nita's two sons, Chris and Wayne were two knockout Kings and Chris had his little scraps with him like Dareese, Meat, Lil P, and a

CHAPTER 21

few more lil niggas. Man, that group of lil niggas was causing havoc in Southeast Raleigh but that's what you get when you don't have any home training. A recipe for disaster! My brothers Lamont and David use to be that same way but being out there long enough teaches you that niggas didn't fight fair. They were bringing guns to fist fights, so it wasn't anymore fighting nowadays. My brothers also started messing with every female out on the block so their whole mentality changed especially when messing with ladies 10 years older than them. Yea, I was rocking the cradle, but 10 years! That was a little steep for me. I had B by 5 years and to me that made a lot of difference. But Nov, Dec 2005 there was a lot going on in them streets. I remember in Dec 2005, my cousin Lewis calling me from UNC Chapel Hill and telling me that he was working on the highway and a dump truck ran him over and I was trying to help his family cope with that situation. Now the week before Christmas the devil was busy around that time because it was a lot of people getting arrested on the block like My Aunt Nita, her home girl we called Legs (Yvette Elliott), and a couple more niggas out there like lil Ray, ReRe's brother that got locked up for robbery and kidnapping. During this time, I was laying kind of low because it was around the time the blood gang shit was getting out of hand.

I never respected a blood member from Raleigh because when Jersey first came to Raleigh he came as a Crip and he ran with a lot of niggas in Crip and Folk. And each and every last one of them "blood" members that's out here was Crip under Jersey. But once Chico ran him off, Chico brought Mel his cousin up here who was a Blood, and he flipped them niggas from Mapel St. and they all became blood. Just that simple! After that a lot of people lost a lot of respect in my eyes. Chico didn't care because that shit was funny to him. After the whole block became blood, my cousin Wayne was the only Crip out there and he dared them to touch him. But they did stay calling the police on him and he is in prison to this day because of it. The police was trying to stop all the violence that was happening on Mapel St.

165

ALL I HAVE

but with all the murders that was going on out there, the Blood Gang stuff had gotten too ugly out there in Southeast Raleigh and we were right in the heart of it and niggas was always trying to make a name for themselves. On a daily basis on Mapel St. at 115 Mapel St. you had Tink, Tommy , Adina, Tim, Ant, Lo, Raspberry and the list goes on and on and whoever else they allowed to be over there at the time. It was considered the blood house. They stayed hating on us, but they couldn't tell how I was moving because I was always solo, and they knew I always kept something and wasn't scared. But on this particular night my brother and a couple of his people and myself goes to "Unas", which was a club that was on Pool Rd. and my brothers and his people had left a little bit before me and ReRe's sister June. I asked her to drive because I'd been drinking a lot and the police were doing a lot of extra work out there that night, so she drove. As soon as we hit Carvey St. we saw a crowd of people and they yell that I needed to go check on my brother Lamont on Mapel St. So, I tell June to pull up on Mapel St. to see what was going on and we see lil Ray standing outside ready to fight. He tells me that they just jumped on my brother Lamont and I asked him who and he said Ant and Lo. Ok, Bet. "June, take me to Flushing St." I told her. She takes me to Flushing St. and two other girls by the names of Angel and Cas jumps in the car. I run in the spot, get my piece and I told June to ride up Ponder St. I then see Lo's car, and I said "Yea, June get me beside that car" and when she did, I points the Mossberg out the window and pumped it. I swear to God like on some movie shit, sirens came from out of nowhere and when I looked around the fuckin police was right behind us in an unmarked car. I freaked out and said, "Damn June drive now!" I'm thinking this bitch was going to at least try to help a sister get away, but this bitch stopped at every single stop sign and stop light on some law-abiding citizen type shit. So, she finally pulls over and I get out to try to run but they already had us surrounded. All I heard was, "Get on the ground and where the gun at?" "In the car" I said, and they made everyone get out and lay on the ground. Of course, they got the gun and took us all downtown. But check this shit out. I was the last

CHAPTER 21

one they came to and when they finally got to me they told me that everyone had already threw me under the bus and they'd already let them go and they were charging me with possession of a firearm. Out of curiosity I decided to try to flip it on them if I could. So I said, "Now I'm also going to tell you something but I want to see what you are going to tell me" so I asked the female officer what they told her and she said they told her that I was the one that had the gun and the officers then asked me what I was going to do with it? I told the officer that she "already charged me with the firearm and that meant that I was already in trouble, so I was going to need an attorney". I then added "Ms. officer no disrespect to you but it's them against me" and she came back and said "Ms. Gilchrist, ever since this blood gang stuff been happening, we have been out in unmarked cars patrolling the area, and we saw everything that happened that night. "That meant that not only did we see when they jumped on your brother, but we also saw you run in the house and come out with the gun". But what tripped me out was when she said that they had to stop me before it went any further. She also said that they knew about all of us and she didn't blame me for what I did but she still would have to take me downtown. I received a $2,000 bond and I hopped right out the same night. After that incident every white person in a strange vehicle was suspect. As a matter of fact, damn near everything moving was suspect because after that night things weren't the same anymore. We had to all stick together and that's exactly what we did. Them niggas couldn't even come outside after that and what made it so bad is that them niggas already wasn't making no money. Now it was on, I was stopping everything going to 115 Mapel St. I'd never been a greedy person but when I'd always say it was enough for everyone to eat, now they get nothing! They'd been eating long enough. But also, the police weren't trying to let anyone eat because they flooded the streets for a while. With all the gang activity and people trying to make a name for themselves, I believed that no weapon formed against me shall prosper but I knew that now would be the perfect time to go on a vacation. I respect the Police Gangsta!

CHAPTER 22

DURING DEC 2005 I fell back completely from the block. I really didn't have to go over there because I always kept a phone and my clients would call me, so I was making ends meet. I would stay in the house a lot and go play Bingo at 7pm. On Christmas 2005, while at the house chilling because I was already feeling some kind of way because my cousin Lewis was at UNC Hospital and everything else that's going on out there, I wasn't feeling it. And now on Dec 30, 2005 I get a call from my sister Tonya from the burn center of UNC. "What are you doing there?" I asked her and that's when she told me that her and Glue, her current boyfriend got into an argument. They were both under the influence and he threw hot boiling water on her. All I could do was cry. So much hatred filled my heart that all I wanted to know was where that nigga was at? But Tonya sounded like she was in so much pain and I didn't want to stress her out any more than she already was but I had to ask her where the nigga was at. She told me to leave it alone because she didn't know for sure what happened. She blacked out! But she did say that he could have poured the hot water on her or she might have knocked the kerosene heater over and that's how it happened. I really wasn't trying to hear all that. I just wanted revenge! My people knew that I wasn't the one to talk because I was about that action! I then told her "Ok, Tonya since you are taking up for that nigga, I'm going to let the Lord handle it and in due time he'll reveal who the real culprit is. So, after I hung up the phone with Tonya, something in my gut told me that 2006 was going

CHAPTER 22

to be a year to remember. The month of December alone I had two family members at UNC hospital where one was in the burn unit and the other one was crushed by a dump truck. I remember making up my mind on Dec 31, my birthday, I was not going outside because I was gonna stay in the house with my son. I wasn't feeling too well, I brought my birthday in at 12:01am watching T.V. and falling asleep with my son. I'd turned 25 years old and it was truly a blessing! But check this, no more than two hours later I got another call from my sister Tonya telling me that Poppy, my daughter Brianna's Dad had just got killed on Mapel St. OMG! It was like a stab to the heart. Charles White? That was my dude! He would call me Bonnie and I'd call him Clyde, and he had just started coming back around us. He had left and went to Jersey for a couple months and he wasn't even back that long and now he was deceased. That hurt! I hated to bring my Birthday in like that! I had to pray and ask Jesus, "What's going on here?" I also remember Tonya telling me "Tina, you have to finish your book because if you don't things are going to keep happening."

I was dreading to hear the countdown but 2006 was finally here and the block was most definitely on fire. The only way that you could make some money was to play the outskirts. So, I went back and cop me a room on Jones St. and while Reggie was still in the back, Bobby played the front and I ended up copping the other two rooms as before. My safe room was in the back and the room I was working in was in the front because I always had to have a window to see who was coming and going, cars and all in order to see the police coming. I stayed away from the block because it was too much fronting going on over there. How did Poppy end up getting shot with one bullet and he was a blood gang member was crazy to me. Where were all his brothers at then? That shit had me pissed! "Fuck em' all"! So, while I'm posted up there on Jones St. I was hearing all types of stories about some New York niggas that moved in on Ponder St. and the people at 115 Mapel St. wasn't feeling them niggas. All the smokers that came to see me would keep me informed on everything that was happening

ALL I HAVE

on the block. I laughed at them behind that because they were the same New York niggas that me and Worm ran up on and made the nigga run out the spot butt ass naked. The only reason why I did it was because my people didn't have anything so I went to the spot and one of the New York niggas took my money and gave me some shit that I wasn't feeling and wasn't giving me my shit back, so I went back and took mines and more. Thank You! So, while I'm hearing all this shit about these New York niggas shooting at the niggas on 115 Mapel St. I said to myself, those are some straight bitches. I was hearing China's brother Dareese, Tommy and Tink then sent the brother of a girl whose name was Kesha in the New York boys house. He was one of those crazy crack smokers so Dareese, Adina, Tink and Tommy pumped lil dude up to go in the New York boys house and soon as they opened their door lil dude pulled out the ratchet, but he played pussy and got fucked because they were 10 steps ahead of him. After that I was told he went running down Mapel St. towards Booker St. screaming help, got to Churches Chicken and fell out. Once I heard all of this, I had to see for myself if it was Dash and his crew because that didn't sound like his motto because Dash was a bitch. So, I then walks to Mapel and I saw my cousin Chris coming from where the New York boys house was at and I asked him was that Dash and his crew that was over there, and he said "no". He told me that it was a whole different crew of New York niggas. So, I continue walking down Ponder St. and I see Angie standing on the corner of Ponder and Mapel St. That was kind of strange to me because I was trying to figure out why was she blocking the money from turning on Mapel St. So, as I walked down Ponder and made a right on Mapel St. It was a ghost town. Not a soul was out there and I'm thinking to myself, these bitch ass niggas done let these New York boys take over Mapel St. The only people that were out there were smokers and they was the ones taking the money around the corner to the New York boys. I was heated because niggas were letting absolute strangers come over there and run them off the block. Ok, it was now time for me to do some surgery because fuck all that! I then talked to Cynt the lady that stayed

CHAPTER 22

at 115 Mapel St. and I posted on her porch to peep the atmosphere. I had Reggie at my house holding the spot down so my cousin Chris, me my mom's boyfriend Alamo, and my uncle Rodney was out there and this shit I had went in no time. I then asked my cousin Chris how the stuff was they had, and he said that it was some fire. So, I asked him to take me there so I could cop me some, but he didn't want to because he owed one of them some money and he didn't want to go there until he had his bread. It shocked me because people feared my cousin because that lil dude was something special. He told me DaDa could go there. She was another smoker that was out there, so I told DaDa to take me over there and she did. They had the lay out right and they had the people going through the back door so when I went in, some dark-skinned big dude who wasn't sloppy big but nice looking opened the door with a gun in his hand. I told him I had $500 just to test the water and the nigga wouldn't even serve me. I could respect that because I was the same way, but I didn't understand why he even opened the door in the first place. He could have said that through the door. So, he let us back out and I said to myself, that was his loss. But they were looking out for my cousin Chris so they were cool with me. I had my own people, but I did shit for reasons. After that day I kept my ear to the streets because when it came down to my lil cousin, if a nigga could tolerate him those were some real niggas!

After that I went back to my spot on Jones St. and I left Mapel St. alone, but that shit didn't stop me none because I had met some niggas through a smoker of mine and they took me to their spot off Raleigh Road. Their names were Dee and Braids. Dee was the bald head, pretty boy type, and braids was his brother who wore cornrows, short plump guy. They had that fire, and plenty of it. As soon as the smoker took me over there, Dee was all over me and he didn't even know me like that. I had this thing after Chico where I didn't want no more pretty boys and he was one that was off limits. I also didn't want no one that hollered at me first. So, he was a turn off up front but with the price he screaming that cheap, and fire, I figured okay, let's get this money, and that's what I did. Brought that money to him. Around that time also it was a drought, so I turned my brothers on to them and it went from there. For some reason every time I turned my brothers on to something they would go and turn the whole world on. From experience, I told myself that I'd never do it again, but family how could I turn them down? Dee and Braids was some cool dudes to me because not only did we do business, but they would come and chill with me at the spot. They also paid for me to get in my house on 4 Mapel St. They told me that out of all the people that they dealt with; I was the realest one. Dee would tell May to tell me to talk to him, but it wasn't no need. But I was thankful that they helped me get the house I wanted at the bottom of Mapel on the dirt road. I could have gotten it myself but why when someone offered to get it for me? I furnished the house, but I let it sit there for a while. I would let them go do there to do their lil plays but I stayed on Jones St. until that got hot and then I transferred everything. Business was going well for me I never wanted for nothing. Even though the block was hot it didn't stop my flow. The only thing to do was make money, spend it and go to bingo. Clubbing I didn't do because I trusted no one, besides I had no friends anyways.

    I Remember one night while at bingo I had gotten a phone call and it was one of the worst phone calls of my life. My cousin Chris had just got shot and killed on Partin St. He was like my brother because we all grew up together. I hollered so loud in Bingo that people already knew something was wrong. I ran out that Bingo so fast and jumped into my car going straight to Mapel St. My mind racing a million-mph wondering WTF happened, but everyone already knew the story. He went to Partin St. with his friend Meat to rob someone and the nigga brother pulled out a gun and shot Chris one time in the chest and Meat left him there to die. The guy that shot Chris was my mom May ex-boyfriend's nephew. His name is irrelevant all I wanted to do was kill 'em. We all grew up with these niggas and that hurt the most because it was the same scenario again but with another blood

CHAPTER 22

gang member getting shot with one bullet and his blood family wasn't there to help protect him. I asked myself where was Meat and why did he run off and leave my cousin out there to die?

I was tired of these people because that was two fallen soldiers alone. They even had the nerve to dress Poppy up in a brown Dickie's outfit and red flag in his casket. Once I saw that I left pissed. Not Chris! Towards the end of Chris's life, I did see the change in him. He had a baby mother whose name was Lyric, and she already had a son by Chris and named him lil Chris. She was pregnant with a girl by him. He was on powder at a young age and I would always tell him that he had to respect his elders. I remember one day before he got killed, he came to me and gave me a hug and a kiss. Thinking back on it now, when he did that it sent chills up my spine. Even towards the end of Poppy's life he would say "I Love you Bonnie!" Damn just writing this down makes my heart heavy because at the end of Chris's life the first song I'd ever in my life heard him sing was a song by Neyo "I'm so sick"! After his death, every time I heard that song I would cry. My Aunt Nita who was Chris's Mom was locked up, so we bonded her out but his Dad big Wayne and Chris's older brother lil Wayne stayed locked up. The Lord must have known that they couldn't handle that news on the outside. The Lord always knows what's best! That loss of Chris was a low blow to the family, especially when who did it use to have sleepovers at our house and vice versa! For a long time, I'd blame Meat because why did he leave him there alone when Chris was a "Big homey"? To my knowledge his scraps was supposed to handle the situation, but two weeks after Chris's death, Meat got shot, killed and threw off a bridge! 2006 was a year for the record books because 2 soldiers were gone, and I was afraid to wonder if anything could get any worse.

It was March of 2006 and my cousin Lewis and sister Tonya was still at UNC Hospital. My cousin Chris was dead, and my grandma Lynda had to take from her retirement to bury Chris. But one thing I can say is that funeral was beautiful. A lot of people had showed up to support the family and some was just coming to be nosey but Thank God for allowing him to go out in style, God is good! He had a beautiful casket and his kids was there, but I couldn't even look at them. I would cry every time I saw them because they were his twins. Especially Chrishire who was a pretty chocolate baby. She hurt me the most, but if they ever needed anything or if their mom reached out, I had them and still do. My cousin Wayne got out a couple of months after and they should have kept him in there because that nigga was the only Crip over there and went one by one boxing with them bloods and knocking them the fuck out. And they took that ass whipping! Wayne's hands were lethal but I've always told him that he should have been a boxer, but he never could stay home long enough because someone would always eventually call the police and he would end up right back in jail. It was hard with everything that was going on around all the killings and shootings, but looking back on how shit was back then, I Thank God for having mercy on me and my loved ones and friends. When I started to see how things was outside, I had come to the realization that we had to stick together and I started with my brothers because I loved them the most and because they were out there with me before the rest of them. I also didn't want to see anything happen to them because shit was hitting too close to home. I wasn't trying to hear anything happening to my brothers. But it seemed like they didn't want to be around me because of the competition. See that was the problem with our family. "Greed!" One was always scared the other was making more money than them. They would also have a bunch of snakes down their ears. My mom May even called me a federal informant! Yo, when she said that shit that fucked me up! But you know what I told her. "Girl, you don't even know me like that for you to come out of your mouth with that". I was going to let the Lord handle her and that she was at a trap house that I opened at first with Easter the lady that got on the witness stand and testified against my baby father! I even added that I'd shoot that house up if she kept talking. After I said that I had to pray and ask God to forgive me. But, that's why I kept my distance

CHAPTER 22

from her because the Lord said, "honor thy mother and thy father", but how could I when she was moving like a snake? Her reason was always hating, Period! At that one house you had ReRe, May, China, my brothers and I'd stopped messing with them years ago. But what really took the cake was when my baby daddy Chico "home boy" Jersey had got caught on Ponder St. with a lot of work and ReRe his baby mama was the only one that knew the nigga was coming. Just as soon as he got there the police hit Ms. Cary's house and took that nigga to jail and right then and there, I knew she was the one that did it. ReRe's mother before she died even told me that I'd better watch ReRe because she was the police. But when Jersey got locked up in 2006 it sealed it for me when Jersey had come across Chico while incarcerated and he admitted that ReRe did it. My motto was always "Birds of a feather…."

So, with Lamont and David having those females in their ears, I just left it alone and went on about my business. Everyone out there would always say that I was the police, but it was only because I was the one that was easiest to blame. I didn't mess with no one and always stayed to myself because that's how it's pretty much been my whole life. Why? I have no clue. But the niggas that I was spending my paper with loved me and I could get whatever I wanted from them. They knew when I called, it's paper and nothing else and that's how I kept it. Business and pleasure, I learned a long time ago didn't mix and that's my motto to this day. Certain niggas that was out there would come to me for legal advice Though. The ones that recognize realness besides, I'm far from a slow leak, Thank God! The times when Chico was locked up, I would go study at the law library, and it paid off. Also, all the run-ins I had with the police I'd always keep me a paid lawyer and at the time it was my angel Ms. Bridget. Yes, a beast! She was Jersey's lawyer at one time and that's how I got turned on to her. When it came to retaining lawyers, I would always ask a lot of questions and because of it I learned how important it was to have a defense. It's all about who could paint a better picture and discrediting witnesses. Dareese China's younger brother

ALL I HAVE

one time came to me and told me that the police had chased him and that the police had finally caught up with him further down the street. Now while he was in the police car they back tracked and found some drugs and charged him with possession with intent to sell and deliver cocaine (PWISD). He then asked me what to do. I told him don't take it because it is a drug area and PWISD is 9/10 of the law and it states that they had to have got it off your person because anyone could have dropped that when they saw the police coming. And guess what happened? He got that charge dismissed! Sean Black had the same thing happen to him where he just got out of his car and walked on the porch to talk to Rick and as soon as he walked up the steps the police hit the corner, jumped out on him, searched him and found nothing, searched the yard found something and charged Sean with it. I told him to take Rick with him to court because their two statements against the officers. His case got dismissed also. The police were crooked and they were not fighting fair but what people don't know out there was that we had Internal Affairs on our side. Although justice is often blind, people's problems stem from giving the police and the court system too much credit because at the end of the day, money talks and bullshit walks. So, if it comes down to it, I'm calling the police on the police. My baby father Chico once told me that niggas out there be fronting like they gangsta, running around with guns, pulling them out and shooting but when you catch the niggas and defend yourself, the baddest nigga is now getting on the stand and testifying against you. So now you gone for the rest of your life. He went on and said that he knew that I was about that life but if a nigga threaten you with a gun, put the law on your side because when the niggas comes at you the next time you can stand your ground. He said that at one time it was unheard of for a gangsta to put them crackers in your business but when it comes down to gun play, you have to be smart nowadays. I'm sure that there are a lot of people that may disagree but it's likely that you have never been about that life or have but still have so much more to learn. I just hope it don't be too late.

CHAPTER 22

My spot on Jones St. eventually got hot, so I ended up letting that go and I opened up on Mapel St. again on the dirt road. It was in the cut and in the perfect spot because you wouldn't even known it was even there. But the messed-up thing about that spot was as soon as I got in it, my boys Dee and Braids got hit. The U.S Marshals had got them not for drugs, but these niggas was up in New Jersey robbing banks and came to N.C. to lay low. Them getting hit made me regret turning any one on to them because it seemed like once I did everyone was dealing with them and once that happened, they were gone. People got on my nerves because your connect was like having a roof over your head with lights and water. It was a necessity, but people were too selfish. I would ask myself why these people are out there hustling if they had to run their mouth to beat a charge. They didn't understand that once you snitch to the police, they were gonna keep coming at you until they use you up and sit you down for a while. But yea, my niggas was gone but I appreciate them getting my spot and paying for my lights and water because that was truly a blessing. In the backyard at the fresh spot was a cut that lead right to Carvey St. store and I used the side door that came out on Carvey St. and I would run the money through the back yard. I had Fatima and my Aunt Nita and Legs (Yvette) down there with me. Fatima had her own room and Nita and legs was close by and they kept their clothes and things in the other room. We worked it out day and night and we got to the check. I made sure there was no loud noise or people standing around the spot since I was in the living room window, I had someone in the kitchen window and a door person. I would pay $10 an hour to each of them and they would all switch shifts. I had me a hiding spot so sweet that the police never found any drugs. I would tell y'all, but the game meant to be sold not told. But we were on fleet and by this time I was dealing with this cat whose name was Boo who I had met through my brother Lamont. Another cool cat but his prices were a little higher than Dee and Braids. It's just the game but I made sure that my face was platinum status, so it wasn't long that I had the trap booming. I had just about every main smoker out there that everyone knew and on that end of Mapel was safer. Yes, it was sweet. But on the other end of Mapel, the police were so bad that people on Mapel St. couldn't even work over there anymore. My brother Lamont had warrants so they would go to Easter house because the police knew that Lamont would be there, but Easter wouldn't let the police come in her yard or the house without a search warrant. She learned from the best, so they stood on Mapel St. for hours. Even the news people came over there talking about a standoff on Mapel St. because a suspect was believed to be in the house. I think it took them 8 hours before Lamont came outside and gave up. They couldn't get a search warrant and on top of that, he was bonded out the same night. You talking about crackers pissed! A whole box of crackers but they turned up the heat for real after that. Nobody was making nothing, me included. Since I believe that I had to trust these people with my life, I was very picky with who I let in the house or had dealings with. I had to have known you for at least 7 years or more or if one of the girls knew you then that would work also. Of course, I would let them deal with them, not me. But other than that, things were running smooth. My mom May, ReRe, Lamont and David had got them a house on Flushing St., Mapel St. Had become a distant memory, but not on my end of Mapel, just 100 block of Mapel.

I truly believed that the Lord had brought Ebony my angel in my life because being on the streets and losing my first two kids the Lord knew I couldn't take the loss of my son so he put people in my life to help me with him. They say it takes a village to raise a child and that's exactly what happened in my case so Thank You Lord! I can say that she loved Chico just like he was her very own son. She liked women and I didn't knock her for that because to me she was truly a blessing. Her and her mom had ended up letting the apartment go that we shared together so I copped my own little place and they went their separate ways, but she kept my "stinka butt" (lil Chico). I continued to pay for his daycare and if it was anything that she needed for him all she had to do was pick up the phone. Around Sept

CHAPTER 22

of 2006, B and me was still going through our struggle and one day my brother David told me that they were at a hotel getting high and B slept with my cousin Chris baby mother Lyric in front of 4 people on the bed. Now, I don't know what that dumbass nigga thought but "Abracadabra" Deuces! He would come to the trap when I wasn't there crying to my Aunt and whoever that was in the trap but negro please! I wouldn't have mind as much if it was any other female but with my dead cousin baby mother! And on top of that, she opened her legs for him when Chris was only buried a couple months prior. Yo, I told both of them that they could kiss my ass! I had been with him by now for almost 3 years and he was already hanging on by a thread. Not too long after that I had let D.J. the one Chico had jumped on after I called Tera's house to get him on the phone, stay at the house I had on Mapel St. since he was going through a rough time in his life. It was a small two bedroom house and where Fatima had one of the rooms, I let D.J. get the room on the right because my Aunt Nita and her friend Legs ended up leaving to go to Flushing St. where they were crunk! And that was exactly their problem because they always had an entourage and they had no order (kin folks). They were too messy, out of order so I kept my distance and always kept them in my prayers. Shortly after, I ended up getting a call from my baby father Chico and he told me that he had won his direct appeal and his trial date was coming up but he didn't want me to come because he didn't want me involved for protection reasons. I respected that because I had no choice and besides, he had stopped reaching out to me long before that. I had also been busy trying to erase my memories of him. I know it sounds crazy but that's how I coped with my issues. I erased it. I can't explain how, but one of the reasons was, I prayed about it and let the Lord handle it. Prayer played a major role in me erasing the past because if I hadn't, I'd be messed up. I tried to erase the fact that my kids was gone, but every year on their birthday I would think about when I went to court for the custody hearing and the state asked my mom May Gilchrist to take the stand to testify. I'm wondering why they called her to the stand to testify. She then got on the stand and the District Attorney asked her was she the one that called Social Services. She lied at first and said she didn't recall but they asked her if she wanted them to play back the tape and she said "no". She then admitted that she was the one that called Social Services on me. My own Mom, she had the nerve to get my kids taken away. No Love! Period!

Chico eventually went to trial and for the second time he blew it with another verdict of Natural life. So, things were rough for me mentally. The things that I had went through would have beat down the average female. Thank God for being with me because he was the only thing that I did have and that's a fact. By me always talking to him no matter what, I am thinking about it now while looking back on my life, half the time I believed that I wasn't praying right. But come to think about it, I had to have been doing something right in God's eyes because I'm still here to tell you my story.

CHAPTER 23

D.J WOULD COME to tell me about this guy whose name was Drama that had been asking questions about me. DJ then told me that he had a spot on the corner of Booker and Flushing street and Drama was sitting on the porch stopping the money from going to Flushing street where my family was at. The shit didn't faze me because as long as they weren't near my cut stopping my shit I was good! Drama would give DJ some weed, and he kept that fire. It was purple haze and he had the Molly's (Ecstasy in powder form: MDMA). So, I would send DJ there to get me some smoke and a few pills, but I really didn't indulge in the conversation because I wasn't ready at the moment to start a new relationship. You see, once I let someone hit (sex), that's who I was going to continue being with because that's just how I am. But every time DJ would go out, he would come in with a bag of weed and cigarettes so I looked at it like DJ knew what he was doing so I couldn't knock the hustle. I eventually asked DJ who was he and he told me that it was one of the New York niggas that was on Ponder street. Once he said that, I knew exactly who he was because one day when I had walked to the Hills St. store and when I'd come off Mapel St. and made a left on Ponder St. someone was trying to get my attention. So, I turned around and he walked towards me and he asked me my name. I started walking towards him and I told him my name and we exchanged numbers. But once I left his sight, I threw the number away because I always said if anyone showed interest in me, I didn't want them because I had no time for the drama. So once

DJ told me where Drama was from, I knew right then who he was. Although I am still hurting from how B had treated me, I still told DJ to give him my number. I was still friends with B even though we had broken up, but since I started to leave B alone. I didn't mind going out to get a couple of drinks, but I didn't rush it. I waited a month or two, but Drama never called so I forgot about him. On a different occasion I was walking to the store and I saw Oge A.K.A Drama again and he pulled over and asked me what was up. We did some small talk and again we exchanged numbers. I asked him if he was sure he wanted to give me his number because I'd came to his house one day and he wouldn't even serve me. I didn't know if he was lying or not but claimed that he didn't even remember what I was talking about. I refreshed his memory and he started smiling and he passed me his number and I walked to the house. At the time Flushing St. had the juice but it was a drought during this time and them New York boys from Ponder St. were back and they now had the juice. The product my people had was O.K. but it wasn't what was on Ponder St. now I was catching the scraps. Sometimes in the game it bees like that. I knew my mom May and them kept some fire and I also knew that they were getting theirs from the New York boys house. I would send DJ to go see the New York boys for me although I already knew who it was, but I wasn't going to call him even though I had his number out of respect. But anyways, I called him up one night and we met up at a restaurant on Gormen St. It was a bar and restaurant, so we ate, watched some T.V. and drank a few drinks and ended up at a hotel in Cary. Both of us was twisted so we laid down and slept the night away. The next morning, he woke up and was trying to get some of my cookies and since we had no condoms, too bad brother. But I was glad he woke me up because I had him drop me off and that was that. The next night I tried to call him again to get straight and he told me to meet him at the Chicken and Seafood place on South Anders. When I left to meet him there, he had me sitting out there for 45 minutes. Essentially, he never came. I called him and I got no answer, so I thought something had happened to him. So, the next

CHAPTER 23

night, I went down to the house where he was at to make sure he was alright. When I knock on the door, the door opens and damn near half of Raleigh was in there and he was serving every one of them. When I saw him, he was around a lot of females, so I didn't want to bother him right then. But once he came my way, I tried to get his attention, but he put me off on his homeboy who I learned was Late Night. Late Night asked me for a ride, and I told him to come on. When we left, the whole time I was driving the nigga tried to holla at me. I didn't know what type of games those niggas were playing but I had no time for them. So, I took him where he had to go and dropped him off. I got the picture. But one thing I knew for certain them niggas wasn't going to last long because the same niggas from Mapel St. that they were beefing with the year before was the same ones in there and a few more snakes. I felt sorry for them and I prayed for them because it's not what you do but how it's done. It's crazy that I prayed for them and I didn't even know them, right?

One day I was sitting at the trap house and Fatima told me that some guy she didn't know was walking through the cut, so I look out the back window and it was Oge. Kind of shocked me because it had been a few weeks since I'd heard from him. So, I went and unlocked the door and I asked him "What's up?" I then let him in, and he said he'd come to smoke a blunt with me. So, we chilled in the living room. By this time Flushing St. was on fire! Them niggas was the only one's during that time that had the best thing smoking. I even had some of their work, but I had to go through someone else to get mine. So, he rolled up and we started smoking but while we were smoking, B walks up and they let him in. Oge even played his position when B came and sat beside me but I knew B felt that I was trying to play him because I didn't want to cause a scene, I get up, got my water out the fridge and sat in B lap so that Oge could get the picture. So after I hugged B around his neck and sat there for a few minutes, I went to make a play in the kitchen and sat back down on the couch, Oge then called me in the kitchen and asked me could he borrow $300 until

ALL I HAVE

later on that night. I didn't have a problem with it because I knew the nigga was making it and besides, he might have been a little short for the connect and that was a small thing to a giant. So, I gave it to him, and he left. The next thing I know, someone came to the house and said that the police had hit Oge spot. I knew that was going to happen because he had all the wrong people in his house. I grew up around these people and one thing I did know from experience like I said before is if they don't like you, they were going to get you out of there with the police. And that's exactly what they tried to do. That's how my love got gone and now Oge might have been gone. The guy that owned the house came to me after they hit the house and he told me none of the boys was there and they didn't find anything. "Thank God". When I asked Oge what he thinks happened he told me that one day he was sitting in the house and the landlord came with a man and they fixed all the smoke detectors in the house. He also said he wasn't feeling the man that came with the landlord so as soon as they left, they disconnected all of them and the next day they came back to check on the detectors and once they did that he knew right then and there it was the FEDS. And that's when he left. Good thinking, so I told him to hit me whenever. When a week had passed since that nigga came and got the money from me, I wasn't really sweating the money, but In the back of my mind I'm like I knew the niggas wasn't fronting on me like that so I called him. His phone was off. Two more weeks had passed, and I received not one call from this dude, nothing. Now I was thinking the dude had done got hit or something, so I called, and I get no answer. By the 3rd week, I'd left it alone, but I decided that the nigga must have really needed that shit for him to play it like that. It was only $300 so I was glad that he didn't ask for 2 or 3 thousand. You live and you learn. Never again. A month later the nigga came popping up at the trap house. Shocked me, but "what's up?" So, he gave me a bullshit ass story, but he had some work and it was good because it wasn't nothing out there for real but "Procaine". Everyone had procaine, fear factor, or Dummies, but my people had the best procaine. All I did was cook it back in peroxide add a cap

CHAPTER 23

full of Clorox just a touch and it was on from there, But this nigga Oge popped up with Ounces of peppermint patty and he had a lot of it. It was nothing anywhere so anything would sell if nothing would. He also straightened me with the $300 that he owed me which took him a month to bring it back to me, but it was O.K. because it wouldn't happen again. It was the principle behind it. Communication is the key because miscommunication leads to complication is my motto. At some point, I pulled him to the side to see what was on his mind and he told me that people had come to him and said that I was the police and don't mess with them Gilchrist because you wouldn't be around long. He said it was a lot of people screaming the same thing and I kind of figured that much because that's why he wouldn't serve me anything. So, I asked why he would come get money from me then and he said that he wasn't going to pay me back, but he thought about it. He told himself that I didn't know him, and she gave me $300. How many people out there would have played it like that and how could I be the one when he wasn't even dealing with me and that's what made him come back. Man, these niggas! But in a way I didn't blame him because it was probably a lot of people screaming that shit about the police because I was solo and didn't speak to none of them unless I was spoken to. I had to learn the hard way that the ones you think are your friends are the main ones talking about you. So, if they spoke to me, then you'll get spoken to. So, he sat and chilled for a while and he asked me to go with him to a Gucci Mane concert that was at a club in downtown Raleigh during the time Gucci Mane had just started getting noticed. I was down for it, and that was that. I threw my Coogi dress on and I was in the building and it was only about 100 people in there. But we were lit and Gucci did a good performance that night. A couple months later when Gucci Mane came, you couldn't even get it. Same thing with Juice Man when we went to see him, no one was there but the next time, everyone came. I began to take notice that Oge loved his music and he was universal with it also. But all that Aye! Aye! That Juice Mane was saying threw me completely off...

ALL I HAVE

Well me and Oge began seeing each other on the regular. I didn't think he had a girlfriend because he carried himself like he didn't but maybe a month or two after we finally slept together he had me drop him off at some apartments off South Anders St. over the train track and he told me that his baby mother stayed there but she gave him the apartment because she didn't even be there. So, I told him that he was going to have to move if he was going to be with me and that was it. She was out of the picture and once I found out who his baby mother was, it kind of tripped me out because I thought she was a dude, and he got her pregnant, WOW! But he told me that she told him everything about everyone and he had sex with her one time, and she got pregnant. Yea, like I believed that one. But anyways...... so after we hooked up, when you seen him you seen me. Niggas was already hating on him because he came around and opened up shop but now it seemed like they were hating even more because he was messing with me. Niggas out there knew how I moved and because I got that check. I noticed that I intimidated a lot of niggas out there. I kept something fresh to drive, hair, jewelry, clothes, shoes, trap house, Domaine so I stayed on fleet. But it was the God in me because things weren't entirely what they seemed. I was barely making ends meet but it's all on how you budget yourself. One thing I knew was if you do the crime you do the time so selling weight, I wasn't on that type of time by then. I sold peanuts. My day would begin just like any other person that went to work and hours of operations because I treated the game just like it was a legal job. I remember asking myself what type of salary I wanted to bring in a month and I decided that a certain amount a day profit was a good enough salary for me. I would go cop what I wanted to make a day and just that cause one thing I did know was greed will get you nowhere fast. So, people just do the math. Yea, and sometimes it would be better days and the only reason I played it this way was because I had no one to help me turn my money legit. I'd got used to seeing parents with kids out there in the streets and they turned their backs on them when the best thing to do was to help them find a way out because they're going to end

CHAPTER 23

up losing them to the prison system or dead if they didn't. So not only did I not know what to do, I didn't know who to trust. With so much against me I always felt like if I made sure I talked to my brother Jesus Christ, respect my elders, treated people how I wanted to be treated, try my best to keep that fire, stay to myself, I'd be alright, but I learned with time that it didn't always work out that way.

Two years had passed and Oge and I were still together and for the most part nothing happened out of the norm. But I would have to talk to Oge and tell him that he didn't need a gun around because we were in a hot trap house and we couldn't afford to keep the gun in the trap house. I told him to leave it outside in the back and we'd have someone to watch it through the back window. But during this time, I did do something to Oge that I will never do to another human being in my life. I even pray about it to this day, but when I was 26 years old we were at the house one day and because Oge only drank brown liquor and smoked fruit, I opened up a Molly and put it in his Hennessey and gave it to him. I knew how the feeling was to me, so I just wanted him to experience that feeling with me. I then watched him drink the whole shot of Hennessy and about 30 minutes later he asked me what I did to him. I just started smiling because it was a funny sight to me, but I made sure he was O.K. But I had to stop him from trying to go under the kitchen sink when it was only me and him in the house. So, when his high came down, we both laughed about it and I told him what it was. I hate I ever in my life did that because it was like from that day forward Molly was all he was looking for. Like the rapper, Future said "I'm looking for her". But one thing I can say about Oge, that's a loyal dude to a certain extent. The reason I say that is because one day I had left to go to Bingo and when I come back, I saw yellow tape and automatically I knew who done it. It was right behind the trap house at Carvey St. near the store, so I go to the house and it was a house full of people and I catch him sitting up there looking flicted (suspect). I immediately asked what happened and I was told that the nigga that got shot was trying to take

ALL I HAVE

something from my sister Tonya and Oge just so happened to walk up and seen what was going down so he pulled out and shot the nigga in the leg and he gave Tonya back her shit and the dude walked quietly to the store. After I heard that I told him that he had to leave, and we left. Once he was safe, he pulled out the Clorox, washed his hands and jumped in the shower. His clothes went in the washing machine and after that, I heard nothing else about it. A smoker picked the two shells up so the police found no evidence. But around that time the spot that my family had on Flushing St. got closed. They City of Wake had bought the houses on Flushing St. and when the police had come down to the trap house one time, they told us that they were coming through there and that it wouldn't be any more houses over that way. I took heed to what they were saying so I knew right then to get prepared for that. So as usual I felt sorry for my brothers and I let them come to the trap house to work but once they came, it seemed the trap got hotter. Once I saw that, I started to find me another trap house in the area. I eventually found an apartment on Waldon St. that was a couple of blocks from Mapel St. in the red zone that was straight to me, so I let Oge go there and I stayed on Mapel St. In one house you had my mom May, ReRe, China, Lamont, David, Nita, Legs, DJ, and Fatima. Yes, we were deep, but it allowed me not to work at night. I let them have it. They only reason I allowed ReRe to be there is because she was David stunt dummy and I didn't want her around me because she had just caught a case with Bernice on Mapel St. But other than that, at least I knew where my family was at. Oge and I were staying at a hotel off Wake Fore Rd. called the Studio Plus. It was the same one me and Chico stayed at a lot of times and we had been staying there a couple of months now. But we decided to move to another hotel because we had been there too long and also one day I stepped out my hotel room and right across the hall, I saw a girl that was going to the Bingo I be going to. It was Adina from Mapel St. so it was most definitely time to go and we moved the next day. During this time, we had been seeing in the newspaper that the police had hit one of the major houses of the blood gang and on the wall in the

CHAPTER 23

house they had everyone's name and who they were up under. Somebody even called Oge and told them that it was Adina house. There was another girl that stayed across the hall from me who was cool people so when the girl saw me, she asked did I want to smoke a blunt. I told her I was good because I was heading out the door, but I told her to have a good day though. The next day we moved up the street to the Hometown Suites that was a couple of blocks down the street from where we were currently at. One day a friend of mines Ava had come by to see me she left and we left behind her, now during this time I had bad tags on my Lincoln because my license was suspended because of a ticket that I didn't pay. So, I leave out the hotel and hop on interstate 440 going towards Knightdale not paying no attention to my surroundings. If I only looked out my side and rearview windows!! I then pulls in the gas station and I get out to pay for my gas now while I'm in the store the police comes running in the gas station and say " put your hands up, we already know you have something on you because your boyfriend said whatever she has on her he had nothing to do with". Straight like that! I couldn't believe what I was hearing. I'm like yeah right, I'm tussling with these mother fuckas trying to get my shit together and my shit falls out of my bra!! Damn!! They caught me off guard. A mistake I vow not to make ever again and just like that I'm in the back of the police car. While all of this going down my son at the tender age of 6 watching all of this go down. The police then asks Oge "Mr. Oge didn't you tell me that Tina had something on her"? and Oge said "no" and the officer said "lock him up for lying to a police officer" and that's when Oge said I'm sorry baby, I did say that" and they let him leave with my child. Damn again, another nigga running his mouth. See some people freezes up when it comes down to the police not knowing they hurt themselves and others in the process. The officers then take me downtown and before they could ask me any questions I asked for an attorney. Now I'm hearing on the radio that they inside my hotel room and they found nothing but some money. The officers went on to say that Ms. Gilchrist we weren't even coming at you we were watching the room

ALL I HAVE

upstairs from you and saw two white people come to your room and when they left you left right behind them' like on some stalking type shit. The police went on to say " we knew that was your car and your license was suspended and we followed you" I called Oge to tell him to hurry up and get me out so I can inform them what the police was up to. I really didn't know the girl like that, but I don't want to see no one gets in that type of trouble if I can help you I will. But by the time I get out and get back to the hotel they were locking that girl boyfriend up. After the police finished searching the room upstairs from ours and left, me and Oge was trying to figure out what was going on? It was a coincidence we happened to end up at the same hotel, this was the same girl that asked me if I wanted to smoke a blunt and I said no. And I'm not too fond of believing in coincidences. But we slept and the next morning we were out of that hotel. After that night we had found out that the police had a special task force that focused on hotels called the Career Criminal Task Force, so people that stays in hotels they focus on how they're paying for their room. They also pull the guest list and check to see if they have warrants or not. But one thing I did know is that girl that room got hit she be at the bingo also, so I was eager to get there and ask what was going on. When it came to Bingo I was in Bingo every night faithfully so the next night that I go, the girl from the hotel all of a sudden came in the Bingo on some Ra Ra type shit and coming out the side of her neck. I mean loud in the Bingo, so I told her to step outside. We step outside but her boyfriend decides to hop out of the car but didn't peep Oge was in the car. So, he hops out ready and the girl began talking about yea everybody talking like I'm the police and I probably set her and her boyfriend up. I told that dumb bitch that I never bought nothing from her let alone knew her fucking business. I also told her that she'd better check that bitch Adina's ass because her house was just in the newspaper not too long ago. I told them people my first middle and last name because I had nothing to hide they was still getting hostile then that's when Oge hops out with that peace maker "Tommy gun" and once they peeped that they started getting in their vehicle I then

CHAPTER 23

told them once her boyfriend got his motion of discovery back, I wanted an apology. After that, they left. A couple of months after that, I saw the same girl in the Bingo, and she apologized. I then told her to tighten up and accepted her apology. Around the same time, the trap house was on fire. Everyone around there was catching charges and snitching like crazy but you couldn't really pinpoint it. So, everyone was suspect to me if they weren't family because what I did know was the police hated my family. But something was telling me in my "know it" the older people would say (gut) that ReRe was the one that was doing it. Why? Because when I went to the ATC program I'd never messed with my mom May, ReRe or China before and only close family knew my movements but while I was getting out the cab and walked around the back, I see the police coming so I slides in a neighbor's house, prop my back up against the door and put my feet against the sofa so that the police couldn't get in while my shit vanished in thin air!! "The game meant to be sold, not told." So, once I had everything secure, I rolled over, and they came in. I was already laying on my stomach, so they put the handcuffs on me, right then and there. I knew it was someone close, but I couldn't pinpoint who. After about a week, my mom May and China was riding in the 55 Universal cab when the police pulled them over and at the same time hitting the house where they cook the drugs up at. Not only didn't I mess with them like that, but I'd never been to their safe spot and I'd only went to May's house two times max, but somehow they had hit both of the houses at the same time. When being pulled over in the cab my mom May gives China the stuff and by China thinking nothing of it, she put it in her pants because she thought it was going to be only a traffic stop. But they took both down and found 3.5 oz on China charging her with trafficking and May with conspiracy to trafficking. While the police had May and China, ReRe walked in May's house off Wake Fore Rd. and the police was right behind her. Bitches aren't shit but what did they do even though I wasn't there? Blame it on me! Dummies, and after all that ReRe started fucking my brother David who is China's baby Daddy after fucking my oldest brother

ALL I HAVE

Lamont. Just trifling! But after all of that, guess what? They continued to mess with her despite all the warning signs. I thought that it was fucked up after my own Mother called me a federal informant and took a girl that fucked both of her sons over her own child's word and I still let them come to the spot like a dummy, but my heart wouldn't let me see them out there in the wild. And on top of that I'm the one that pretty much let them keep it and got me another house two blocks over. I always let the Lord handle things for me. Well not always but through the years, I've learned to pray and sit back and watch the Lord handle it. So, in this case that's exactly what I did. I prayed about it until it didn't matter anymore about what people thought of me. But for the ones that truly knew me know what time it was, and their word was the only thing that truly mattered. Not to boast but I Thank God for bringing me this far. Only God is the one that is perfect so I truly hate that May felt that way and tainted my brothers in the process. I'd hear what came out of their mouths from what other people said but all I'd do was shake my head and try to hold my head up and talk to God because I knew that one day I'd look back at it all and smile. But as usual, they just let the people do whatever they wanted with no regard for their life because if they did, they would have their own shit in order. On this particular day, no one was on Mapel St. but my brother David, DJ, and DJ's baby mother Grace. My brother David was laying on the couch sleep and DJ and Grace was in the back room when the police with a search warrant kicked down the door to the trap house on 4 Mapel St. My brother David had been up for a couple of days but Thank God he was clean. I guess they thought he was fronting because the police took the butt of the gun and hit him in the face with it and also hit DJ a couple of times in his face and kicked Grace in her stomach while she was 8 months pregnant! They beat them up bad and prior to this, a new chief of police from upstate came down here and brought some city slickers down here and they were doing all types of illegal shit. False documents and beating up people, wild dumb shit. They even ran up on me on Mapel St. one day and charged me with bogus charges that

CHAPTER 23

ended up getting dismissed. As a matter of fact, I called Internal Affairs a few times because they were doing disrespectful shit. They were showing us that they were the biggest gang out there and their shit was legal. So, fuck that, I was calling the police on the police (Internal Affairs) and they told me to take pictures and make sure to get proof of the date and time. They beat the shit out of David, DJ, and Grace but then DJ called me and told me what happened, I told them to take a phone and take pictures where their injuries were and to make sure the date and time was on the phone beside the bruises and bumps that was on them. David and DJ had 3 big ass knots on their heads, so I told them to go to the hospital right then. DJ and Grace did, and Phillip went later. The police did all of that for nothing. I knew the police had a job to do, but when people are asleep and you still use excessive force like that, I'm not feeling that at all. And they were doing that on the regular! After DJ got discharged, he called me and said he was staying at the hospital because they were admitting Grace because they said her stomach was swollen from the kick! Bingo! So, I told them to take pictures and everything because we had them. The next day DJ went to Internal Affairs, we contacted the N.A.A.C.P and attained an attorney for the case but check this, the Raleigh Police Department turned all the way up even more after that. Every other day they were coming down to the bottom of Mapel St. just sitting there of course. We had them by the balls. A sin is a sin in God's eyes so there is no sin, no less than the other one. The police can lie to us and to the magistrate "A court judge" to obtain a search warrant and that one lie is the same as a person killing 100 people in God's eye. The police are no better than we are. They just had better cards dealt to them than us street people but keep it 100%, most of us black people on the streets know the Lord. Grandma took us to church. So, I would tell people that were still out here to don't fall victim and play their cards different by putting Jesus "The Lord" in the equation. He listens to us so all we have to do was go through him in prayer for whatever our needs are. Yes, Lord was listening because he knew what the police was doing. He heard our prayers and I would like to

ALL I HAVE

Thank God for using me to help him because one month after we contacted Internal Affairs with the evidence that we had, the chief of police resigned. But making that move caused a lot of damage like I said before because not only did the police turn the volume up, one day I just happened to go to 4 Mapel St. just to check on everyone because I'd been hearing about what was going on. Come to find out, they'd hit the house every two days and that alone was a sign to let it go, duh! But people slow! So, me and Oge go there and it was a house full and then Tink's brother Jimmy comes to cop something. Now that was kind of strange to see him there so being nosey, I decided to see what he was up to but as soon as I get in the house with Oge, I heard someone say here they go (police)! Boom!!! "Police search warrant" !!!Remember it's a house full in there, so all I could do was lay on the ground. It's freezing outside and the floor was made from concrete and I'm told to sit on the floor with no coat on and the heat was not working. I'm shaking because I'm cold and because it's a lot going on around me, anxiety kicks in and suddenly the police get off everyone else and bring all their attention to me. One of the officers must've said she might need an ambulance because she might have swallowed something. Next thing I knew the ambulance come, they took me to the back, and a black and white guy that was the ambulance workers checked my heart rate. She has anxiety the black guy says and that I had to go to the ER now because my blood pressure was down, and my heart rate was going too fast. When the police left out the room the black worker said "look, we have nothing to do with the police. If you have swallowed something or have anything, let us know now." The police had searched the whole house and the lights were not working in the room we were in. Only the hallway lights were, so once again my shit disappeared into thin air! "The game meant to be sold not told." They got the stretcher and brought it to the back and put me on it. But check this, one of the officers said that he was riding with me in the ambulance car and when I asked "why"? He said because he was about to get a warrant to go get what I had inside of me out. Now hold up! This dude was talking

CHAPTER 23

crazy! I didn't have a clue about what he was talking about but so be it. I didn't have nothing to hide. When we get to the hospital, the police went with me to the back but sorry Mr. officer he came back and said, you got it this time and he left. And, I left against medical Advice, Thank You God! That night no one went to jail, but I knew one thing, someone in that house was talking to the police for the police to come at me only. But I figured who it was. It was a girl whose name was Tiny that I knew growing up. She had started smoking crack but how I knew it was her was because after I came in the house she came and got something, went straight in the back room went to the window and she did not move. When the police came, they came through the back and Tiny was the first one that seen them and said "Police"! It was like she signaled for them to come, but the Lord was with me....

We eventually got our new spot on Waldon booming and Oge people from New York came down to visit him. For some reason, I wasn't feeling one of the niggas aura. He was moving like a snake to me and plus a lot of snake shit had been going on, so everyone was suspect in my eyes. But, Oge grew up with the negros so I let it be. In time we would see. After Internal Affairs got involved the police had caught me off guard but now, I'm feeling threatened for my life. So, from then on Bridget Agguire was my best friend and Ally. She knew everything that had been going on and over our relationship through the years, she has become a good friend of mines. Even though she was raised right and played the hand she was dealt right, she knew I was good people. I was just lost. But the police were still out there like they got hatred for us unfortunate people. It's to the point that I feel that psychologically it's not healthy. One lady officer even told my brother Lamont that he was the reason she woke up and got ready for work, she thought about him in her sleep. I mean come on, what was that? Is that healthy? The police were doing way too much but that's not the half. I hadn't been on 4 Mapel for a while but one day Oge and myself decided to pop up because things had slowed down over there a lot. My kin folks were still there so I was going to come through to see if everything was ok but 10 minutes after we got there, the police came and hit the house again. It was a house full but out of everyone in the house, they locked me up because on my car key chain I had they keys to 4 Mapel St. They also locked up Oge, Brose and one more person and because someone in that house threw their drugs on the floor, they automatically said that it was mine also. They also got a shotgun, scales, razors, baggies and took what money we had in our pockets. Oge and I both had $50,000 bonds each. Oge had a PWISD cocaine, and felony maintaining & dwelling and a Firearm by convicted Felon. I had the extra $50,000 for the firearm by a felon and maintaining & dwelling. Brose had child support, but the police took his money anyway, the other was a female smoker that I didn't know and so I made sure the police left the search warrant because the police are liars. So, I called Bridgett and my girl was downtown on our 1st appearance and got both of our bonds down to $60,000 together and I paid her not one cent. I love that lady, but I did end up paying her later. While still on probation I was told that I had to do weekends and take N.A. meetings from the first charge at the gas station. When we got out, I go get the search warrant after I asked who threw their dope on the ground and I found out who it was that did and was pissed because Legs knew better. But I had no time right then to argue with her because I was trying to figure out how they got in the house in the first place. So, while reading the search warrant, it said "We sent an informant to go into 4 Mapel St. and purchase cocaine and the informant was searched prior to going in the residence and we gave them a $20 bill to make the purchase. They went in and we observed it and they came out and handed us two pieces of crack cocaine. The informant also said that they had got the drugs from a girl whose name was ReRe AKA Vernita Gilchrist. I knew it was a lie because the date they said that Vernita Gilchrist sold the informant the drugs, Nita (My Aunt) was admitted in the hospital in order to help me get out of doing my weekend that weekend. What happened prior to all of this was that I paid Nita to go get me a Doctor's note

CHAPTER 23

and she went under my name Tina Gilchrist and she had congestive heart failure and the only reason why the hospital ran the test was because they said she was too young to be having the symptoms she was having. Remember she used my name at the time I was 28. So, I already knew that they lied to get that search warrant. The only one other person that people called ReRe, was Renata Gates. Got em! I couldn't wait to holla at Bridgett the next morning. I then left Mapel and went down the street to Waldon to tell Oge what I'd just read and to show him the paper and when I walked in the spot, ReRe was going out and I stopped her ass. I told that bitch that I knew that she was the one that tried to set us up, I knew that she was the police and we weren't taking no charges so she had better get ready to get on the witness stand. That bitch eyes got so big that before I knew it, she was running out the door. I asked Oge did any of them sell her anything and Oge said he didn't, but his homeboy said he did. I broke everything down to Oge and I told them to be careful and shut the house down. I then left and went to Bingo. But sure enough, a couple hours later I got a call that the police had just went in the new house that we had just gotten on Waldon and took Oge, L, and Tee to jail. Once I get Oge on the phone he tells me that L had threw his dope down the vents and the police went up under the house and got the dope. I asked him how much everyone's bonds were, and he told me that his was $100,000 and the other two signed themselves out. Something didn't sound right, so I was like WTF was going on here, and Oge told me that both of them put the blame on him and they were charged with weed charges. So, they hit Oge with trafficking and maintain & dwelling. These were supposed to be Oge homeboys and they told a lie on him ASAP. But I already knew who was the one that got the police to come in the house in the first place that was ReRe Gates.

I was getting tired of them MFs, the police hating, niggas out there in the streets snitching, and fake ass wanna be gang bangers fronting. I had a trick for all of that because they had the right one! I started praying harder than ever because the Lord was allowing the devil to come at me from all aspects and I needed some answers. The devil was hitting me hard and it was beginning to wear me down a lot. I was trying my best out there but what was I doing that was so bad? I didn't understand! Another big bond that had to be posted and once I got Oge out, he went to look for his people, but they had already left and went back to New York. You live and you learn, and I had to rub it in his face because I told him I wasn't feeling that dude. Why? Because the nigga was talking slick behind niggas back but different in niggas face.

I finally made it to go see Bridgette and when me and Oge went because I wanted her to represent both of us, she said she couldn't do it because we were co-defendants and that would be a conflict of interest. She also said that she needed to talk to me about my case, but she would rather talk to me alone. She said it's about a plea agreement that the DA offered me. I told her Oge was good and that she could talk around him and she looked at me and said that the DA would drop two of my charges, firearm by felon & PWISD and plead to maintain dwelling but I had to testify against Oge. I told Bridgette "No Way!" I also told her about the warrant, I brought her the medical records and the search warrant. I also told her about the ReRe AKA Vernita Gilchrist, and I told her I wanted the search warrant suppressed. I had got the suppression tactic off a movie I saw. Thank God he allowed that part of the movie to stick with me. Bridgette then looked at me and said if I'd go get my paralegal degree, she will give me a job!

While we were in her office, we went to Saparallis office and hired him for Oge's case. Oge's case was simple, the PWISD (possession with intent to sell and deliver). Possession is 9/10 of the law and that means it must be on your person. The drugs on Waldon St., the police found under the house and the maintain & dwelling charge couldn't stick because the apartment wasn't in his name. So, we advised Saparralis that we were taking everything to trial. But the harassment didn't stop because one day we rented a yellow Mustang

CHAPTER 23

drop top and while riding down Garner Rd. with the top dropped chilling, we see the police go by on the other side and bust a U turn and come behind us. As we pulled in front of my sister Punky house, we stopped and started to get out and they jumped out. Detective Harcia and another officer said that they had smelled weed, so they searched the car, find weed and lock Oge up because they found it on him. Now prior to this, Harcia was the officer I called Internal Affairs on when he ran up on me on Mapel St. and gave me resisting arrest and breaking and Entering charge. Ms. Clara came to court with me and told them that I didn't do no such thing and they dismissed it. Harcia was also the one on the warrant on 4 Mapel St. when he fabricated the warrant pertaining to ReRe, AKA Vernita which was a lie. But every one of those charges got dismissed, Thank God! When the 4 of us got locked up and they hit me with the firearm by felon on Mapel St. Bridgette did get the search warrant suppressed and everything was dismissed. Bridgette even asked me if I wanted the gun back, but I said No, and Brose went and got his money back. Brose said that was the first time ever he had been able to get his money back. Oge got his money back as well. Everything was dismissed on Waldon St. also but the police kept Oge's gold teeth. I guess it was to get his DNA. But sorry, nothing. Oge got his money back also from Waldon St. In the case of the yellow Mustang, the police were on the other side of the street when they bust a U turn and harassed us, so all charges were dismissed! Bridgette B. Aguirre is a beast! I called her to Thank her and once I did that, she told me that she was leaving to be a district attorney. My heart dropped! She laughed and said she was going to Asheville N.C. But to this day, I still call and say hello! Prayer answers all things people. The Lord is very merciful. He loves us and he is our father and even though I was out there doing illegal business in these white people eyes, he knows my heart. He also knew that it was a bunch of shady stuff going on with those officers and that's why he answered my prayers. I'm justified through faith, I'm righteous because I believe in him, Romans 4:3

CHAPTER 24

DURING 2008 I was finally able to relax for a while and get my mind right, even though I was still on probation for the gas station incident but I was able to go through the fire with the help of Jesus Christ who took my prayers to God and not get burnt. We had gone ahead and let 4 Mapel St. go and the landlord boarded it up and we let Waldon go also. We went and got a room on the 300 block of Mapel St. and we just chilled on the low there and just let whoever call the phone. I didn't really have no one there but Fatima there at the room. When I had my Aunt Nita go to the hospital the doctor had told her when she was there that if she hadn't went to the doctor when she had she wouldn't have made it because on top of congestive heart failure she also had an Aneurysm. I'm glad that the Lord used me to get to my aunt, Thank You God because I love my aunt! She is the only aunt that I have. But Praise God because she's been clean ever since. From time to time I would let her running partner "Legs" come and chill. Legs "Yvette Elliot" was from New York somewhere. Her son Stacks and I would conversate over the phone every time Legs would mess up my baby love (money) up, she would call him, and he would send the money to me. Stacks would tell me how crazy things were in New York and before I started dealing with Oge I would tell him to come down to N.C and chill for a while but he never got a chance to come. But once Oge and I started dealing with each other hard, then Stacks decides to come. When I saw him, he was a handsome fella, but I was already taken. But, may his soul rest in peace because he had

CHAPTER 24

got killed back in New York. Not wishing jail on anyone but I was so glad that Legs was locked up when she got that news. It's crazy how life goes. I didn't even know Stacks had the fan base that he had but it was ironic that on one of his songs, he talks about his Raleigh people and Shout out Oge's name. Legs told me that she thought the rapper J.J was the reason her son was dead and when she went to the funeral, she said that J.J had the nerve to show up. I told Legs that the Lord was going to handle everything because if he was the one that was responsible, then he was going to get his. After that, I saw Legs trying to change. Mr. Joe was her boyfriend and instead of her staying out like she used to, she would call Joe and he would come and pick her up. But I can say that after Stacks left the world, Max was that dude! Oge always had an ear for music and that's how I came across Max music before he hit the radio. Once 100 block of Mapel St. closed once the city bought up the properties, everyone like Easter and her husband Bull that stayed on the left side of the 100 block of Mapel St. had to move out. Now with Easter's house gone, niggas were basically standing at the Carvey St. store. We had to transfer the money at the end of 4 Mapel St. and when we did all the hustlers moved that way. Then I decided that I was going to transfer it to the 300 block. Follow the leader....

And what you think they did??? Started hustling on Ponder St. I didn't mind because I looked at it like as long as the niggas standing out on the corners that will keep the police from looking at the houses and besides, they can't stop me!!

Legs and Fatima knew this lady whose name was Sanya that had got the apartment on the left side. I had the front room and a lady name Twin had the back. We had the front room booming and I looked out for the lady that stayed in the back because she had two boys staying with her. Things was kind of rough for her and her two boys but once I did that, I didn't hear a word from her. She was a cool lady and her sons ended up being a part of the family. They even come around to this day. I did have to knock a couple niggas out. But Oge was right there and I knew they weren't going to swing back. A few times I had to run up on niggas with the hammer and if it wasn't for my mom May, it was a family member jumping in front of the gun which stopped me from shooting them. Those niggas weren't built like that for real. But at the same time, we had the spot on Mapel 300 block, it was some "Jafakeican" niggas across the street. Everywhere I went it seemed like it was people hating. The Jafakeicans that was across the street was new in the area but people were getting scarce around there because if they weren't dead, they were getting locked up. Everywhere I went, my people came to me so they were the least of my worries. I'd hoped that they'd mind their business, and everything would be alright because the more decoys, the better off it was for me. But as time went by everything worked out besides a couple of hating ass niggas here and there. The Lord made sure I had someone out there on those streets that always had a queen back because those New York boys that was putting in that work, yea I ended up with "Oges" and boy let me tell you. I don't see why I attracted those type but one day God is going to reveal it to me. Gunplay they weren't ready and as time went by, I allowed my brothers to come and join me on the 300 block of Mapel St. They went on the side where Sanya was at and I stayed on the other side but after that everything just got worse. For some reason I always gave in to my family and they always messed things up for me. I didn't have problems until they came around and on top of that, they weren't loyal people. Police wise yea, because I bet you won't find "Gilchrist" on no ones Motion of Discovery, Period! But my family seemed like they were always in competition with each other and would talk about each other behind each other back and I thought that it was Wack! I think I know where they got all that Bitch stuff from! I love her but May I'm sorry! Why I'm saying that is because if there's anyone that has what she wants she kisses their ass. Jamaican Mike was the one supplying most of them niggas out there with shampoo once upon a time, but I knew that them niggas really came down to Raleigh through Jersey people Antwon and them niggas was do boys. Now

CHAPTER 24

suddenly you get a connect and you gangsta. But it was a few times that I dealt with him because I was gambling badly so I went to him and got credit or something. I can't remember if I spent money and he threw me something, I'm not for sure but as I can recall the next day, I got a phone call saying that Stinky (my cousin), "My Pops" had got killed in a fire in Chester, Penn. and that just tore my nerves all up. Carol which was Stinky's Mom said he had made an invention out of the motor of a lawn mower and put it on a bike and he tried to sell it and she believed that he got killed behind that invention. I can't recall if he put the motor on the bike or the skateboard, it was one of them but anyways, I was a wreck behind that. But, at the same time I didn't know it until later down the line that Mike (Jamaican) had got beat out of some work. When he started blowing up my phone, I didn't want to talk to anyone at the moment but because he was blowing up my phone so bad, I figured that something was wrong, so I answered. The dude came off all hostile and was asking me when can he get his money? Really? So, I responded like who you talking to like that? While he was still speaking loudly, I told him when I get ready or I might have said that he was beat but at the moment, the timing was wrong on both ends. But the nigga called me back and said that I was a dead woman! So, what do I do? I go get my gun! At the time I had a spot that was across the street from Dice house so I went and sat on his porch so I could hit who ever went on my porch with ease. I figured he was going to go to my spot, so I put my gloves on. No one knew what was going to happen but that night I had planned to take advantage of the stand my ground law. Everyone was inside the house when I saw Jamaica Mike's car ride by slow but no one got out. So, I went in the house and Jamaica Mike came through Dice side door. I whipped my piece that was already cocked out so quick that I saw the fear in his big ass eyes as he stood there with his hands up. My mom May was yelling, telling someone to get me out of there and her boyfriend Moe said "Hell No! Get him out of here." My brother who was scared to death asked me how much I owed, and I said "nothing!" I watched both my Mom May and brother Lamont standing in front of the nigga and began peeling out money for him. Stupid people! He didn't get a dime out of me. But I saw him a year or so later and he paid homage. But, Thank God because he could have allowed that to go any other way. I love you God...... Yea, they'd turn on you quick when it came down to a connect. But I still loved them though. My oldest brother Lamont who I got a soft spot for was on the other end of the block but one day he came to me looking all pitiful talking about how May and them was fronting on him and this and that so I gave in to him and my youngest brother David. The next thing I know, May and every smoker on the Southside "Lincoln Park" followed us. It was never hard for the police to find out where the Gilchrist were at because all they had to do was follow the traffic. BOOM! That simple! But with me turning 12 years old on the street along with my brothers who were only 8 years old give or take, most of the smokers had love for us because they practically saw us grow up. So, we were the last people they would tell on because we also treated them like they were our family which most of them still feel that way to this day!

So, things are going O.K. down my way. We would argue from time to time but Oge didn't like how May would come at me and especially when I allowed them to eat at my spot. But out of the love I had for my brothers was the only way I could put up with it. So not only didn't I never want to see anything happen to them, in my eyes and I bet their eyes, I was their Mama! "The lioness and her cubs" But at the time our mom May was influencing them and I'd wished she would have let me handle them because with them following her lead, led them to a dark and dangerous place and it's no coming back from that.

CHAPTER 25

ONE YEAR LATER......

My brother David always kept him something on his arm but around 2009 he hit the jackpot when he began messing with this girl whose name was Cristy. Cristy mother was white and her pops was black. When I first met Maggie, which was Cristy Mom, I met her when she had pulled up at the Carvey St. store one day while she was looking for Christy. She knew who I was, but I didn't know her. But that wasn't nothing new because it had always been like that with me in the hood. I told her where Cristy was and then she asked me did I do my taxes that year. I told her no. She then asked if I washed cars or braided hair etc. or if I knew anyone that did. But I couldn't get off into it now, so I told her I would call her later because I had my friends out who was rushing me. But in the back of my mind I was thinking hard about what she was talking about. So later on, that day, I called her, but it was after I'd talked to David and Christy. When I called her, she asked me a few questions and she told me to send her my information which I did and a little while later she told me that I was getting back $3,600 give or take. But it wouldn't come until the next Friday. She said I was O.K. just as long as it was approved by Wednesday night and sure enough every cent hit my bank account. She took out her $500 fee, but it didn't make me no difference because I was good. No one believed that it was going to get done but once they saw it happen for me, like always everyone followed my lead. After that

ALL I HAVE

it was all she wrote because the whole Raleigh was doing income taxes. Every smoker, dealer, shooter so if you had a name, social and birthdate, let me get it because everyone out there has a hustle, think about. A smoker actually makes more profit than some low-level dealers do because all the rocks they smoke in 24 hours, think about how hard they had to hustle to get it. So, I collected the information, sent it in and just like magic, it was there the next week! I'd give her 10 names at $3,000 apiece and I'd split it with the people, so I was good. An idea came to me one day of what would happen if I went ahead after it had been approved and paid them $500 jump street just to see if they take it, and sure enough just about everyone did. I was sitting lovely but check what Maggie do, she goes all out and says she can get $6,000 per name OMG, I was rich! I don't know what she was doing or how it was getting done but it was like magic. People in the hood was really going to the bank getting $25,000 cash money. It was like robbing the bank with no weapon and from the middle of Jan 2009 all the way to May 2009 it was on and popping. First my brother David bought a 745 BMW shittin on niggas, so I wasn't trying to hear that, so I went and got a Silver 2006 Range Rover. Next thing I know my whole family came out with something foreign. All you saw lined up on Mapel St. was Lexus, Benzes on each side and the outsiders had not a clue on what was going on, and come to think about it, I really didn't know either. I would just send her 20 names and she would tell me that half of the names was rejected but the whole time, I figured she was stealing them. But where Maggie messed up at was "GREED". Once the people that I'd sent to her began wanting their money that's when they called the IRS (Internal Revenue Service) and that's what opened and investigation on her. We were steady sending her people's names but she would say half of them was rejected and I found out that she was doing $12,000 per name. Damn, she messed me up with that one! But she was the expert, so I paid the people what I owed and the ones that she claimed was rejected they called the IRS to find out why. But I know one thing, I've never done so much traveling in my life. Oge had went somewhere and got robbed

CHAPTER 25

blind for a couple thousand. No, I'm not going to say robbed because allegedly, someone tried to set him up with the police per say but that was chump change at the time because I'm just going to say that it was real out there when all the smokers around us had racks on top of racks in their pockets. Those smokers were smoking ounces and you couldn't tell them nothing! Every Friday we would go up in the bank and take out at least $30,000 cash and that was rare. But I wasn't no slow leak because I knew that someone was going to come back and visit us one day. I was hoping that they wouldn't, but in the back of my mind I knew that they were. I had a gray drop top mustang and a grey $36,000 Range Rover truck but I had enough sense not to pay it off. I should have but if I did, I knew they was going to take it if it was paid off. But, New York City we burnt it down, Jewelry, Casinos, clothes, and after we got the Range, that same week, we drove to NY went shopping, drove back to NC and hopped on a plane me, Oge, and my grandma and went to the MGM in Las Vegas. I had been to Vegas before, but this time was different because our spending was unlimited. We were charging everything to the room. Roberto Cavalli shades, Gucci, Versace, you name it we charged it. VIP status at the club on top of that, it was the Mayweather & Pacquiao fight week and we were in there. Also, on May 2, 2009 on Legs Birthday, me and Oge got married at the MGM and we charged that also. My grandma Lynda was there, Oge's sister Kosha and her baby daddy and because she was my girl, the trip was all on me. She was pregnant at the time and that girl was on fire out there. I couldn't get nothing to shake but I did hit for $1,200 betting 25 cents on a Kenny Roger machine. I couldn't believe that because that was some T.V. type shit. I put the .25 cent ticket in, bet and BOOM! That's exactly how that went down. The casino was packed because of that fight and it only lasted one round. All the Philippines out there was pissed! Pacquiao couldn't take Mayweather. We stayed out there for 5 days and we also had to borrow a couple thousand from Maggie. I know we spend every bit of 40 racks (thousand) out there. That might be chump change for some but I ain't the fronting type. I'm from the hood and to me, that's a lot of bread to blow in 5 days. I had a ball out there to the point that I got tired of spending money. I couldn't wait to get back home. Don't get me wrong, if the money was legal then things would have gone differently but common sense told me that the alphabet boys (F.B.I) was coming. We weren't the only people that Maggie was dealing with. I just broke the ice for her, and greed took over the rest. But we finally made it home safely, Thank God and I dropped my grandmother off at home and headed to the house not believing that I was married. It was crazy but stuff like that happens in Vegas.

I get back to Raleigh and go pick up my son Chico and I pulled in the parking lot of the apartment complex where I stay at. When I looked things looked kind of different, but at that moment, I wasn't putting two and two together. But, I get Chico out the car and I go in the apartment, go to the kitchen, turn on the lights on and I just knew I saw someone running but I wasn't thinking clearly until I saw that my apartment was ransacked. Someone had broken into my apartment! I didn't keep anything there, but they took my son's PlayStation, his games, and they tried to take the T.V. but couldn't get it off the stand. I caught their ass in the act, and I think they came in through the closet from the neighbor's apartment because that was open once I looked there. I called the police because I needed some answers but once the police came, they didn't even make a report. Instead they asked me if I sold drugs. These people came into my shit so what did that have to do with anything? The officer even had the nerve to say that his reason for not writing a report was because we needed to stop selling drugs. Fuckin crackers in NC! It is one racist fucked up state. Now I had to take matters into my own hands. So once Oge got there, we took it from there.

Even though we spent all that change in Vegas, we still had $24,000 coming the following week. So, we just sat back and relaxed a little. But these niggas out there on the streets were on some hating shit! I didn't blame them though. Niggas was Icey, riding foreign, going to Vegas and getting married and all the while I was still

CHAPTER 25

on probation. The weekend before we had left for Vegas, I had to do a weekend in jail, so I went and got my hair and nails done because once I got out that Sunday night, we hit the highway. It isn't what you do it's how you do it but niggas were already hating on Oge because they were intimidated by him but now, they couldn't stand him. He appeared like a nigga that had more that they had but on the low we had maxed out and we were only working with the little change we had left, while waiting on the 24 racks that was coming the following Friday. But when that Friday came, it was no money. So, I called Maggie to see what was going on and she said it was supposed to be there but when I called the bank, the bank said it was a freeze on my account. I knew right then and there that it was going to be a problem. Everyone associated with Maggie's account got frozen including hers. She even called me asking for the money that she let me borrow but I was trying to get my $24,000. The truth was that, I couldn't pay her because I was banking on that 24 racks to hit my account. But now it was over. They had everyone's shit on hold and now everyone was scared. I made sure all the people who I helped got notarized papers because I wasn't playing with them and on top of that, Oge's sister Kosha had gave him 50 racks so that saved me also. After the bank put a hold on everyone's account, things weren't looking too good. So as usual we had to go back to work. All that splurging niggas had done, now niggas were wishing they had that shit now. Things was already on fire on the block but things were about to get even hotter.

1 month after I got married....

It was summertime and it was such a pretty day that everyone was outside. My ex-boyfriend B walks in the other side where my brother Lamont and them was at and I couldn't do anything about them being over there because the girl that was staying next door had done took a liking to Lamont and as usual they played me. But Oge was in the house and once he saw B, he came outside and told him that he needed to leave. I couldn't fault Oge for that because we were there

ALL I HAVE

first and that's when my ex B started talking shit. So Oge whipped his ass and B left. Oge told me that he needed to go get his piece, but I told him no because B was pussy. But no more than 20 minutes later, B comes back, and he tells me to move out the way. I then see Oge runs in the house and my sister baby father Brad in front of Oge At first I didn't but he says it again and I saw the look in his eyes like girl you can get it to so I hops out the way and he started shooting through the house. He unloaded and then ran. I go in the house and I saw that Oge was laying on the floor and couldn't breathe. Fatima was hit and Bradley, so I pick up the phone and dialed 911. I told them 3 people was shot at 304 Mapel St. The news people even got there before the police did and on the front page of the Newspaper there was a picture of me and Oge on a stretcher from a triple shooting on Bloody Maple. I couldn't believe what had just happened. I had just got married to this man a couple weeks ago. And my best friend hit also. OMG! They wouldn't even let me go in the ambulance with Oge, but they took me down to the police station. All that was running through my head was "Lord please don't do this to me. I just got married a few weeks ago so Lord please don't allow me to endure this pain" Then I would think about what Chico my baby father told me. He would say "Tina I don't care what people say to you. They can call you the police all they want but I know you a rider so if a nigga put your life in danger, you have to put the police in it because if you come across them and have to defend yourself, then as long as the police know about the situation, if you shoot them in a crowd of 1000 people in broad daylight, your shooting would be justified. "There's a lot of niggas gone out there that lived by the street code, but most of these Raleigh niggas are bitches so they were telling as soon as the police looked them in the face. Chico got natural life behind a wanna-be, but I lawyered up and they finally let me leave. They took me to the emergency room, and I called Oge's sister Kosha. Immediately they were flying on a plane. Once we arrive at Wake Center Hospital, I go inside and tell them I'm Oge's wife. The police vouched for me and they take me into a private room. When I pulled up to the emergency

CHAPTER 25

room ReRe was standing outside being nosey, but anyways, bitch bye! The police were there a short period of time, a chaplain and a nurse were in a special room with me. The nurse told me that it wasn't looking too good for him because the bullets that he got hit with was a small caliber and it bounced around inside of him, She also said that the chaplain was there to help me with any concerns that I may have had. Now I wasn't trying to hear nothing this woman was saying so I told her I wasn't worried about it too much because deep down in my heart, I knew the Lord wasn't going to do that to me. So, at the same time, I'm talking to them, I'm praying to God. "Lord please let him make it through because he's my best friend and my husband." All I could think about was what had I done to get this treatment. It's like I could never be happy and deep down inside, the only reason why I got married was because I was trying to do right by God. So, I continued to pray. "Lord handle this situation because I'm sorry for whatever I've done wrong for you to allow this to happen or maybe it's not me and I'm just caught in the middle, but whatever it is, I know you love me also, so please Lord hear my prayer!" Then comes the nurse. I'm not fully understanding what she was saying because my mind is not fully registering but I did understand when she said that it was taking longer than normal for him to pull through. I then told her again that I didn't want to hear anything else because God was in control and to just let me know when I could see him. The nurse was acting like she didn't believe in God because she kept telling me that this was a serious matter. I told her that I knew that, but I told her again to come let me know when I could go see him. By this time, his sisters Trina, Kosha, Coco and his Aunt Barbra had arrived. Out of all the sisters, Kosha was the only one that I had met but his Aunt Barbra and his sister Trina was looking at me crazy because they thought that I had something to do with him getting shot since my ex was the one that did it, going off what his baby mother was saying. She told them I was the reason he had got shot but at that moment I had no time for negativity. It had been 15 hours and the doctors had been working on him nonstop and before you know it a nurse came in and said he is stable!!! Thank God! He was laying in the hospital bed with a lot of tubes coming out of him but when he came to, I wanted his son to be there when he woke back up. The message got to Mia his baby mother and she brought his son to the hospital. This was my first time seeing his son, that lil dude look just like him. Mia had a fitted cap on his son's head that made Michael and Oge look like twins, just like lil Cheek and Chico did before. Michael bent over and gave his Dad a kiss and he seemed like he was happy to see Michael. At the time I couldn't go check on Fatima because they were both under aliases because that's hospital procedure when you're a gunshot victim. Oge was in ICU, so visitation hours were over at 7:00pm. But, once I came, I went to find out what room she was in. Oge couldn't stay awake for long because they had him under Fentanyl which is the highest pain meds they had. He even had a push button so every time he pressed it; he was out. I waited on the doctor and they told me that one of the bullets bounced all over the place, causing broken ribs where they put screws and metal there, his shoulder had metal plates and the hand the bullet came out of had screws there also. He had punctured his left lung, so they took a part of that out as well. So, he was lucky to be here. No, he's blessed to be here by the grace of God!

When I finally got the O.K. that he was going to make it I felt a lot better. I let his family chill with him, and I left and went home. I couldn't believe that B would do such a thing. See these young people these days are punks. During the time I was younger we wore a lot of ass whippings and gave some as well. Why did people resort to gunplay and know that they weren't built like that? B. was going off his emotions and hating but like the old saying goes, you never know what you have until it's gone. So, it was all his fault. Dude was the one that fucked my cousin Chris's baby Mother. But Lamont and my family should have respected the situation more and kept B. from the house also. They knew that I was the one that turned them on to the spot but like I said, dis loyal niggas. People showed loyalty to the wrong niggas. When watching the news, they put B's whole name

CHAPTER 25

as the suspect of the triple shooting on Mapel St. and how about he turned himself in and was under a million-dollar bond. Yea, that was his best bet because Fatima's family was pissed, and I was also because all of this could have been avoided. But, could it? The Lord says, "Heaven and Earth shall pass, but his word shall always stand", and then I got to thinking, Oge was on probation for a shooting charge and at that very moment he was going to violation court. We had hired another attorney for his case and I also contacted Randy Hill that was his initial attorney and I informed him that Oge wasn't coming to court for a while because of the shooting. Mr. Hill. was cool about it and was very concerned for Oge, and he told me that he was going to handle it for us. Mr. Hill worked in the same office as Bridgette, so he got his court cases put off until further notice. I'd been hearing a lot of damage "work" that Oge had dished out in the streets but Oge is a Capricorn like I am, and I know or think I know that most of this stuff was justified. But the Lord also says that "if you shed blood, your blood shall be shed", so everything Oge was going through at the moment could have been worse. But I'm Thankful to God that he showed us his mercy and grace, and he heard my prayer because God knew mentally, I would have been a wreck. My husband and best friend by the hands of my ex-boyfriend OMG! That would have done a lot of damage mentally.

I had got up with Fatima's Mom Mrs. Ora, and I met her at Wake Center Hospital, and I went to visit her in the ICU. She was hanging in there and was doing better than Oge was doing. She was more alert, but you could tell that she was still in pain. My baby girl was a fighter and I loved her so much! We had our ups and downs but after everything we had been through, that's how I knew we were besties because we would be right back together stronger than before. Fatima even reminded me of a dream I had, and it clicked in my head. After looking at the whole thing I realized it was what my dream was about. Fatima said "Tina, I don't like when you be having dreams!" What she was saying was real because it seemed like when

ALL I HAVE

I have certain dreams of someone getting hurt or shooting, it be trying to tell me something. But at the same time, I was trying to find out how Fatima got hit because she was asleep on the mattress that was on the floor. She even told me that when she was asleep, she woke up to a lot of noise and she went to sit up and that's when she got hit twice in the chest. One of the bullets the doctors managed to get out but the other one was too close to her heart so they weren't going to bother that one because to do the surgery, it could have done more damage to her. She didn't stay in surgery as long as Oge did because he was in surgery 15-16 hours compared to her 8 hours max. She got lucky a little because she had no broken bones or anything major like Oge. Two days after the incident happened, they had their room and Fatima was around the corner from Oge. I even popped up one day on them and I saw Fatima walking towards Oge's room! Fatima didn't mess with Oge like that but after that incident they had become good friends. Some days she would be sitting in the room with him keeping him company, but she was released in about 3 weeks. Oge stayed almost two months. He had lost a lot of weight because he couldn't eat anything. They were feeding him "Ensure" through a tube. He also had a bag that the nurse had to change. But as long as he was alive, I didn't care about any of it. Thankfully two months later, Oge was ready to come home. I stayed at the hospital with him as much as I could, but I had to keep things going. It seemed like niggas was happy Oge had got hit but it's just hating ass niggas. But only the strong survive and my nigga came up out of there like Stephen Segal! Once he got out of the hospital, he did everything the doctors told him to do and while putting his sugar on top, before you knew it, he was at 80%. He still had the sling on his arm so I couldn't give him 100%, but despite the circumstances, he did what it do, Thanks to the Lord! He started gaining his weight back. But if it ain't one thing it's another. There was something he still had hovering over his head and that was his probation violation. Oh yea, after he had healed up, we had moved from the apartment that we had off Green Rd. because I didn't like the fact that niggas knew our movements. Mr. Randy Hill

CHAPTER 25

had got his court date pushed back about 5 months after the shooting and we had to finally face that he would have to do 18 months. That was on his dumbass because he had the best probation possible. Unsupervised probation. All he had to do was go in and say hello and pay his fees which were $5,000. But he was so stubborn that he couldn't do that! But it was also a reason why he couldn't do that and that's because his P.O. had quit. I told him several times to call in and talk to a supervisor to find out the hold up, but when it came down with the police or people in the Judicial System he would want to run. Like the charges that we beat prior to this, he would say "I'm leaving", and I would tell him "nigga, you are running for no reason". All this shit can be beat. My thing was if you out there in the streets you must play by the rules because you're going to run across these white people. Just let them know that they aren't messing with no dummy. They have a job to do just like you have one. Money talked, bullshit walk, Bottom line! We left voice messages on the supervisor's answering machine several times and when it was his first time to go to court, I prayed to God to soften the heart of the judge and the DA. The Lord knew that we tried to get in contact with his probation officer because this time the blame wasn't all on us. But judge Fox, I will not forget his name was that day the most laid-back black judge I'd seen in a long time. And, the officer, P.O. that came also told the judge that Oge left numerous messages and that Oge played his part, but his P.O. quit and that is what messed everything up. Once Judge Fox heard that, he dismissed the case and told the P.O. office to get it together, Thanks to God! So, he got another chance to redeem himself! God is good! But a hard head makes a soft ass! One day he would learn....

I can't front on Oge, he held my family down. It's not what you know but who you know and Oge knew a lot of people that were scattered up and down the East coast he stayed on the move. When other people would experience a drought, all we had to do was go the extra mile for a few hours and Boom, it was like we had never

ALL I HAVE

went anywhere. If my brothers had any beef with anyone, they knew to come to me because they knew that not only was I about that life, but my companion would come with me. For instance, after the income taxes, a cat named Nick was telling a couple of people that David was broke and that he was coping flips from him and riding around in that 745 like he was balling. So, I called Nick and asked him to pop up on me because I wasn't feeling how he was coming at David. For one thing, I knew that Nique was fronting because I'd been knowing that cat for years, but why was he running around hating when he knew that he wasn't built like that I didn't understand. So, the nigga pops up on us during the time Oge wasn't going anywhere without his lil friend (gun) and after what had popped off, I didn't blame him. So, he comes around talking like it wasn't like this that and the third, coping pleas. I defended David by saying, "So what he not no shot caller, but guess what? The ladies love him, and he got what you don't, period. The Lord got him!" But what people didn't know was that I made sure my family knew, if they couldn't do the time then don't do the crime because that selling weight shit is not worth it. Them other niggas could have all that because if you don't know what you going to do in life or don't have any goals set up, then it's no need. Go back to school people. I don't wish prison time on anyone but shortly after that dispute I had with Nick, two weeks later the FEDS picked him up and right now he got 38 years FED. The sad thing about that, was the nigga wasn't making that kind of money, to get that type of time. But after the incident with Nick some niggas had kidnapped David over a bitch and Oge had to go straighten them cats. So Oge looked out for my people but what use to make me upset with my people was that they didn't show the loyalty back. The reason why I feel like they didn't was because of the people they grew up around. Just about every one of them cats turned out to be bitches and my brothers got tainted also. When I sit back and looked at what they had become, it was sad to see them that way. I had to come to the realization that I had to be on my own. I'd keep them in my prayers, but I had to let them figure out which direction they

CHAPTER 25

wanted to go for themselves. Their business was out of order and they were greedy and disloyal and on top of that, May was with them because she acted like she was just as lost as they were and that's their Mother. But once the shooting happened with Oge and Fatima at 304 Mapel St. we didn't stay there long. May and my brothers went to the Northside off Greenwich Rd on Capitol BLVD and I went and got 4 Mapel St. back! This time all my family members were gone off the Southside of Raleigh. It was just me.

CHAPTER 26

I RECEIVED A phone call the summer of 2010 from a good friend of mine whose name is Tamara. She told me that the FEDS were outside, and they were looking for some Gilchrist. I'm like damn what the world they are doing coming to 4 Mapel, Shit! I'd just moved back down there. I told Tamara to open the door while I was on the phone and she told them that she didn't know any Gilchrist but the federal officers had already done their surveillance. They told Tamara they saw my truck come down there a couple of times and they just wanted to talk to someone. They ended up leaving their card and told us to get in touch and if we didn't then we were going to make it harder on ourselves. Damn I tell you! She read off the information on the cards, Internal Revenue Services "IRS." I was like here we go because I was expecting them but dang, not this quick. I had to think, so I contacted Maggie and told her what had happened, but she already knew. The best thing I knew to do was go ahead and face the music because one thing I did know was once the FEDS come, it's real. I knew I'd done nothing wrong, but my nerves couldn't take that suspense. If I needed to get an attorney, I wanted to know early on because while they were starting their investigation I could be working on that ASAP. I then calls the number on the card that Tamara gave me an a woman by the name of Ms. Julia answered the phone and I informed her of who I was and she asked me could I come down to the federal building on New Burn Ave. I wasn't feeling going to a federal building without an attorney, but I'd been in the streets for a long time and one thing I learned, Thanks to

God for the knowledge, is that if it was any questions that would incriminate me, I would plead the 5th amendment. So I asked the lady if I was in any trouble and of course, like all the other officers I'd come across she lied and said no and that she only had a couple of questions that she needed to ask me. Mainly about Maggie Willis! I told her I would be there the next day at 1pm. After that phone call, my heart was racing because I knew that if the FEDS wanted you they'd already done their homework on everything from your criminal history to what song you liked in Elementary school, so once I got there I was going to take it moment by moment. But first and foremost, I prayed, "Lord, please forgive me for my sins and Lord please be with me when I go down there to talk to these Federal Agents. Lord if you help me out with this Lord, I will not indulge in this type of activity every again." Shoot forget all that! I woke up the next day and prayed to the Lord early that morning I thought to myself if Maggie would have kept it 100% and not took those people money, then none of this would have ever happened. I was upset for her putting me in this position but one thing I had to my advantage was that I made sure I got notarized papers. We also had the paperwork from when Oge's sister gave him $50,000 once she got her settlement. I ain't no slow leak, so I had to try to be 10 steps ahead. But you also must have God with you. Once I'm dressed that morning, I didn't even feel like leaving the house because I just couldn't think straight. My mind was strictly on that interview and how the FEDS was about to come at me, so I knew I had to be very careful not to play myself. So, I did what I always do, I prayed about the situation and I headed out the door, jumped in the Rover truck and headed to the federal building. As I was pulling in the parking lot of the federal courthouse I thought to myself, why did I drive this truck up here? That was the very reason why they called me in the first place. I wanted to turn around and take the truck back, but I thought to myself, they already knew that I'd bought the truck. It's the FED's, duh! When I walked in, I noticed that it was an older building where everything was locked down. I entered the building and went through the metal detectors and in my head and heart I was still praying to God because I knew that it was a lot of money being exchanged but I also knew that in all actuality I or we didn't do anything but take money out of our banking account. But I was ready to see how it was going to go. Once I got to the secretary after I got off the elevator the whole time I'm talking to Jesus because at that moment, he was the only one that could help me with this. I think it looked even better for me because I'd come there solo without a lawyer. So, after I spoke to the secretary a couple minutes later, a little bitty white lady with glasses on, by the name of Ms. Valdez came. She was the special agent that oversaw everything because I had her card. So, we shook hands and she walked me to the interview room. Now in the back, I'm nervous because I wanted to know what's gonna happen and then Ms. Valdez told me to hold on a minute because her partner was coming in also. OMG! My hands started sweating and I'm asking the Lord what should I do? How should I handle this whole situation, and something just told me to tell the truth because all I had done was take money out of my bank account. Her partner finally came but also with another little black woman by the name of Ms. Smith. They turn on the tape recorder and the interview began. First thing they do is record both of their names and they said that they were in the interview with Tina Gilchrist in reference to Maggie Willis. I asked them did I need an attorney there because I knew that I did have the right to remain silent so if this was going to be an interrogation, I knew what I said that day could come back to haunt me then I was definitely going to need an attorney. Those federal agents told me point blank that they already knew who they wanted and to just tell my story and if I wasn't hiding anything then I had no worries. That right there let me know that Maggie had a serious problem on her hands. So, they pull out all my bank transactions which I knew they would, and they asked me how all of it came about. I went ahead and told them the truth but I'd also talked to Maggie prior to the interview and she told me to say that she was riding around looking for clients, which was true and that's how we got together on the taxes thing. I also told the FEDS that she was the Mother of my brothers' girlfriend and I ran across her at the Carvey St. store and she asked me did I know anyone that

CHAPTER 26

needed their taxes done. She also said that if they braid hair, wash cars, little odd jobs then they're able to file taxes also. I told them that I told her that I needed my taxes done and Maggie gave me her number and that's how we linked up. I texted her and she told me to send my information, I did and the next thing I know I had 3 bands (thousand) in my account the following week. After that, it spread like wildfire. Ms. Valdez then asked me if I had helped Maggie with preparing any of the income taxes? Once she said that I told them right then and there that I already know that they'd done their homework because they are the FEDS so I already knew they knew what's up with us Gilchrist. I went on, I had a GED and I'm a recovering addict. I then asked her if they had my criminal record and they said "yes". Then I said so you already know my D.N.A I know nothing about no filing of income taxes. I continued, so after I got my taxes done, I turned everyone else on to Maggie. Ms. Valdez then asked me how I was able to get all the transactions to my account and I told her that I got my peoples information and sent it in a text message to Maggie's phone. My people said that they worked, and I told Maggie what kind of work they did and sent their birthdate, social and name and Boom! I also let my people's use my account because they didn't have a bank account at the time. I admitted that I didn't know it was a federal offense to allow a friend to use your account. That interview went on for hours but once I walked out of the federal building, I went ahead and called my people and told them to get ready because they were coming and I believed it was in their best interest to call them before they caught anyone off guard. The FEDS knew about the money going in my bank, everything I spent the money on, and my trip to Vegas. Hell, they also asked if my truck was paid for and I told them no, which it wasn't. They knew everything! But they asked did I pay the people and I told them "yes", which I did. I also told her about the $50,000 that Oge sister gave him for the wedding, and that we told the people that if they wanted the money now, I would go ahead and give them half once it got approved and we would keep the other half and they was cool with that. I also told her that we got them to do a notarized paper. I gave the info to the FEDS and proof of the 50 bands Oge's sister gave him, and that was it for that interview. But I can say that Maggie was a smart woman. The FEDS said through her account alone she deposited over two million dollars. They said she bought 5 houses and multiple vehicles. Oh, she wasn't playing any games! But what messed her up was greed. I would tell you how she did it but again, "The game meant to be sold not told". But man, that lady snapped! She was killing the game and only if she would have slowed down, none of that would have happened with the FEDS. But now they were saying they were not going anywhere until they talked to everyone that was linked to her. Dang Maggie! I liked that lady, but she was just another white woman that thought she was getting over on us niggas and ended up messing herself up. They say don't bite the hand that feeds you! I called Maggie and I told her everything that was said and I advised her that she might need to get an attorney and I also told everyone of my people to tell the truth of how Margo was preparing our taxes, looking out for us little people that washed cars and braided hair. The FEDS went one by one interviewing everyone that was involved with Maggie. Even the people that we didn't know and the word I was hearing on the streets was that Maggie was about to go to jail. Her daughter Cristy told us that they took everything she had but she was able to pay for her attorney. Cristy also thanked me because she said out of all the people that she dealt with, I was the only one that looked out for her mom and she appreciated that. But after all of this was over, Maggie ended up with 3.5 years FED. If she would have had that money buried in the cut somewhere, over Two million dollars, I would have done every bit of that and would have come home sitting pretty! But thanks Maggie because that right there opened my eyes on that white-collar shit. All my life I'd been out there risking my life over peanuts but people like Maggie was scheming millions and getting less time than us people selling nickels and dimes. I must start mingling more. They say it's all about who you know but one thing for certain, I wasn't doing anything like that anymore. That shit was for the birds!

CHAPTER 27

BY THIS TIME, things were looking bad. Oge wasn't doing what he was supposed to have been doing for probation, but I was reminded that you can't help nobody that don't want to be helped. Oge was a grown man and it was on him but at the same time, I was the one that caught the back lash. He was going back and forth to jail and 3 times I posted $100,000 bond. I even had to sell the Range Rover to get him out the last time. See me, if I'm with you then that's what it is because if the tables ever turned, God forbid it, I didn't need any problems. The last time I got him out, he missed court and I couldn't get him a fourth, so they went ahead and activated his time of 15 months. With him only having to do 15 months and 9 months post release that wasn't bad. But it took them a while to give him his time. He had been on probation since 2005 and his probation was only two years but since he couldn't do right, it took him 6 years. But people make things harder on themselves when all he had to do was pay the money. If you out there doing wrong, pay them white people. Do what you must do but stop giving these white people y'all freedom because I done saw time and time again people go in the courtroom intimidated by a white person in a suit. People you must have a defense. Period! The legal system is all on who can tell the best story and who is the best person to tell your story. I tell a lot of people to stop giving up and if you are doing wrong you need to tighten up because these white people will hide you just off them making up a theory. Look at my baby Father, Chico. The D.A. which by the way

ALL I HAVE

was white and who presided over his case (Jeff)put on a 3-piece suit and made up his own story and sold it for Chico's life! His version was nowhere near what happened, but Jeff didn't care about the truth, these crackers do what they want. So, pertaining to me, I rebuke them haters in the name of Jesus. Around this time, we had left the bottom of Mapel St. and had went back and got a room back at 304 Mapel St. That shit was a dub once the Feds came, I wasn't about to take any chances. I got Legs to get it for me. I would have stayed at 4 Mapel St. but things happen for certain reasons. It was Legs, Tamara, and myself but the landlord didn't want to see me down there because he already knew what it was. So, I would slide in and out while Tamara and Legs held the fort down. In the house it was only 4 rooms there with two rooms on each side. On our side which was the left this time it was a man whose name was Frank that stayed in the front room and we had the back room. Automatically I had to have control of both rooms because I had no time for no jealous neighbors wanting or threatening us with the police. So, when it came to Frank, I peeped his whole character with one look and conversation. I hollered at Tamara to get on that for me and once she had done that, I had him. The oldest profession in the world for a woman. Tamara was a young petite lady that liked to enjoy herself and the men couldn't resist. I could have put Legs on him, but Legs was a special character. She would probably drove him crazy. After her son, Stacks had passed like I said, she had started to change for the better, but she was still fighting her demons. I remember Legs would go in the bathroom with a razor blade and she would come out with bald patches in her hair. I had to snap her out of that. I would tell her that I wasn't going to be her friend anymore if she continued to cut her hair and that helped a lot because after that she didn't; she started to humble herself and Mr. Joe her boyfriend would bring her over to the trap in the morning time and he would come and take her home at night. It got to the point that I didn't even have to sweat Legs for my change, and she built up the trust that she would have my money when she came out in the morning. It took a long time for Legs to get to the point, but it was working itself out.

CHAPTER 27

With Oge being gone and me not having anything to do with my time, I would go to these internet cafes and sit there and gamble all day and night. At first, I would hit on the regular but all of that was a setup because once they got me hooked, they had reeled me in. I couldn't make nothing happen anymore. With Oge being locked up and my son Chico staying with Tang, I was basically on my own. With no friends by choice but my buddies. I wasn't supposed to be seen on 304 Mapel so I gambled to pass time. One night I had been at the Sweepstakes and had spent almost all my money. I as banking on the money Legs had. When I left the Sweepstakes and go to the house to see how much change Legs had, when I got there she wasn't at the house. So I called her phone she picks up and I told her to come to the house because I needed some money from her so I could go back to the Sweepstakes and get my money back that I had lost. That's how my mind was. When Legs came to the house, all she had was a few dollars. O.K. I then tell her to go get the work that I gave her so I could check and see what's going on. She hesitated and once she did that, I knew something was wrong. She went and got what she had left and she damn near smoked all my shit up. Everything in my being had to hold me back from putting my hands on that woman and the reason why I didn't was because the city was buying the house that we were in and the room was in her name and I needed that change. They were going to pay her rent, lights and water for 5 years in 3 installments so I knew I could have put my hands on her, but something told me not to. So, I took what she had and mushed her in the face and told her I was going to let the Lord handle her. I told her to get out. A couple of days had gone by and sure enough my brother Lamont baby mother Lonette came to the trap and told Tamara that Legs had died in her sleep. When they called me and told me that, my heart sank to my feet. I couldn't believe it because she had started to change completely. I love that lady and even though we had our ups and downs I considered her a friend. It was two years after her son died. It was deep and the money we were getting off the room from the state, was gone out the door. She had a nice funeral here in

ALL I HAVE

Raleigh. I didn't want to go but I had to pay my respects to my friend. Gone but never forgotten.

Luckily, I was looking at the duplex at 203 Mapel St. Mr. Ben had just moved out of there and it was two apartments side by side with the back room connected to a door in the back! Mr. Ben was a smooth criminal (old coon) and he was going with this lady whose name was Cynthia and they use to watch lil Chico for me. When I called him, he gave me Mr. Luke number and when I called Mr. Luke, I told him Ben had gave me his number and $1,200 was all it took. I was in there and it was also the perfect trap for me. Once we got the keys to the house, we moved in the same day. Someone turned everything on illegally and Boom! We were in there. But the next day we went ahead and arranged for the lights and water to get turned on. It was the perfect spot for me. It had two addresses to one house so if the police were to come in, they could only come on one side. It allowed us to be able to see them coming and we would slide through the back door and lock it. You see the police couldn't come over because they had no search warrant for that side of the house. It had been just what I'd been looking for and I had it in my possession. If I had played it right, then I would have had longevity in that house. At the time, it was only 3 houses and Clive grandparents who lived across the street. The City of Wake was coming through there purchasing all the other property over that way moving us black people to the country but Mr. Luke had already said that he wasn't selling his house, so I was good. Let's get it! The addresses I had at the house was 203 and 203 1/2 Mapel St. 203 I kept for Oge because when he came home he was going to need an address for his parole and also I knew he was going to get right to that check so I painted 203 and put carpet down. I hooked that side up just in case I decided to come and chill or whatever. I did know one thing; a nigga better not had come up over there and played pussy because they were going to get fucked. They saw the traffic going to the right side so run up over there if you wanted because you weren't going to make it off the porch because I was on the left and they wouldn't even see it coming. Looking at how the streets was looking then it was the best way because everyone that was out there on Mapel St. got locked up or 6ft under. But, Thanks to the Lord, he made sure that I was protected. No one came to bother me at all. The only problem I had was out of the smokers and I could handle them on my own. I would often sit and think about all the nights I was out there in these streets alone, as a female 10 toes down with females hating as well as niggas. But the only trouble the Lord allowed to come across my path was the police and the drama I had with the men in my life. Also, God made sure I had a real nigga with me, well let me rephrase that, a shooter so I always was protected. God knew what he was doing, but coming to think about it, he probably brought them to me for a reason because he might have chosen me to be in the environment for a reason. I'm going to always pay homage to my Lord and that's how I'd always talked to anyone that came across my path. That's why I tried to keep my circle small because people who weren't on my level might have tried to take the way I talk or the love I show as a weakness not realizing that my faith in God has always been a powerful weapon. All I ever had to do was pray about a situation, sit back and watch the Lord handle it every time. Now check this out! During the time when I was at 203 Mapel St. Oge was locked up doing his probation time, I made sure that he was straight, and Scott Corrections was the place to be. He wasn't even there a week and he had already had a C.O. bringing him in Bojangles and whatever he wanted to eat for that week, but I had to get a $100 VISA gift card and give him the card information and they would also bring him in tobacco or whatever. I held him down, but that didn't last long because hating ass niggas snitched him out and they moved him. What I would do was send him a money order every day because during this time my gambling addiction was at its worst and if I needed a couple thousand, he would send it out to me. It would take 3 weeks so that made me tighten up a little bit but overall, he was good, and I was also, but this ain't the half. Before Oge had got locked up he had finally figured out who had broken into our

ALL I HAVE

apartment. We just knew a lot of people, although I'm not necessarily a people person but he is, and we found out that Dareese (China's brother), Jimmy, and Aleman were the niggas that did it. Oge wanted so badly to do something to them, but I knew that what the wrath of God puts on a person won't compare to what a human can do, and I told Oge to let the Lord handle it. Those niggas were faking the funk like they were ready for the streets but instead of the niggas running up on a nigga, they wanted to break in someone's crib. Oge had put so much work (earning a reputation) out there on the streets that the reason why he was locked up was because he called two guys whose names were Ronnie and Dank to bring him some Marley (weed), we set it up to meet them at the Internet Cafe, and when I saw Ronnie and Dank pull up, we handle our business even after I told Oge about them cats. But right when they pulled off the bondsmen showed up and arrested Oge. I knew that most of these niggas in Raleigh were pussy and that's one of the reasons why I didn't mess with niggas from Raleigh. The other reason was because it wasn't no telling who was your family. My family is so big that I only know a select few of them, but before Oge got locked up, Dareese was trying to be all up under us a lot. His sister China got two kids by my younger brother David, but when it came down to Dareese, I really wasn't feeling him because of the history that Oge and him had. Before, Oge was letting loose on him on sight but during this time, it seemed like Dareese was coming to the realization that he had been on the wrong team out here. The reason why I said that was because Dareese was under my cousin Chris before he got killed and with me on the outside looking in, he took the gang stuff to heart. With other people it was for show. But to me Dareese was lost. He thought that he had a family that had his back out there but they didn't. When niggas got in any beef, they would go get Dareese and he would rock with them but prior to him coming around us, he came to realize that he was on his own because the two different times Dareese got shot, no one was there to hold him down, but after the last time he got shot, I believe it was a wakeup call because Oge and him began to be cool with one

CHAPTER 27

another. Oge would ask me what I thought about the situation and I told him that real recognize real and Dareese was young, but he was maturing. One night about 4am while Oge was locked up, the house on Mapel St. was full that night, and because it was hot outside (police wise), while I'm sitting in the front window, I saw someone with a hood come from the side of the house. I couldn't see the persons face, so I grabbed my piece and stood behind the door. I asked who it was, and he said Reese. O.K. Dareese. It was kind of strange to me because he had never done that, so my guard is up at 4am. I looked back out the window and he said, "Sis, everything O.K.?" Something in my heart told me that everything was good, so I put my piece in my back and opened the door and he walked in. He took his hoodie off and said "Sis, I just need somewhere to sit for a minute." I could tell something wasn't right with him, so I told him to give me a minute and let me put some shoes on. So, I goes next door, get myself together and I went to the other side using that back entrance. I threw my coat and shoes on, locked the back door and came out the other side to let him know. You never knew what could be up over there, feel me? So I called him to the front porch and as both of us sat out there on the front porch, Dareese was just telling me how he was tired of going through the same thing because he had just had a baby making it two kids and things were not what they used to be. I told him that we were getting older and that we had to be an example for our kids. I was talking to him about God and getting a job and going back to school. The conversation that we was having kind of threw me off because listening to him at that moment and hearing what people on the streets said about him, how they hated him and how the two times he got shot, they were glad that it happened. He was a ruthless young guy but during that moment I saw a whole different cat. I saw someone that was tired, someone that needed someone to talk to that he could trust. It made me feel good because that let me know that he respected me a lot and I told Dareese to pray about it and let the Lord handle it because it wasn't about us anymore. We had kids now. Dareese just looked at me and said, "you right Sis." Suddenly

ALL I HAVE

someone on the inside called me and I told him to give me a minute and to let me run in the house right quick. So, I went in the house and when I was walking towards the front door, I saw Dareese run off the porch towards the old spot on 4 Mapel St. on the dirt road. I called him and I run behind him and I saw him run towards Criss St. across New Burn Ave. I turn back around and started to walk back to 203 Mapel but right then I heard a lot of gunshots. The first thing I thought was Dareese! So, I ran to Criss St. and when I get over there, I saw Dreese's body laid out on the ground. A police officer pulled up, jumps out and tried to stop me as I said "that's Dareese, help him!" The officer asked me, "How do you know that's Dareese?" I tell him that he had just left me and to help him. But then the officer said, "Ma'am put your hands behind your back!" OMG! Things had happened so fast that I didn't even have time to think. One minute we were sitting on the porch talking about life and children and the next minute he was lying dead in the middle of the street. It didn't take long before his body was covered up and yellow tape everywhere and as I thought about the last conversation we had, I felt better because we did talk about God and he wanted to make a change. May he rest in peace.

At the police station, two detectives come in and asked me how did I know that it was Dareese? I told them that he had just left Mapel St. and he left running but then I heard gunshots and recognized his clothing. They had me down at the sub-station for hours. The police tried to say that Oge, my husband probably put a hit out on him, or he might have done it, and I told them that Oge had been locked up for months by then. Whoever they had in that other room had it all wrong. I knew for a fact I was good, but I got tired of them coming at me sideways. I told the police they needed to turn up out there on the block because it had been a lot going on out there between Dareese and plenty of niggas because they were barking up the wrong tree. But 12 hours later, they decided to let me go! My condolences to the Terry family. But the crazy thing about Dareese was like Chris and

CHAPTER 27

Poppy, they had none of their homies with them. They died alone and all of them was blood gang members! Another black man gone but one thing I can say is that I didn't even have to think about Dareese because God brought him straight to me. I don't wish death upon anyone, but the Lord said vengeance is his. As for Aleman the other guy that was with Dareese when they broke into our apartment, he got killed on St. August Ave. right in front of the apartment that Chico and I first met. Only one more to go! Oge couldn't believe it when I told him what happened, and I could peep the way Oge was talking that I had done rubbed off on him a lot. When you have been with a person long enough and when what that person says to you comes to light, then you have no choice but to sit back and think about life. Me and Oge would argue all the time and he would do dumb stuff like take my money most of the time because niggas that I deal with know that's what hurts me the most. But I'll let him bury himself also, because I'd pray about it and sit back. It's kind of scary once you live through it, but I know it's the work of my God! So, I must tread lightly because I must try to obey and keep it 100% also. Things was going good so far. But something keeps telling me that it's deeper than that. In time will tell.

My family was out there on Greenwich Rd. I was hearing that they were doing big things over there. I would go over there to see how everyone was doing but every time I'd go over there, it scared me. They had that apartment off the hook, but I kind of figured that also. Everyone was breathing so I couldn't complain but I wished that they could get a little organized. But they were grown so they were going to have to learn from their mistakes.

The city of Wake managed to buy every house on Mapel St. except 203 Mapel. I was the last man standing out there. They tore down every house out there and that made me feel special because only the strong survived and with me keeping the Lord in everything despite the circumstances, he was the reason why I'm still here. It wasn't no need for anyone to be nowhere on Mapel St. because I had

ALL I HAVE

the only house. By this time Oge had come home and he was glad to be out. But that dude Oge is a character. Whoever that worked in the mail room at the last prison sent me a letter that he wrote to his baby mother, Mia and whoever they were, knew exactly what they were doing because they put my name on the front. I'm guessing they saw the money orders and the letters I was sending, and they called themselves dry snitching. Good looking! So, once he got home, we had already got off on the wrong foot. He also got out like I owed him something. I do know that it's my fault that he started popping pills. Like I said before it hurt me so bad, but I repented for that mistake and it will never happen again. I've never in my life saw no shit like it! So, once he got home, it was like I couldn't do anything with him. After I'd seen how weak minded, he was, it kind of threw me off with him. He would say all he did was smoke weed before me, so he had a pass to do whatever he wished. But me being a God-fearing woman, a married woman at that, and not wanting to continue with this marriage because I'd saw his true colors, but I love him. When I would look at him and saw the person he had become, I knew it was my fault. That's what I told myself. But, Thank God for putting my baby father Chico back in my life. If it wasn't for Chico I wouldn't have someone I could trust to talk to. Regardless if it hurt or not, he kept it 100% with his word! Even though he was a THOT! But I forgave him for the past because it was time to move forward. So once Oge came home, it was tough. It's in a woman's nature to be worried about her family and that's how it was with him. Niggas would get into some beef and would always come get Oge but when B hit (shot) him, I didn't see no one coming to help him. I also knew his temper. He analyzed everything and if a nigga said something wrong, it was a problem over the smallest things. He was out smoking boat and popping pills and would stay gone all kinds of hours in the night. I wasn't no dummy, but I didn't hear anything, so I left it alone. When Oge got home he was doing his parole from 203 Mapel but every time the P.O. would come to the house he was never there so the P.O. put him on house arrest and he had to do it from our house on Grand St. The P.O. didn't stress him about getting a job because of his injuries he had, so he was excused from that. While he was on house arrest, he couldn't leave the house, so I knew where he was, but I never stayed home. I would leave early in the morning to go gambling and wouldn't come home until 12am - 1am leaving my son Chico and Oge at the house. While Oge was on house arrest I would tell him to finish writing in hopes that he could do something because Oge had an ear for music. When he was locked up, he had been writing and wrote a couple of songs while he was in there. We needed to find our way. With Oge's mom and pops both deceased from heart disease as a result of being heroin addicts and me not having any parents neither, both of our options were limited but prayer answers all things, so patience had to be a virtue.

CHAPTER 28

ONE DAY OUT of the blue my Uncle Reggie came calling me telling me that a girl whose name was Destiny was trying to get in contact with me. He claimed that she was saying that she was my daughter. OMG! 8 years later and the Lord allowed them to find me, so I asked Reggie what should I do? He then told me to create a Facebook page. I'd never knew anything about no Facebook, so it was a first for everything. So, I created a Facebook page and I scrolled through all the Destiny's, but I couldn't find her. I then told my Uncle Reggie my Facebook name and told him to tell her to send me a request and sure enough I saw the little girl that I once knew and she looked exactly like me with buck teeth that were yellow! That was my child! So many emotions flooded my memory because I wouldn't have never thought that the Lord would bring her back that soon. I was thinking about the age of 25 or 30 not 11 or 12 but my God is a good God. Thank God for Facebook! We did a little catching up, but Destiny was the only one I'd talked to. Brianna my other daughter didn't want to speak to me. But Destiny would only call me when her parents was away. That was understandable because she was only 4 years old when I last saw her. I asked Destiny how she found me, and she told me that one day she was rambling and came across their birth certificate and sure enough my name was on it. Of course, it was God's doing because all their parents had to do was go get their birth certificate changed and they probably would have never known. My father God is Amazing! I love him! But the shocking thing about the whole situation was that

CHAPTER 28

Destiny gave me the impression that she already knew that her adopted parents wasn't her real parents. Wow! I remember when I went to visit them at Social Services and that was a hurting feeling to have to let them go. So now I had to take it moment by moment because at least God brought them to me early in life so I wouldn't miss too much. My problem was that I had to tell my son Chico that he had two sisters. When he was little, he was saying that the other kids would tell him he had sisters, Chico would come and ask me did he have any sisters and I would tell him no. He was young and I figured once he got up in age, I would tell him but shoot, I didn't think I would have to tell him at 8 years old. Thank You God! I held back so many emotions thinking about them girls. I tried my best to try to erase the memory of me having two girls because it hurt me so bad, and he showed me mercy. I will forever be grateful to my Lord. So now I'm in contact with all my children and I couldn't wait to see them under the same root. But I wasn't going to rush anything. I was going to take it moment by moment and when God was ready, he was going to make a way. He always does! I eventually told Chico about his sisters and I love my son because he was very understanding. Even though he was 8 years old, I talked to my son like he was a grown man. But he also knew not to play with mommy. I didn't sugar coat anything. There wasn't a Santa Clause or Tooth Fairy. You do right in school, and I'll do right by you, plain and simple. Things that I'd wished my parents would have taught me, I tried to instill in him. I also tried to give him the things that I never had. People think raising a child is a lot of work, and it is to a great degree but with Jesus in the equation, life is a whole lot better. In a way, I'm glad that my childhood ended up like it did because I learned to depend on the Lord at a young age, and he has kept the enemy off me as long as I can remember. Because of that, I've instilled this into my son. As long as you put the Lord in the equation you have nothing to worry about. There's going to be trials and tribulations but ask yourself "what would Jesus do?" I would tell lil Chico to pick and choose his friends because that's why his father was doing natural life for not choosing his friends wisely. I ain't going

ALL I HAVE

to front, my son Chico has come a long way. At one time he was in a B.E.H. (Behavior) class because they said he was mean. This dude went to school once and the gang police visited, and he thought it was cool to tell them that his stepdad was a gang member and that he was doing all types of illegal activity. It shocked me to hear that he said them things because when you think you are hiding things, you are wrong, so that taught me a valuable lesson. But DSS (Department of Social Services) took him, but the Lord put people in my life for a reason and Tang held him down for me and once them crackers were out the way. I then got my baby right back

Once I moved in my new place, my whole family came right behind me. My Grandma Lynda moved across the street at 538 Grand, I stayed at 541 Grand St, my brother David moved down the street at 600, and my cousin Candy moved one street behind us. Yes, it seemed like we always stuck together. But sometimes it does get annoying because all day long it's a bunch of little people knocking on your door because it's so many of us. But for some reason everyone gave me respect. I don't know, maybe I just demand respect? If I give it to you then that's what I want in return. But in a way, it's kind of cool because all the kids can grow up together just like we did but with different households. The first couple months when we moved to Grand St. things was alright. I had just copped me a Cadillac CTS, but I was still doing my gambling. Oge had got off house arrest so now he was free to roam. Like the normal stuff, police hit the spot and although the police didn't find any drugs, Tamara had served that same Ebony chick that I told her not to mess with, I know for a fact that she was the one that tried to get me out of here. Tamara said once the Ebony chick left the house, the jump out van hit the corner and went up in the house at 203 1/2 Mapel St. They got the $20 bill off Tamara and locked her up for the charge. I went and bonded her out, but Tamara's record was so messed up that we automatically knew that she was about to do some time. So, we had to come up with something else. I told Tamara not to mess with that girl, but a hard head

CHAPTER 28

makes a soft ass. Tamara's court date came, and she didn't go to court, so she wasn't out long. Someone had told the bondsman where she was, and they came and locked her up. She ended up getting 15 months in prison. That's my girl so that one hurt. But, luckily Oge had one of his "scraps" who was a follower that needed a job, so it all worked out for the good. His name Dizzy. He also knew how to spit them bars but I made sure to tell Oge to not do anything with that dude because I had seen too many times where a nigga trying to make a name for himself ended up getting you life in prison. I did say that we needed to keep him close because with Oge's ear for the music and him spitting them bars, we could make a nigga blow and also, I always wanted to be on television some way. I had gone through John Modeling agency with a couple others but for some reason the streets kept calling me. I also encouraged my son to try and follow my footsteps with acting and modeling. I paid for his acting and modeling classes and a talent agency in New York they were interested in him but at the time I didn't have the funds to make it happen for him. But if God had that in the cards for him to do it then as much as I play the lottery, I figured that God would have allowed us to go. So, I came up with another plan and had my homeboy Buddy Klein who was a local rapper who was doing his thing and he knew a few people. Buddy had signed to the actor Vin D record label at one point, even making a song on one of Vin D's movies. He also was on 108 & Park a while ago and I kind of figured that he knew someone that had a studio that could help us out. It never hurts to try because we were making the money so why not do something with it. We had Oge with the ear who also had a way with people, Dizzy who could spit and Buddy Klein. We also had lil Chico and my nephew Rob rapping who were both 11 years old so let's get it popping. I figured that we could instill the words to a song to them while Oge picked out the beats and see what it does. Everyone was with it and Buddy Klein had the perfect guy to help us out and that was Jarul. We then put our minds together and a friend of mine whose name is Mallory, her husband Desmond knew some people that did the videos, edit and make flyers. So, we had a project to do! Everyone played their position and Desmond also found an attorney and we got an LLC for Black Diamond ENT. "B.D.E." and that was our record label. Oge and Dizzy got together with Buddy and they made a song called G Shocks and Jordan's. Chico and Rob learned the song in no time. The next song was Cali Swag. Studio time was $50 an hour and a minimum of 4 hours and they went once a week. But then after Dizzy had laid down his first mixtape, everyone wanted to be down. They even played his music in the club so things were looking good. Chico liked the attention he was getting, my brother David and his girl Ash sounded nice together. It made me believe that this could work. But something was stopping this project from taking off because all the time and money for the video shoots, flyers and paying for the club to shoot the footage ETC, God wasn't allowing it to take off, or was it us? Everyone that saw the movement including the DJ at the club said the track G-Shocks and Jordan's was a layup but there were some things I didn't know about. The whole time I was keeping things 100% with niggas, busting my ass to make sure my family was fed, a roof over our heads and business ran right, I was dealing with disloyal ass niggas. I was so naive. Not communicating with outside people kind of messed me up. Prime example: One night at 1am in the morning I hear Oge's phone going off. I mean someone was blowing his shit up! I'm thinking it's an emergency, so I go and open the phone and it's a text message. The text said, "Are you going to come back and make me cum?" That shit right there messed me up. I woke that nigga up out of his sleep and guess what this dumb ass nigga text back? He tells her "He's tired!" Right then and there, I knew it wasn't going to last long between us. My heart cracked just a little because I knew that Oge wasn't a loyal ass nigga because after the mistake that I did with his drink and how he went all out behind that, he was weak! I can't deal with a weak ass nigga, but I married him and stayed with him because I'm a God-fearing woman. But once I read that text, I started to go out and fuck with a nigga that night. My mind had been on a lot of devious shit, but I knew that I had a higher power to deal with. It

CHAPTER 28

would have been different if I wasn't married but I was unfortunately. I was glad that I made my own bread because I could never let my guard down with this dude. I was hurting behind that situation because this nigga didn't have to do shit. All he had to do was keep it 100% and that nigga couldn't even do that. In a way, deep down inside of me, I felt kind of sorry for him because I felt responsible for his life being messed up at the moment, but it was only one ecstasy pill. Come on now! Shit, I was popping 4 and 5 of them. He was supposed to have been an O.G. Blood let them tell it. But if I would have ever known that, I wouldn't never have dealt with him period. So, after I caught this nigga doing me wrong, he wanted to flip the shit on me, talking about I'm never home and that I didn't consider him at all. With all that crying like a bitch, I didn't wanna hear none of it. I told him "Just get out, that's the bottom line." One thing I can say, the nigga didn't touch me, but mentally I was done. The nigga did pull out a gun and took my shit. Yea, on several occasions this nigga took my shit and would stay gone days at a time and come back broke. I was beginning to think that the nigga was smoking crack. I remember one time going to the trap house and one of my friends who was HIV positive told me that Oge came in the house high and wanted to trick (have sex) with her. But she refused him because she knew me and told me when he came in the door right in front of him. He gets mad and tried to jump on her but come on now, what if she was a messed-up chick and had sex with him just because? So, after that, it got to the point that I was scared to death to let that dude touch me. This was 6 years after we met and 3 years since we got married. I was stuck because although I wanted to get out of this relationship, I was scared to death of the wrath of God. So, I prayed about it remembering when my sons father Chico would always tell me to be careful about what you asked for. I would just talk to Jesus and tell him how I felt and how confused about what to do because I got tired of the nigga taking my shit fuck everything else. Sometimes I would just give it to him and tell him to leave and don't come back. But because I would hear people telling me that Oge was doing stupid dumb shit.

ALL I HAVE

They would say he was tripping and would ask me to come get him. I knew that I was the only one in Raleigh that he could turn to because everyone else couldn't handle him. Sorrow would take control and I would open the door. But after everything that he took me through to this day, he has never kept it 100% or apologized about anything. Don't get me wrong, he came through a couple of times because when I would go gambling and lose my money, he would keep something up his sleeve, but in my eyes, it was my money he took tricking. After every argument I would tell him that he was gonna reap what he sowed and trust me, it never failed.

CHAPTER 29

SUMMERTIME 2013, I get a phone call from Brose telling me that Oge had just got shot by Peter Gray. He said that he had got shot in the back. WOW! I slammed the phone down and flew to Mapel St. and when I got there, I saw yellow tape and them putting him in the ambulance. They had pulled off, so I asked Brose, who else was out there with Peter. He said "Jimmy, Tommy, and his wife Tink." For some reason, they always hated on Oge and Tink, never liked me for some reason. I had never done anything to her or never spoken a harsh word towards her, but some people just be hating, and I think that my spirit just irritated her Demons. Or maybe it's because her husband ate my cookies a while back but that was before they were ever married. They didn't have the guts to come at Oge face to face, they had to get a stupid follower to shoot him with his back turned. When I get to Wake Center Hospital for the second time with Oge, Thank God this time he just got hit in the shoulder, but I was getting tired of them nothing ass wannabe's coming at us sideways. We had run up on Tink one time but if it wasn't for her kids, she would have laid stinking." After that, we had saw Tommy's brother at the barbershop one day and the nigga was talking big boy shit when we caught him on New Burn Ave. Oge hopped out and was about to do some damage in broad daylight, but I told him not to because it was way too many people out there. But check what these gang bangers do! They sent the police to the trap house! Yes, they came deep and asked for Oge and we told them that we didn't know an Oge. But my brother

ALL I HAVE

Lamont did say that the only Oge he knew stayed in Southgate just to throw them off. So that's why I wasn't taking no chances with these wannabes. If we were in Chicago, Cali, or Florida, that was really about that street shit, it would have been a lot of stinking ass niggas laid out in these streets, niggas not loyal for real. Fuck all that, I'm getting tires of these mother fuckas fucking with us and it's long overdue. It's time to turn up out here. But something in the back of my mind kept telling me that you reap what you sow and all the shit Oge was taking me through I looked at it as Karma!! But Oge came out strong, he stayed in the hospital for about a week. He wasn't feeling too good, but Karma is a bitch! And, I didn't even have to touch him. I know Oge could have easily got them niggas touched but just as fast as they sent the police down to the trap. If something would have happened to anyone of them, they would have done the same thing so as usual I told Oge to put his trust in God lay low and watch the master at work. I know it's rough but have patience. Look at B, he gone 5-7 years so sit back and observe.

I can go on and on about me and Oge relationship, but the bottom line is I should have gone off my instincts when it came down to him. Something in my soul tried to warn me not to begin a relationship with him let alone get married. I believe to this day that if it wasn't for his sister Kosha, I don't think we would have even done it. I should have listened to my gut. When he took off with my $300 and didn't answer the phone for a month, I should have taken heed then. When he would have different females bring him to the trap house, I should've asked questions, but we weren't together then, so I didn't. And, also when I would drop him off at home knowing that it was his baby mother's place. But ever since I've been with Oge, it's just been nothing but confusion, pain, and heartbreak. I was a God-fearing woman so I would try to forgive him for taking my money and leaving to cheat on me. He wasn't even trying to get a job or do anything to try to help me, let alone show me that he cared. I knew that I made a terrible mistake and he most definitely gave me the impression that

CHAPTER 29

I owed him. With females calling my phone specifically on Christmas morning, yes 4am to be exact, a female called me "His wife" crying talking about how sorry he was and that he's a liar! I felt sorry for the chick because I knew she wasn't lying, but at the same time my nigga, you supposed to have your hoes in check. What made this chick think she had the authority to call his wife's phone let alone, how did she get my number? We had plane tickets set for 12-31 but right after the incident, I couldn't. The same girl also sent me messages on Facebook and one time when we went to Vegas, how she knew we were there, I haven't a clue but I asked this chick why she was still calling me with this bullshit, call his phone. After all of that, one of his people even sent a female to me one night while I was at the bar. The chick came up to me and said that she shouldn't be telling me this, but now that she saw me she just wanted me to know that my husband left her in a hotel room and she had no ride to get back. I looked at Oge's people his name is "5" because I knew that he had sent her, and he came to me and said he just wanted me to know that my husband wasn't shit. He went on to say that he knew that he should have been told me, but I knew that when a nigga trying to get pay back on a nigga, they tend to act like females. I learned that Oge had been taking females to the hotel rooms, getting high and he did that on the regular. 5 told me that I deserved better which I already knew that but at the same time I had to figure out how I was gonna get out of this marriage. By this time what little bit of affection I had for him was gone. Now it was sympathy because I felt like it was my fault but why run around fucking everybody? I was a good person and I tried my best to keep it 100% and did the best I could do with what I had. Now I knew why Oge was so quick to take my change because he was getting high, tricking my shit away. I felt that I couldn't just leave him because he would always do stupid dumb shit. One time this dude put sugar in my gas tank after I'd just copped another burgundy Range Rover Sport HSE. I'd put it in the shop for something and I had just paid $2,000 to get the truck out but he went behind my back and picked the truck up and then poured sugar in the tank and left town. He swore up and down he didn't do it, but the dude left the bag of sugar on the counter with the cup he used. But thanks to his sister who made it possible for me to make moves. As time went by my marriage had become a burden. By me feeling sorry for him, I tried to figure out a way for him to be alright to the point that when I did move on with my life, I needed to know that I made sure he was good once we departed ways. How that was going to happen, I had no idea as well. But in the meantime, I was scared for him to even touch me. I went months without him touching me and after a while, I didn't even care who he was with. It wasn't an easy task, but God put my baby father in the position to be there for me. He became someone I could ask questions about how men move and the reasons why they did what they do and because I trusted Chico, he became my best friend. I remember driving all the way to Dash Correctional (1 hr.) from my house and barely making it back home just to get a peace of mind.

Chico's sister Knee-Knee came to N.C. for the holidays and he didn't want her around, Oge would say because she's a jump off etc. But he was the problem because now I see that he couldn't trust himself around her. During that time Knee-Knee had come, our relationship was towards the end. I had sent him home for Thanksgiving and he was in New York a couple of weeks before Chico's sister Knee-Knee came up from Alabama. So, while he was gone, I decided it was a good time to bring Knee-Knee to N.C. because I really didn't want Oge to come back yet. During this time Mapel St. had got closed because the City had come and bought 203 Mapel St. and the city paid me $36,000 to move. Yes, the last man standing, and the City of Wake paid me. They gave me 3 installments every 6 months of $11,500, so during the time Knee Knee came, I had got an installment. I also got me a new spot. Things were looking good but Oge acted like he was jealous of me for some reason. Here I am married to this dude so why would he apply pressure on me? He would threaten my family and It had gotten to the point that I started to not like this dude at all but I felt obligated and determined to get him back on track so he could

CHAPTER 29

move on. One day I got a phone call and it was from his sister Kosha. She told me that I had to come to New York because Oge was in the hospital and his bone had come out his foot and they wouldn't work on him unless he had his insurance information. I'm like what do you want me to do about this situation? She asked me to come up there. Now I was dreading to go up there, but I would always be back to the Lords teaching. Where it said, "Forgive and forget", and "Do unto others as you would have them do unto you" so that was what I was struggling with! I felt like I was trapped, confused and man it was starting to take a toll on me. I had to come up with some answers because I knew it was a way out. But a person could only take but so much. So I went ahead and caught a flight to New York City, I was feeling some kind of way anyhow because the reason for him even being there was because I was tired of him and there I go again playing myself, and come to think about it, I don't blame him for coming at me sideways because if I was anywhere like he was an ran across a nigga like me, I think I would've done the same thing if he let me because that nigga aint shit, he is one of the worse husbands on this planet hands down! We had been together 11 years and out of all that time, he never worked a day in his life. That dude didn't do absolutely anything. He never had to because I had him. Like I always told him "If you shed blood, your blood shall be shed" and I believe deep down in my heart with him, I'd already played my position. Both times he had got shot, if it wasn't for my faith in my Lord and the fact that God showed me mercy as well as him, I don't think he would have made it out alive the first time, let alone the second time, and now he was in the hospital a 3rd time. This dude needed to tighten up, but this third time was different because now I saw a way out. The Lord was finally working things out for the better. So, if Kosha's steps weren't messed up, then his bone wouldn't have never come out. Once I got to New York, I contacted an attorney and I made sure it was on 5th Avenue, and that same day the lawyer came to the hospital and checked everything out. I took the lawyer to Kosha's house and once he saw how the steps were messed up just like that, he took the case. Thank God because the insurance that we had, which was OBAMA CARE, only covered a certain amount. Yes, Oge had insurance but after that call to the lawyer, that got the ball rolling for him. Now we were cooking in some grease. Oge's sister didn't even have a clue that I had contacted an attorney and we didn't decide to tell her until right before we were about to leave. His family seemed to be big on marriage but I'm the type of person that's anti-social, I don't like to put people in my business. I swear I didn't want him to come back to Raleigh with me but Kosha had 3 flights of steps at her house with front and back porch steps and she the one he the closest to and I guess this was my position to play. So, I got a rental car and drove back to North Carolina and that was one of the worst mistakes I could have ever made. The reason why he was in New York in the first place was because we argued and he put sugar in my tank before he left and I believed that when my rear view mirror got broken off my Range Rover truck, was because he was fucking in it. But there I go and get this dude and bring him back and when I do, all hell broke loose. Once we got back to the house, Knee-Knee and I decided to go to the Stars Bar, this nigga popped an attitude because of that. The next night Kevin Gates the rapper came to town and we went there and after that, me and Oge had an argument. Me and Knee-Knee and her kids left and went and got a hotel room at the Super 8 in Clayton. I left him and my son there because lil Chico had school besides by this time we had got a 3 bedroom in Benson N.C and again my whole family moved out there with me again, and my grandmother was right next door with my cousin across the street. So, I really wasn't too worried about lil Cheek he was good but on the other hand Oge swore up and down, I'd left him to fend for himself. Oge is a grown ass man and he out here fucking so I figured one of those Thots that he was messing with should have had him, right? He wasn't showing any appreciation so what was I supposed to do? He continued to be out for days at a time and when he did decide to be out I would call him to at least see if he was alright because it's been plenty of nights I heard him say that he had to run down on some guy or he was coming in the house

CHAPTER 29

pouring Clorox on his hands and jumping in the shower. Remind you, he'd been shot twice so me being a woman alone, I was going to be worried, it's in our nature. But not answering my calls at 2am come on now! When he did come home, he'd thought that shit was going to be peaches and cream. It would be different if he was going to work or at least paying like he weighed and he was easily 270lbs, but no I paid for everything. At first, I didn't know the nigga was on nose candy but when you start to move like someone using cocaine, then that peaked my suspicion. So, one day I popped up on him with my brothers and sure enough, he was on the nose candy. Deep down inside, I knew it was my fault but enough was enough because I was tired of it all. I was tired of him using the fact that it was my fault that he started with other drugs but come on, a whole 11 years later and I'm still carrying that same burden. This dude didn't care about me because if he did, he would have stepped up to the plate and tried to help me out instead of bringing me down. Every time we argued, I wanted him to leave so bad that I would pay him to leave and he'd stay gone and once he spent all the money, I would feel sorry and let him back in. But once I left this time, I made up in my mind I was done because I couldn't take it anymore. It was really no need for us to continue with this marriage because if a nigga loved a person aint no way he would disrespect you to the point of trying to fuck with any and everything moving. I had asked my baby father Chico what he thought about the whole situation and he broke it down like this "He can't handle a Queen like me, period! So he goes out thinking with the wrong head and sleeps with other women to make him feel good." Chico also said, "Tina, I bet the girls he is cheating on you with don't even look as good as you!". I love Chico, always will. So, with Chico helping me through those trying times, he never poured salt on Oge, and he never judged me. Chico was just all about making me stronger mentally and I believe deep down in my soul that the Lord brought Chico back into my life to help me mentally because I was breaking down. It's like I was getting hit on every cheek I would turn. Back to back even and I really needed Chico because Oge didn't care. I tried

ALL I HAVE

my best to hold on to the marriage, but it took two, so I was beginning to let go.

First, I let go of the record label after they made the video for G Shocks and Jordan's because things just fell off with that completely. Once I read that text message, I knew right then it was over. I had started looking for a way out then but was struggling with how going about doing that. I had gone ahead and let Dizzy go from working cause he wasn't with me his loyalty was to his big homey, so he had to go. I began to distance myself from Oge and anything that had to do with him. But Oge did come in handy when it came time to re-up like I said, he knew a lot of people but Oge would throw that stuff up in my face talking like, if it wasn't for him then I wouldn't be getting the shampoo but I would tell him that I'm paying for everything. He began to be petty because he knew that I didn't have anyone to have my back. My brothers and sisters would pour salt on my name and my mom May showed no love so God and Jesus were the only two I had besides my Grandma and I love her life to death. I would tell Oge I was going to let the Lord handle him and he would say "you think the Lord loves you more than me?" I'll say no but I had faith in my Lord to know that he got me. I'd done absolutely nothing to him to get the treatment that I was getting from him. I never asked him for anything because I knew he didn't have it. Everyone that I was dealing with or could deal with didn't want to mess with me because they didn't trust Oge. But once I left this last time, in my mind it's over.

CHAPTER 30

CHRISTMAS OF 2016 came around and we decided to go to Raleigh to stay at the Residence Inn because the rest of my family had got a room there. They had upstairs and downstairs apartments. I felt that I needed to be around family during the holidays. I would often wonder about my family sometimes. But I do know for a fact that the Lord got us because we are still breathing on this earth, Thank You Lord. But I didn't think they know the meaning of family. Why I say that is because, they already knew that Oge and myself was going through a bunch of issues so why would they all let him know that I had a room at the same hotel? I didn't understand that. He had got him a rental car and went to the emergency room to get a soft cast on his foot so that he could walk on it. So, Christmas morning, me and Knee Knee leaves the hotel room and I get inside my truck and Oge came pulling up behind me blocking me in. He jumps out and came to the driver's side and pointed a gun at the window while telling me to roll the window down. My first instinct in that situation was to pray and the dude goes in my bra and takes my money out and walked back to the car. Dizzy was driving the rental car and they pulled off fast. I then gave Knee-Knee the keys to go back in the room and I speed off behind them. I catch them near the Subway on Wake Fore Rd. we turn right there and luckily there was no traffic on the road. So, I'm flying behind them in my Range Rover and finally they pulled up in the parking lot. I know this dude had a gun, but he also just robbed me, and I wanted my money. They then pull out of the parking lot

ALL I HAVE

and I see the window roll down and he was pointing a gun out the window. I mashed the brakes and turned around quick in the street. The light they were at had just turned red so I backed all the way up and boom I hit the back of that rental car that they were in. When I mashed the gas, I tried my best to ram them into the utility pole and I hurried up and turned the truck around. When I laid eyes on that car, OMG! The trunk and the backseat ended up in the front. The shit was funny to me because I saw the panic in their faces. I'm right on their ass so I called the police because I saw Oge picking up the phone and because I didn't know who he was calling, although knowing him it was the police and sure enough he texted me saying that he just called them. When we pulled up at the corner store on Capitol Blvd. Dizzy jumped out and went behind the store, done something and came back out, I'm guessing it was hiding the gun that they had on them. When the police pulled in, the officer went to them 1st and when Oge and Dizzy was talking to the police, a girl pulled up looking frantic. I jumped out and looked at the chick and she pulled across the street and didn't even get out of the car. Yes, I knew she was fuckin him but look where he was at Christmas morning harassing me, and the rental car she got him, how was she going to explain that to the rental car people? Opps, she couldn't! The police then walked up to me and said, "Ma'am why did you run into the back of the car?" Oh, he is snitching huh. Okay, since they played it like that, and they blood... OG gang bangers!! "Oge pulled a gun out on me and took my money and one of my phones, search the vehicle" so the officer searched and found nothing. But the officer did get my info and let me go. "Yea bitch that's what the fuck you get for fucking with a married man!! Now you pay for the rental you bumb bitch" man I was talking big boy shit in my mind but I'm tired of this mother fucker. I wasn't even thinking about him and now he all up on my shit!! It's time to bounce. I ultimately checked out of the hotel and went to a different county. This happened on Christmas morning but thankfully I had already given the kids their Christmas presents early. So, I had no worries there.

CHAPTER 30

During this time, I had left Mapel and got a new trap house on Artist Ave. and the trap was booming as usual it didn't take long for that to happen and on top of that, I didn't have to be there. "Thanks to the Lord." The real reason Knee-Knee came to North Carolina was to work. But Oge always has been a hating ass nigga and I was his wife. How could you hate on someone you married to? But that's what type of nigga he was. It wasn't my fault that when he met me, I was independent. Nothing changed. It wasn't my fault that he got lazy and comfortable to the point that he didn't have to come out when all he had to do was keep his stick in his pants. I could overlook other things, but he thought that he was going to fuck whomever he please and I was supposed to continue to fuck with him. No, hold up pimpin, I had a trick for him. It was time to play chess! Prayer answers all things, "I know it's my fault for putting myself through this but Lord, I need your help with getting out of this situation."

About 10pm on Christmas day, I get a phone call telling me that a guy I know had just got shot in my driveway at the new house and I'd already knew who was behind it. WOW! This nigga was playing them kind of games. I was really getting tired of this hating ass nigga. I mean, who was I supposed to call when the man you married sending shots through your trap house? No one. So that night I laid in the bushes across the street, praying that the nigga pulled up and try that shit again because I was going to light that whole muthafuckin car up. I stayed out there for hours and nothing. Nishan was my dude because he held it down for me because when the police were all over him he remained silent. That didn't stop anything because on 12-31-16 the day of my Birthday at 1am I was told that somebody had just came and shot the house up. The police and the CCBI were there and it was bullet holes everywhere. I was beginning to truly hate this dude with a passion because he was bringing all this extra stuff my way because I was tired of this dude. Why niggas can't take no for an answer? All this extra shit he was doing, I thought that I was going to have to kill this dude. Now I'm planning on how to do it. With the

ALL I HAVE

CCBI and the police involved, I was going to take a warrant out on this dude because he was taking this shit too far. When I went into the house after the CCBI people left, I noticed how those bullets came through there and where Ms. Ellis was laying, if she would have sat up, she would have got hit like Fatima did. The Lord was truly with them. Like I said, all this happened on my Birthday early that morning and the day had just started. Could it get any worse? Chico's sister had only been there 3 weeks, and all of this went on while she was there, and I couldn't even blame her for wanting to go home. I rode with her down to Alabama to drop the kids off and she had a nice apartment in a nice neighborhood, and she was also trying to escape a domestic relationship. If I would have known all this drama was going to pop off, then I wouldn't have never told her to come to N.C. with all that drama. Now here I go again stuck in a nasty situation that I put myself in just because I brought this nigga back to N.C. On my Birthday, I rented a burgundy Range Rover Sport limo the same as my truck and I rode in it from club to club. I didn't stay long because I knew that this dude was on some hating stuff. I had got numerous phone calls that night but I had already paid for the limo and didn't want it to go to waste so I picked the kids up and we enjoyed the city until it was time to turn it in at 3am. After I took the warrant out on that dude, I thought maybe I could get a little bit of peace but that didn't happen because he continued to come at me sideways. So, I just closed the store down and I copped me a 3-bedroom house off interstate 95 in Benson N.C. which was 15 minutes from the old house. I bought brand new furniture and put flat screens everywhere which made it a beautiful house sitting on the corner off Maine St. After I got the house, Knee-Knee and her kids went back home to Alabama and it was just me, Chico and my sister Tonya two kids because she was in prison doing 16 months, so I took them in and I let the tension cool down for a while. Out of sight, out of mind! I tried my best to keep in contact with big Chico my baby father because he made me look at things different but every time, I would talk to him, it always brought back memories that I had buried. So, when my feelings started to

CHAPTER 30

come back, I would begin to feel sorrow and would block his phone calls until I thought that I could cope or handle the situation that he was in. It would be disappointing because of the fact of how I knew that he was a God-fearing man. I could see it all on him from the way he talked, and he still looked like he was 26 years old. His conversations always made me look at life differently and during that time, I needed someone like him that could give me a biblical sense of what was happening in my life. And he had done that for me. Every time I would communicate with Chico, it seemed like we were having bible study but it was pertaining to my life. Every time I would listen to him talk, my heart would get heavier and heavier because I would think to myself, if that man was out here now the things that we could do together. Then there were times that I would listen to him speak and confusion would kick in because in my mind, I knew that God could do anything in this world without a doubt I do, but I would wonder why God wouldn't allow Chico to come home to his family? Looking at his only child, his son looked just like him. So once I started thinking that way, then sorrow would take over and I would stop answering his phone calls because the pain would hurt so bad, He was the only man that I would ever love with all of my heart and soul and he was gone for natural life and I thought that there was nothing I could do about it. I would feel defeated and try to bury me ever knowing him period. But I then would have to turn around and deal with an ungrateful, disrespectful nigga like the one I married. I explained to Chico the reason why I felt obligated to Oge because of the drink incident I had done to him a while ago but enough was enough. Chico would then say that Jesus said that any man that keep looking in the past is not fit for the kingdom of heaven. If he keeps looking back how could he move forwards. Tina, you must let go and leave it to the father. After the incident when the trap house got shot up, this dude began running around threatening my life and I had to go take papers out on him. The magistrate's office took the warrant out on him, but the courts contacted Social Services with a blink of an eye, and they were calling my phone. But, Thank God he had things prepared for me this go around to handle these Social workers because the money that the state was paying me for the relocation program, I still had the paperwork for that. And I'd just rented the house and I also had hit the lottery pick 3 for a couple thousand. I'd always keep records and I'd show the Social worker. I'd pay the rent up a couple of months so when she would come to the house two times a month for 3 months, Thanks to God she closed the case. Also, my truck was wrecked in the back after that accident with Oge and shout out to Progress insurance because they came right out and paid for my damages. Progress is my Auto Insurance but the insurance that was on the rental car was Nation. I told them that they hit me in the back and that it was also behind domestic violence, so when I showed the agent the paperwork, Nation didn't pay out anything, so whoever got the rental car for him was short because she had to come out of pocket! But that's what she gets for messing with a sorry ass married man! I don't mean to drag him (Oge) through the dirt, but I'm only telling the truth. If he did love me then how could he take me through this? He might think he does but at the time I really didn't care if he does or not. It's been a lot of damage done and I just wanted to be alone. I didn't care who he was having relations with, but I'd hoped that he didn't try to mess with anyone that I knew. He could have at least went outside of the box because it was bad enough when people from the outside was already looking at me different and feeling sorry for me because the people that knew me knew that when I'm with my dude, I'm there through thick and thin because I'm a ride or die chick. Yea, that's me but what can you do if the whole time you been sleeping with the enemy? Nowadays in my eyes, it's about the children. I'm going to try to talk to these kids about what to do, what not to do and make sure they keep Jesus in everything because it would take them a long way. The crazy part about this whole situation with Oge and myself is that throughout all of this drama that I'd been going through with him, if he was to call me if someone else was to call me and tell me he was in trouble, I would drop everything and go

CHAPTER 30

see if I could stop it before it went any further. And that's exactly how he got into the new house that I'd just rented.

I made sure that I laid low until I got Social Services out of the picture because I wasn't willing to let no "boy" come in between my child, The Lord says that "your husband supposed to be after the Lord and then you and your children." But if your husband wasn't playing his position, he doesn't get that recognition in my eyes. To me, Oge was just another child sort of. Someone that had been around for years. But when I allowed him to come to the house, I had been wanting to live right by God. I've always knew that's what I wanted to do but I thought I could cheat life by applying bits and pieces of the scripture (Bible). Faith wise, I knew God could do anything that could make life much easier, but how things were going, I could tell that it was a lot that I knew nothing about. I started watching T.D Jakes and Joyce Meyers on Television but the one I clicked to the most was T.D Jakes because to me he breaks down things a lot better. That's the reason why Oge was able to get into the house because of my faith in being a God-fearing woman. He came to the house but something inside me wasn't happy. It seemed like the love was there for him, but the sexual desire had left for me. I knew it had already left with him because if he desired me like he was supposed to, ain't no way he could've cheated on me. With me knowing that I couldn't satisfy him anymore, I did like I'd always do and beat myself up with a lot of negativity, It seemed like with my relationships, it wasn't hard to do because for some reason every man I've ever been with has cheated on me first and I'd finish it. But this time I had to move strategically because I had to worry about the wrath of God. I'm married and the Lord don't play about adultery, so I had to figure out a way to get out of this relationship. God forbid him when he tried to come around me wanting to have sex because in the bible Paul wrote that "A wife cannot deny her husband of sexual relations and a husband had to do the same." but I didn't want anything from him. Not even a kiss although in the very beginning we did but after marriage, it was very rare. Now it was no kisses at all, and I didn't want him to touch me anymore. The marriage was basically over but I felt that the reason he didn't divorce me was because he knew that I was a go-getter. Thanks to God, but I'm no fool. I'm just a lost sheep in training and I'm going to be able to do as my shepherd say in a minute. I would pray "Lord please continue to have mercy on me. Thank You and Lord, help me with this marriage situation that I'd gotten myself into". I would ask the Lord plenty of times to please forgive me for taking myself through all this extra stuff because if I would have obeyed God or done something different, then I feel that my life would have turned out better. I was the reason why I was going through what I was going through. So now I'm looking for my Shepard to help me get out of this situation. "Seek and you shall find!"

After I opened my door and let him in, things went Okay for about a month or so. His cousin Hyphese came and stayed with us for a week. He was from New York and he brought one of his people with him. I guess he was going through some changes up in New York and every time someone was going through something, they would always come to holla at Oge. I think that Hyphese was just trying to lookout for his cousin, but Hyphese was in N.C. one week and as soon as he got back to New York he got shot up. It was something up with his family members because Thanks to God he came out of it. God was with that man but what got me tripping was how he came to us 1st. Looking back at life itself and trying to figure out why it seemed like everyone that clung to me didn't be around long, I've come to accept that it's a reason behind everything and now at this moment there's no such thing as coincidences.

CHAPTER 31

OGE HAD BEEN at the house a couple of weeks and my oldest daughter Destiny decided to come to the house to visit and see how everything was going. She had come down when I was staying on Grand St. and the first time I saw her she looked like a tall goofy me! But her hair, I wasn't feeling that at all. I had to get that done and she also enrolled in Athens High School. She was with me a couple of months the first time but then she bounced and went back home and came back this time with a baby. So yes, I am a grandma at the age of 35. But for a long time, I felt some type of way because I felt like she'd ruined her life behind having a baby at 18 years old. But she did graduate high school, so I give her that much. I also took her over to the trap to meet her god mother Fatima. Fatima was so happy to see her. I introduced her to a lot of people because just about everyone didn't know I even had a daughter that age, let alone two daughters. I was so glad that the Lord allowed my best friend to see my daughter. Fatima's daughter Nique is my god child and she would call me Ma for a long time, but she'd gotten older, so it was cool. If Nique ever needs anything, all she have to do is come and ask but Nique had got out there too far in the world. After Fatima's mom Ms. Ora died Nique took a turn for the worst. She'd began using drugs and prostituting. Fatima used to tell me that I'd better watch that lil bitch, but I didn't understand what she meant by it. I love Fatima just like she was my sister, but damn Fatima always had a way with words!

ALL I HAVE

So, while Oge and myself was going through our problems, I couldn't trust his scrap to hold down the trap any longer so I asked Fatima could she help me out. It's kind of crazy how Fatima and myself started back speaking because I had stopped speaking to Fatima because she allowed her boyfriend to "smoke" my packs up. Fatima had quit smoking and that's why I started trusting her again. It had been almost two years since I last spoke to her but one day, I was walking from Carvey St. store and she was sitting on the porch with a little girl. I hadn't even heard that she was pregnant, but she was there holding her new daughter. When I walked past her, I didn't even look her way because I was upset with her but she said, "Hey Girl!". I responded by saying "What's up Ms. Lady?" and I walked over to her and she asked me for some help! She didn't have anywhere to go, and she had her oldest daughter Nique with her and the little one. Although I was feeling some kind of way towards her, I always considered her my best friend. Like I said previously friends have their disagreements but if you have the heart to forgive, that's a true friend. I had my flaws also and that's why she was my bestie. I decided to allow her to move in on Artist St. and she showed me her loyalty but all of that was short lived. I had heard that Fatima had been in and out of the hospital but to what extent I didn't know and because I'd always considered myself jinky, I would never go visit anyone in the hospital unless it was an emergency because it seemed like once I went and saw a person, the next couple of days they were gone. People would tell me Fatima was in the hospital, but I thought it was something minor because we were the same age although she had me by 10 months. But a couple of months after she stayed on Artist St., she had gotten her own apartment through a program that she was in. She seemed like she was trying to settle down and wanted to be a mother to her children but a couple of weeks after she left Artist St., she ended up in the hospital again. Again, I didn't think anything of it but something in my soul was telling me to go and visit her. Once I found out she was at UNC Hospital, I knew it was critical because only the worst of them went there. Come to find out she was there for

CHAPTER 31

her heart. That hurt because I knew right then something was seriously wrong. I didn't want to go but I knew that I was her best friend so I knew she would want to see me. The first time I went, I took Tamara with me and once I got there, I saw my baby with all kinds of tubes coming out of her. I asked Fatima what was going on, because thing's wasn't adding up to me. She told me that her heart was functioning at 5% and the doctor's said that there was nothing they could do about it. It had been about 8 weeks since she had left the house on Artist St. and she told me she'd been in the hospital for two weeks. At first, she was at Wake Center Hospital, but they transported her to UNC Hospital. When she told me that, what little strength she had left, was gone. It hurt me so bad. I tried my best to be strong in that hospital room, but it seemed like I couldn't find the strength. I then found myself running out of the room into the bathroom to talk to the Lord and crying until I couldn't no more. I don't think that it was registering completely because I figured that it was always a way out. But once I got myself together, I went to smoke a cigarette, I went back in the hospital room and I told Fatima don't worry about anything. God got this but by the looks of Fatima, it seemed like I was trying to convince myself because Fatima looked like she was at peace with her situation. I remembered her going to church every Sunday taking her tithes there because I would give her money to put in for me also. I remember telling Fatima that the lord said have faith as small as a grain of salt and it will be done. You, should have seen the glow that came across her face before she said, "That small Tina?" I said "Yep, that small" I also told her God got this and that he was in control baby girl. Fatima then looked at me and said "Tina, what happened? You were using drugs before me." I said, "Fatima keep me out of it!" I couldn't bare staying any longer because it seemed like the longer, I sat there, the heavier my heart felt, and I needed to be strong for my baby girl. I thought about my statement to her about having faith as small as a mustard seed but it was messed up in a way because although I believe that God could do anything, in some strange way, I didn't believe he would do it. But after that first day I went to see her,

ALL I HAVE

I made sure I visited her every day. Some days I'd get there, and she would have company. Mostly her family and other friends and I would try to leave while other people were there but she didn't want me to leave so I stayed. Sometimes the church people would be there, and I would stay then also. At the same time Fatima was in the hospital, my brother Lamont was in and out of the hospital because of heart failure as well. He was also in a medically induced coma and I didn't go to the hospital to see him not one time. I had broken down to Jesus in prayer "Lord it's too much going on Lord. You are giving Satan too much lead way. Lord this is your world, you are the Alpha and the Omega. This is getting too real now. Have mercy Lord Jesus please. My best friend and brother need your help and help me with the other things that's going on in my life that I don't understand". At the time I was just trying to hold myself together for them but also for myself because it was getting harder and harder. My constant prayer was "Lord, I need your strength." While I was visiting Fatima, one day out of the blue she wanted me to call so she could speak to my brother Lamont and I called Duke Hospital because that is where he was. She talked to him and told him what to do about his heart because during that time Lamont's heart was at 20% and he was only 32 years old at 300+ pounds. People leave the drugs alone because this is the outcome! Lamont had a chance if he would change his ways, but Fatima didn't, and I felt that Branson (B) my ex-boyfriend that shot through the spot was the reason why my friend was in that state. The Lord says, "Vengeance is his!" and I'm going to leave it at that. But after a week of me driving to Chapel N.C to see Fatima, she went home, and I tried my best to be with her as much as I could. Moonk, Fatima's daughter had her Birthday on Nov. 9 the same day as my son's Birthday and I went to K-mart and bought her some Roller Blades and a few other things and she loved them dearly. Me and Fatima sat on her balcony and we would just chill and she would just be smiling, and I knew she was at peace because she had a glow that I can't explain. But thinking back on it, I saw it a few times before with Poppy, Chris, and Dareese. I remember hugging Fatima so tight and kissing her on her

CHAPTER 31

forehead and I went home. Two days later, she was gone! My baby died in the doctor's office. Fatima's brother Amir's girlfriend told me that she had went to use the bathroom and left Fatima standing in the hallway. But before Fatima left, Fatima asked her to take her to Artist St. to see her friend. So, while she was on the toilet, she heard a thump and she hollered Fatima's name, but she knew that she was gone. That right there was a turning point in my life. So many losses and it was all around me, but that loss did the most damage. My cousin Chris hit me but Fatima and myself raised each other basically. Both of us was on the block early and when you saw one, the other wasn't too far behind. Everything that was going on in my life was enough to drive anyone crazy and I believe that the Lord knew that and that's where big Chico came in at. I had a lot of questions that I needed answers to because I didn't understand why one person could go through so much. On top of all that another friend of mine husband whose name was Jerome had passed and he asked me to take care of Ms. Ellis and I tried my best. Ms. Ellis had taken over once Fatima had left but before Fatima even got out of the hospital. Ms. Ellis was at the same hospital at UNC Burn Center because her body broke out with burn spots all over her legs and the doctors couldn't figure out a cure. I was getting hit back to back and the things that was going on were major blows. I had to look at things from a different perspective and keep reminding myself that things could be worse. I try to talk to Jesus and pour out my heart in confusion but at the same time I get scared and ask him to forgive me if I'm being selfish because I'm only living in the flesh so I tried to hold it in. He knew everything so I let everything out to try to soothe the pain a little and ask Jesus for his strength because I was scared and thankful all at the same time. I just had to figure it out because at the moment I was completely lost! I was on pins and needles because I didn't know what was going on. It was getting so real that It was at the point of giving up completely. Just about everything it seemed was going wrong in my life and I wasn't even 35 yet! I had to tell myself, "Tina you have a lot of thinking to do." Things happened for reasons and after all those events happening, that's when I started looking at life differently. But, Thank God for the people he put in my life to help me along my journey. Especially big Chico because without his positive attitude and me listening to him, when I knew God was the reason that he was like he was, he gave me hope. The reason being is because although he was doing natural life, he always paid homage to God and I know that's how I wanted to be. That's the type of spirit I needed, and I knew that I needed to do a little bit more work. Well, a lot more. So, I couldn't complain about anything because although he was gone for now, let Chico tell it, God got his hands in it so therefore, he was coming home.

CHAPTER 32

WHEN PEOPLE SAY if it's not one thing it's another, that statement is a known fact because things went South within a blink of an eye and I was tired. So once Ms. Ellis got out of the hospital and we got the spot-on Clark St. I tried to fall back, but the devil is always working and that's why after the things my husband was taking me though, I needed to rest my brain a while, and I started dealing with the kids a little more. My daughter Destiny had been around a week or so, and when she came Oge made it seem that every time my daughter came around, I would start acting funny. I didn't understand where that came from and it's kind of got me thinking or feeling some kind of way. Destiny didn't stay long thankfully because while she was there, as usual me and Oge would end up arguing and he took my money from me again , bounced and days down the line, didn't have anything. I got the feeling that the only reason why he even came around me was to take from me and give it to the next woman. The love he once had for me had done turned to hate and I got it. I googled on the internet about adultery and it said that once a person committed adultery, in God's eyes the marriage was over and it sent me to the verse in the bible and that right there was all I needed to see because after that, it was all a waiting game. I knew it wasn't going to be easy, but it had to happen! When? Only God knew but to me the sooner the better. I was beginning to see how most married people ended up not caring about what their spouse was doing or having open relationship but with me, I was the type that if and when I did decide to

ALL I HAVE

mess with someone, I preferred to continue being with them. I'd grown out of the things I was doing when I was younger whenever someone cheated on me, I would go and do me that same night. If he stayed out one night, I would stay gone two because I had no time for that. I'd gotten older and I wanted to be with someone that could help me sometimes. I was tired of wearing the pants. Now don't get me wrong, I was built ford tough but I was tired of trying to be strong. I wanted a shoulder to lean on or someone that I could get into their arms and feel safe to let my guard down with, but these days I feel it's kind of hard to find that. I'm not a bad looking black woman and I know there are plenty of men out there that fit the category, but it seemed that I had to look harder. Someone like myself would have been nice but for now I was going to have to be patient because I had to figure out how I was about to play it with Oge. So, I had to take it moment by moment. I already had in my mind that it wasn't going to be much longer because I was getting to the point that I was erasing memories of us. I was installing all the bad memories that we had together. All the nights he's been out, and the Facebook messages females had sent me. I was building myself up to not even like looking at this dude period. For some reason, hatred had always got a person out of my mind but first I had to get them out of sight. It's not as easy as it seems but if the nigga cared about me at all, then I wouldn't have to take myself through none of this. Oge was bringing all types of drama around me and he thought that I had to put up with his shit. It was like he was bullying me or something because I would tell him to get out and he would take anything he could put his hands on, leave to go tricking and come back with the bullshit because he knew my heart. He knew that I wouldn't just leave a person out to dry, but I'd open my door, he'd sleep for a couple of days and we would start arguing again and the same thing would happen. Now don't get me wrong, I would sometimes call to see if he was alive and well because knowing that man for 11 years isn't easy for me to let all that time go. So, I do consider myself a friend of his, even though he's not a friend of mine. Things were not getting any better. When the house got shot

CHAPTER 32

up and Nishan getting hit in the leg, the incident that happened on my birthday, right after he took my money, the ATF hit the house on Clark St. and Thank God that my people was on point when they came. I always kept extra locks on the doors because them extra seconds will save a life and that day it did. This was about April 2017. A week before the ATF came, things weren't sitting right with me. I remember one day, pulling up at the trap on Clark St. and while I was going down New Burn Ave. I could have sworn that I was being followed so I pulled into the Zone Bar & Grill, jumped out and went in ordered me a Jose Cuervo. When I walked to the door, I looked out and saw two police who had parked at the Papa Johns across the parking lot. That right there let me know something was not right and I told them to be on point. So, when they came in that day, we were prepared. The ATF found two guns, but they found them in the crawl space outside. They were shotguns and Ms. Ellis had no felonies. However, about a month later, the FEDS sent Mrs. Ellis a letter telling her she could come get the guns if she wanted because they were not stolen and because she wasn't a felon. But that didn't sit right with me neither because why would they send a FedEx letter to the house with Ms. Ellis name on it? There's no such thing as a coincidence. I had already told Ms. Ellis that I didn't want her son Lorenzo there with a minor because Lorenzo was 32 years old with a little girl that had just turned 16. But a hard head makes a soft ass because Lorenzo and his girl began stealing from Ms. Ellis but Ms. Ellis always made it right. They were cutting her throat and she would always say that Lorenzo wasn't doing nothing in the house, but I already knew that she was lying because other people had already told me what he was going on there. I had hours of operations and I knew from past experiences that you had to respect the neighbors. Cut off at 11pm, but with Ms. Ellis's son Lorenzo being there, they would go all night long and that was their downfall. One week after FedEx dropped that letter off at the house, the police raided the house, Nishan had sold to a confidential informant whose name was Laurie. I'd known Laurie for 26 years, but I told them not to mess with her because I knew she was the police. But they did anyways after I'd told Ms. Ellis to stop allowing her son to work out of the house. One night, I remember it so well. Matter of fact, I would stop by the Zone bar to get me a couple shots and ordered some wings before I hit the beltline and go home. But one night I stopped on Clark St. because I needed to borrow some money so I went and picked it up, went straight to the Zone and 10 minutes later Lorenzo came calling me telling me that the police had just hit the house. So when they said that, I knew that they were waiting for me to come before they hit the house, but I knew that Ms. Ellis was straight because I wasn't working that day so I had nothing to worry about. After that loss I took with Oge, I couldn't get anything at the moment, so I really didn't have no worries. I told Lorenzo we were good because Ms. Ellis wasn't straight, but Lorenzo act like he knew something that I didn't. So, I told him to call me once they left the house and then I would be there. 45 min-1hr later, he called and told me that they took his girl, Ms. Ellis and Nishan to jail. That truly was bad timing because of the loss I had just took with Oge and during that time, I had just gotten back from Biloxi Mississippi from gambling up my money. I'd hoped that it wasn't that much but when I called down there to see how much her bond was, it was set at $100,000 for trafficking cocaine, maintaining & dwelling and sell and deliver cocaine. Ms. Ellis's bond alone broke my heart. They had charged Nishan with sell and deliver cocaine because he was outside when they pulled up although he wasn't in the house and Lorenzo's girlfriend, was charged with a robbery charge. I didn't understand the trafficking charge but once I got face to face with her son Lorenzo, that's when everything had come out. That's why I say, "Never bite the hand that feeds you." So I asked Lorenzo could he be in court with Ms. Ellis and go pay for the lawyer to get her a bond reduction because I'd called Randy Hill's cell phone and he was going to meet him down there the next morning. I just knew that them crackers had wasted their time but I was wrong because now they were thinking that I was the one that dropped that pack off to them, but one thing I knew Ms. Ellis was going to hold it down, Nishan also. But with this

CHAPTER 32

16-year-old baby you all got up in here is suspect. It made me think back on when I was 16 years old and when I was in love, so I gave her the benefit of the doubt because I knew that she loved Lorenzo. She also knew whose stuff that was but she didn't know me like that. But at that moment I said to myself, "weak link!" I told Ms. Ellis not to have that girl in the house, but it was too late for that. I had to get my girl out and at the same time I knew that Oge was behind all of this because if he hadn't come at me like he did, the police would've never known anything. But when you are sending gun shots through your wife's house, I mean come on! What type of nigga does that? And now look. You never know what a person is capable of because I would have never known that dude would stoop that low. We were together 2.5 years before we got married and this is 8 years later and it's like I'm still learning what this dude was all about. But I've seen worse, so I often chalked it up and do what needs to be done.

Ms. Ellis's court date was the next day at 2pm and the lawyer was waiting for Lorenzo to come with the money which was $500. That was all the change I had on me and right then I knew that once the police hit the spot, the search warrant was valid for 48 hours so they could come back without a warrant anytime within that window. So, I locked the house and sat by the phone to wait and see how much the bond was. Somehow, I dozed off, but I woke up about an hour later and I had several missed calls, but none was from Lorenzo. But I had two from the lawyer. So, I called him back and he told me Lorenzo never showed. Now I'm blowing up Lorenzo's phone and with him not answering, I'm thinking that this nigga done took the money. But it was his mom, so I wasn't really taking that to heart. I'd say, one hour later, I get a collect call from Lorenzo, I accept and sure enough they charged him with the same thing as Ms. Ellis but his bond was $150,000. Amazing! Now all I could do was post Nishan bond because his was only $10,000 which I did. So of course, I had to get to work. Things was looking kind of tight but thankfully, Lorenzo signed the $500 that he had out and I decided not to let the stress of them being locked up take me through a lot of changes. I made up in my mind that I was going to take it one day at a time and see how it was gonna turn out. One thing I learned a long time ago was "if you can't do the time, don't do the crime", and like I said earlier, peanuts add up doing a 12-hour shift. That's what it is, period. It was all on how you maintained it. But when it came down to me, gambling is my addiction. I was out there alone with absolutely no one to help me, especially when my own husband is an enemy. I couldn't trust him because now he was the reason why I was broke. But it was O.K. because I was gonna sit back on him because I hoped whatever he took from me lasted him forever.

After I got Nishan out, he was kind of scared to help me out. I didn't blame him because he knew who had shot him or who was responsible for it. Yet he held it down and I couldn't knock him for that, but when one door closes another door opens because Tamara had come back from New York right in time and I knew she was going to help me hold the fort down. I was in the building and I had to turn down a lot of people and I also had to do traffic control because I was precious cargo and I was out there. If I hadn't been knowing you 10 plus years, I can't help you. And the ones I'd been knowing that long, if I wasn't feeling you then oh well. If they were a street walker, I couldn't help you. I was dealing with only working people, people that had something to lose. It was what it was because all money ain't good money. I wasn't going to be greedy when it came to the game, which is called street life, they could have my scraps because I didn't care if they had $300, goodbye, and nowadays, I wasn't trusting that much period. It was too many niggas gone for less. I was just going to continue to keep praying, seeking God and hoped God would help me find my purpose in life. The crazy thing about all of this is that I'd already knew Oge was about to be straight. His bone had come out of his foot and since I was still married to him, I figured if I stuck around and put up with the drama, maybe he'd help me out. Or maybe not. How things were looking, I thought that I'd have to take him

CHAPTER 32

to court to get something out of him. But on the other hand, I had to ask myself if it was worth the drama? The insurance policy max is $700,000. So, to me, it was worth a try. I had gone through all this drama for almost 11 years, so why would I let someone else enjoy what I think I deserve? So essentially, it had become a business arrangement. During this time, I made up my mind that I wouldn't question him about what he was doing and where he was going because I just didn't care anymore. During this time, he had left and went to Sandford N.C. to his homeboy Pee's house. I liked Pee because he was an old school cat and he was a real nigga. So, I knew he was in good hands but even if he wasn't, how things looking right now, it didn't matter if he blew his head off. I had too much going on with me it seemed like everything was going wrong at the same time and I couldn't understand it. But I couldn't let it get the best of me. I had to keep my head up and get out in front of the situation. So, I went to work. It had been a while since I had to put my work in, but I thought that it was better because I knew I could control the traffic until I could come up with someone I could trust. But on the other hand, really all I would have to do was maintain until Oge got that check and then I would be straight. Then I got to thinking, what if he decided to go another route? Only time would tell but one thing I did come to realize was this street shit was coming to an end. It was not like it used to be because people nowadays didn't have any loyalty or any morals. The police didn't even have to do their job because the snitches were doing everything for them. But I'd rebuke all of them MFS because they were no different from me. They lie to people to get a confession. They lie to get convictions, they murder in cold blood and the list goes on, so they're sinners also. It's just that they had better cards dealt to them at the moment than I did. But in my mind set if I could keep God in the equation and play my cards right, I knew I could end up in a better position than they would ever be. A sin is a sin in God's eyes so one sin didn't outweigh the other and God despises a liar. Relaying back to Romans 4:3, I'm justified through faith, I'm righteous because I believe in him. I'll put it like this, if cocaine and heroin could be taxed, the United States would have that stuff on the market! So, after the police hit the house and Oge taking what lil change I had, it seemed like everything was going wrong and I began getting into the word of God heavier than ever. Just about every morning at 7:30am I would turn on TD Jakes for 30 minutes on Daystar and Joyce Meyers also and I was talking to Jesus even more. I would talk to Jesus anyways but since I was getting older and getting tired of doing the same thing, I would look at everything that was going on around me. I had every opportunity to be a Queen Pen, but it wasn't worth it because like I said earlier, it was a different breed out here. All the real niggas were either doing football numbers or 6ft deep from messing around with fake niggas. I had to think about myself and whether I wanted to continue to go through the bullshit with Oge. In my eyes it wasn't worth it, so I would ask God for his help. My mom May is in her 50s out here and I had been out here since I was 11 years old and all she had to show for it was her kids, grandchildren, anxiety, losing her money at the sweepstakes. I love May to death and over the years I began to appreciate her life but it's the truth. My prayer was often "Lord help me because I want more out of life. Help me find a way to accomplish my dreams and goals in life." Big Chico would say "Faith without works is dead", But I always thought it was simpler than that. So, after talking to Big Chick my eyes opened wide on a lot of things and it began to be scary to me. When I did pray I prayed for knowledge, wisdom and understanding and little by little with me seeking the Lord and wanting to make my life better, I got deeper into the word, and once again I have to pay homage to the Lord for giving Big Chico wisdom and allowing us to connect so I could continue my journey. I once looked at what I did for a living as a job just like everyone else with jobs as long as I treated people how they wanted to be treated, gave the people what they wanted and made a safe environment for everyone, then I thought that I could hold off until something else came through and that's what it was. So, before I left home, I watched T.J Jakes, got ready, said my prayer and went to work. Tamara was living at the house and she

CHAPTER 32

had come a long way, maybe because she was getting older and I was rubbing off on her little by little. I had told her to go to New York to get her health together because she told me that she was diagnosed with stage 4 lung cancer and it was nothing they could do for her, but I told her that the doctors in New York might could work it out for her. So, she went, and she told me that her T levels had went back right but ever since she came back, she had been drinking a lot. But Tamara was a grown woman, so all I could do was try, but it was up to her to change. I knew one thing, I had to find a way to get Ms. Ellis home. Timing is everything and I hated that everything was messing up and on top of that, it had been a drought, I couldn't go to work. I knew Oge knew someone and I was trying to make him my last resort. I figured that all the nigga might do was sell me back what he had already taken from me. Whatever he had; it was from my money, but it was O.K. I was going to let the Lord handle him and as always, I was going to sit back because vengeance is his! So what I ended up doing was going through one of my smokers and I got me another connect. He was a young dude whose name was Willy. He was scary at first and I didn't blame him because of the stories I'd heard about myself out on the streets, but I bet you he knew that I knew how to get to that check and I believe that's why he gave it a shot. But I always went through the same smoker because I wanted him to feel safe as well as myself. Another thing I didn't like was a nigga moving reckless. When you came to see me, just bring what I want and nothing more because anything could happen, and I wanted everyone to be safe. On the other hand, I would have rather came your way. But Willy he was alright, but he was too scary for me. He told me what people was saying about me but anyone that really knew me wished they would have known me way earlier. Also, a lot of niggas didn't deal with me because of Oge since he had done just about robbed every dealer out there. Oh well, in my eyes I wasn't with him so that was that. Now don't get me wrong, I did keep in contact with Oge but laying down with him was out. I didn't want the dude to bring me nothing and because he hadn't, it is what it is. Months had passed, and Ms. Ellis

ALL I HAVE

was still not home yet but I made sure she had canteen on her books. What I was trying to do was get the search warrant suppressed because on the video they had, Laurie had the camera in her hat, and you could only see the top of someone's head. You couldn't see Ms. Ellis or Nishan face and the police do lie. So, I went and hired Rosemary Godwin. I had called Bridgette Agguire and she told me that if she was to ever get in any trouble, Rosemary Godwin was who she would hire, and I went with it. I told Rosemary what I was shooting for and she said she would work on it. But Ms. Ellis kept calling people and I don't know what she was telling them, but I tried to understand her complaint but if shit didn't go right, then it didn't. So, one day her son Donnie came to the house talking shit and the nigga pulled a gun out on me. Now this dude had just gotten home from doing 18 years and he points a gun to my head. He caught me off guard because I wasn't expecting that but like I told him, he got that one but what did the nigga expect? His mother loved me more than him because she didn't even know him and with Google that nigga's apartment was surrounded that night waiting for him to come out. They sat out and waited for a while and we knew he was home because we saw his gold car with tinted windows. Oge came through for me then because that shit, he didn't like. But something came across me, and I told Oge to tell them to leave because I wasn't feeling right. One reason was the guy he had with him earlier that day was in his work truck. Dummy! It was also two other people around when the incident happened, but they were smokers and it was 3 boys out at his house. I was concerned with the idea of what if something would have gone wrong and the police ran up on them? To me, it wasn't worth the gamble and I prayed about the situation and I was going to let the Lord handle it. But, I did tell Ms. Ellis what her son did and I also told her he was lucky it was her son because Ms. Ellis out of all people knew that her son could have been dead and stinking. But vengeance is his right? While at the same time "faith without work is dead"! It was getting real and after he caught me slipping that time, I knew I had to step it up a notch because it wouldn't happen

CHAPTER 32

no more. Locked and loaded. I'm glad that he didn't try that shit again. It was a lot to think about and it was deeper than anyone could imagine. You couldn't nowadays just do a drive by or go hit a nigga because it's DNA and cameras everywhere. You pray, then listen, and be patient, but I looked at it like what's the difference in me taking my own vengeance out or letting the Lord handle it for me? Or was that the treatment I deserved? I was the one behind a lot that was happening on Clark St, bullets had almost hit his brother and mother so I sat back and put myself in his shoes and I prayed about it and I gave it to the Lord and I believed that he was going to handle it. I had to fight just to keep it out of my mind, but I didn't let my guard down either because if I ever saw that cat again, I was asking questions later. I was going to stand my ground and I had witnesses that could tell the police why I had to use drastic measures and see how it would turn out. But for real, after that I was no better. The devil tried and Thanks to God he didn't allow it to go any further. But after that incident I allowed Oge back into my circle because he was the only one that did have my back. I knew that he had enough love for me not to allow another nigga to play games with me like that again. But the only reason why I didn't sweat it, was because I didn't want to see it go any further. I'd lost my baby father behind someone else not thinking so I wasn't willing to take the risk at that moment. Patience is a virtue.

Oge is back around but me trusting him would never happen again. What little money I had was never kept in the house. Nothing of value because that's how real it had gotten. I hated to have to put his business out there let alone mine but that's just how it was. And I truly believe that my steps are ordered. The only nigga that I didn't have to hide my money from was B, but I was going to leave the past in the past and focus on the moment but then I was always on guard because it was always something.

All of this happened the summer of 2017. By the end of 2017, things didn't get any better, but I would make sure Oge go to all his doctor appointments. He had also received Medicaid and we was

ALL I HAVE

working on getting his disability but me, I was trying to get him established back home where he was from. His addiction wasn't getting any better and he would stay out all the time and if anything was to happen to him, I don't want it to be on my conscious. He had to go to the Doctor once a month for his foot and it had been over a year since the incident happened, and I noticed that once he went to New York he would stay gone longer and longer and it was cool with me. I needed the mental break anyways.

CHAPTER 33

MS. ELLIS HAD GOT out in January 2017 and that was a big relief on me. Ms. Ellis out of all people knew how Oge treated me and she understood. But she finally got her own spot and she hasn't been back since. But what really took the cake with Oge and myself was when one night he stayed out getting high and I had gone to Clark St. and the whole house was wide awake. I saw Brose and my Goddaughter Nique at the house and with all of them up all night getting high. So, something told me to pop up early that day. Oge had come through high but he left for some reason. Nique wanted to stick around although now she looked like she was scheming but I took it as she was high off nose candy. So now I'm at the window which was my usual spot and while Nique had her phone on the charger, I got up walked to the living room and noticed that Brose and Nique was knocked out on the couch. Her phone kept blowing up and something said pick up her phone. So, I did, and I looked through her text messages and for sure, it was Oge's phone number in her phone and they were going to meet up, so he could fuck with my god daughter. In the text messages, she was telling him that she was ready, and he was on the way, so when he popped up and I was there, it must've fucked him up. And he was with my cousin Mike-Mike! He was the lamest nigga I've ever encountered in my whole life and this nigga claimed to be a triple OG Blood gang member but he is fucking my God daughter. I then took her phone, went in the living room and while she was laid up on my couch, I tried to knock her head off her shoulders.

ALL I HAVE

She jumped up and ran out of the house and next, I called the lame. I knew he was going to say it was my cousin who texted her but my dude, you got to go and that's exactly what he did. But I knew the nigga was down bad, so I wasn't going to leave him hanging. I did make sure I held his daughter down, if she needed anything and I also held him down. And if he tried to front when he got his settlement, I had Western Union receipts to prove it. I also helped his sister out if she needed me because I love Kosha just like my own sister. She could get anything from me if I had it and besides that's basically all Oge had besides his sister Trina. So, all I did in 2017 was trying to find myself. I knew the Lord loved me but I wanted to know the Lord more than what I did at the moment, and Thank God because I wouldn't be here writing this, I knew I didn't want to be married any longer because too many boundaries had been crossed. I already knew that the nigga was going to blame it on the drugs, but my nigga come on, he was selling his soul, dignity and loyalty. I'm your wife but in my eyes, he had become scum. I wasn't a queen in his eyes because you don't disrespect a queen in that manner, but you never know what you got until it's gone. One day hopefully he would find out. He will never find another Tina period. For 12 years, I kept my shit tight and he never heard nothing about Tina. I'm a rare breed but I saw that Oge wasn't ready to be my king. I just hated I wasted 12 years for nothing, right now I have a point to prove. When looking back on my life and realizing that God has been with me all this time and all the close calls I had, he could have easily allowed the devil to take control. So now I had to find out what my purpose in life is. Every time that I'm into the word, the Lord is opening my eyes even more as I want to learn more about the word of God.

Chico had been in prison for 17 years and within the first couple of months he had begun to turn his life over to God and having him in my life at this very moment is for a reason, but when I talk to him, I still feel the same way I felt about him 16 years ago. My feelings had never changed about him, I only buried them and it was kind of hard

CHAPTER 33

at first to open up to him, but I'm getting older and I have to figure out what the Lord has me here for. I really wanted to know because I knew that if God is with you then no one can be against you. I'm still drinking milk at this moment when it comes to the word of God but moment by moment I want to be able to eat meat because once I get there then I know I'm gonna be on one accord with the father God. Chico would tell me I wasn't ready for certain things but the more I seek God by listening to his word and reading the bible, I would get to where I need to be spiritually. I have come to the realization that it's not that easy, it seemed like my whole world came crashing down. I always thought that if I just knew that God could do it, it would be done but it doesn't work that way all the time. God used Chico to explain it to me and I was told that you had to sometimes work towards what you ask for. God did say if you tell the mountain to move from here to there with faith, it shall be done and now I had to come to the realization that it was only a metaphor? That broke my spirit down. I knew Chico didn't want to do that but after that, I panicked, and it seemed like something had opened me up to looking at life different. Then I started thinking about all the lessons I wrote down in my notebook and everything that I'd ever learned about God and I was upset. I felt betrayed because I believed in his word or what I assumed his word meant. I do believe that Jesus Christ is the Son of God, I do believe and truly love the father God and I also believe that God can do anything in this world, but what Big Chico told me and after I Googled the meaning of faith without works and it said it's a metaphor, I dropped everything and stopped studying after that because now in my mind, I'm like how could that be false. God said Heaven and Earth shall pass but his word shall always stand! How could this be? Damn, it had got real and after that I fell back completely for a short period of time. I wouldn't even accept any phone calls from Big Chico because I didn't want to think about it because to me it was like a child getting disappointed by her father. I didn't want to take it any further because I needed to think this out. But I couldn't let something so small stop me from finding out more about God's word. The bible

ALL I HAVE

has always been an interesting book to read because I like watching real life things on television and I hate to say this but whenever I had to go to jail, that's the book I choose to read. Well actually, a long time ago is when I came to the conclusion that everyone that gets locked up the first person they call on is the Lord and that's why I seek him on the outside because God gets very jealous to the point of him sitting you down just to get your attention. I was going to spend time with him every day so during 2017 it was my goal to get my mental right. I had bad asthma and I must make a change because I'm not getting any younger. I'll be 37 years old this year and I want to be on the winning team, I'm seeking God. I have a lot of people depending on me so what I do is talk to Jesus like he's right in the room with me, but I don't speak. It's all in my head and I tell him what's going on with me because at the time I was lost, don't get me wrong, I'm still learning. I could sell cars with hopes of one day renting but also my whole life, I wanted to be famous and write a book about my life. I just didn't know where to start. I was not going to let one thing scare me away so I started back watching TD Jakes because I really wanted to get down to the bottom of this because if I could fully understand the word of God and line up with his will then I knew nothing could stop me. I took everything day by day. So, all I did for a while was go to work and go home. I had no friends at all but smokers and when anyone saw me, I was always by myself because people always took my kindness for weakness and that eliminated a lot of problems. A lot of people were not on my level and things to me had started to look scary because all my enemies I never had to touch. All I did was pray about it and left it for God to handle. The Lord has blessed me to the point he has kept my enemies at bay. I basically stayed to myself, I'd talk to Jesus because he is all I ever had. With my marriage situation I'm going to let the Lord handle everything because he knows what's best and he does things for certain reasons. So, during 2017, I was alone with my son. Oge was in New York City doing ain't no telling but that was on him. I did send him money when he needed it because I am his friend. I just really didn't know if he was mine. But I'd kill em with kindness. I was happy to finally be able to get my mind right, and with him being at his sister's house he was in her hands now. He was their worry, not mine.

Summertime 2017 after my cousin Zae got killed at the City Hotel on Capitol BLVD a week before my Birthday 2016, I wanted to let the family know that anytime any of them was in Raleigh, just come through the trap if need be. That hurt me to find out a girl he was messing with was the one who set him up to get robbed. But what hurt the most was finding out that the mother was the one who told him not to mess with this side of the family. I found out when Zae had Kris on speakerphone and the people that were riding with him, overheard the conversation. So, when that happened to him, that hurt my heart because I felt like he was trying to make his own or find his own way and got caught up in the process. During the end of his life he came through and asked could he hold a couple of dollars and he was going to bring it back, but I never got to see him alive after that. At his funeral I was upset with Kris because regardless my people had been around for years and all of us was still here by the Grace of God. Why would she say that? But Kris told me she'd never said it, but he was gone by then. (RIP) Zae!

4th of July I had a cookout and I told everyone ahead of time so there wouldn't be any excuses. I paid for the D.J, bouncy house, two grills and the food and drinks were unlimited and Thank God it came out successful. A lot of people showed up and we partied from 2pm - 11pm and still had plenty of food left. It was like Mapel St. reunion where no one got to fussing or fighting. Oge and Dino had come down for the cookout and Oge had made his Jerk Chicken for the people and they loved it. But half of the older ones that dealt with the nose candy was in their own world. They had left and went to my sister Punky's house and I stayed on Clark St. until the D.J got ready to leave. Everyone enjoyed themselves and people talked about that party for a while. But one thing I did notice was the police posted at the park down the street, they didn't come near the house. I don't

ALL I HAVE

believe in coincidences, but I had to be on point because it was too many Gilchrist's in one spot. No one was working and I made sure of that. Destiny and my grandbaby came, and they went to my sister's house with everyone else and after everything was cleaned up, I went back to the hotel. I had been staying in a hotel because the house I stayed in off I95 bats, squirrels and everything possible had found its way in that house and I was paying $1000 a month. My daughter Destiny and the baby only came for the party and they left two days later. But check this out, after the 4th of July party which was on a Wednesday two days later that Friday the 6th they ran up in the house on Clark St. Thanks to God, I wasn't there or Oge or Dino. Dino had just walked to the store and he told me that when he was walking back from the store towards the house, that's when he saw the police in the house. He then walked right by the house and he caught a ride and came to the hotel. I already knew Tamara was good, but I was trying to figure out what probable cause they used to come up in the house? So, after one of my people called me and told me that they were gone, I came on to the house and then heard everything that went down. The police found a bag of weed and it was 4 other people in the house with Tamara which they let 3 of them go but they took Nose and Tamara. While I was riding over that way, I saw Nose walking down Rock Rd. and that's when he told me what they found. They got 5 stems (crack pipes), a bag of week and residue that someone left on the phone. That was good to me because I knew they wasted their time like always. Thanks to God! But anyways, Tamara finally called, and her bond was only $2,000 for weed, paraphernalia and maintaining & dwelling and crack pipe. So, I went and got her out and the following week I had to pay the rent for Clark St. In the back of my mind I didn't want to stay there but I was already used to the house. The rent was $1,100 so that following Thursday when the rent was due, something told me to call the landlord and ask if he was going to take the rent. Now at first, I felt some type of way because they found no drugs, but things happen for a reason. And sure enough he wasn't going to accept the rent. Luckily It was a house across the

CHAPTER 33

street that was open and Mr. Sanje also rented out that one, so I got one of my other people to get that house for me and we hopped out of 412 Clark St. and into 409 Clark St. Piece of cake! The Lord knew what he was doing, but I needed to tighten up because on the other hand, it was almost two years since Oge had that incident with his foot, so I didn't have too much further to go. In my mind all I wanted to do was get a rental car service going and once I could get that, I was going to work that just like I did anything else. After I did get it, I was going to fall back completely. After the 4th of July party, Oge and Dino just stayed in Raleigh. I had moved into a new house just across the street from 412 Clark St, but the city of Wake and other real estate companies was still riding around buying houses and empty lots. Before the police raided 412 Clark St., it was a white couple that moved into the house across the street that they had just built. While the house was being built, I would pray about the people that moved in the house because we'd been over there for a couple of years and I didn't want no community watch person to move in there to make it hard for me. I'm a very respectful lady that didn't allow no hanging out or loud music, period. But my prayers at the time didn't turn out how I wanted it because later I came to find out that the big white lady's name Tracy that moved in the new house she had two black adopted kids and one was white. I didn't know if that was her child or not, but I did know that she was married, but that lady kept her drapes open all day long and I could tell she was going to be a problem. What she didn't know was that the neighbors that she talked to about us came and told us what she was saying about it being a drug house and that lady didn't even know what was going on there. But I kind of felt that it was just a matter of time before the police was going to come. I had to sit back and evaluate the situation and I did not blame her. Even though all we had was traffic and it was very limited, but she also had the only house that was brand new surrounded by a bunch of niggas. But on the other hand, when she left for a couple of days, her husband had black girls that were going in and out of her house and he kissed one of them on the front porch. Remember,

ALL I HAVE

I stayed in the window also! She was a bitter woman and I knew that she was part of the reason why the police did come. We were now two houses down on her side of the street instead of across the street so how was she going to act?

In Benson back again we ended up moving into a fresh spot which was my honeycomb 3 bedroom. So, I was blessed at the moment. I didn't have to work because I had Tamara and Dino so that was a blessing. Now I could take time out for me to try to get my mind right. I still would go out every morning to be nosey, but I loved staying in Johnston CO. So, I moved back to Benson N.C. like I said before, wherever one moved, everyone followed suit. When I first moved to Johnston Co. my grandma Lynda came right behind me and she loved it there. She's retired now and her rent was $600 for a 3 bedroom. Then my cousin Candy moved in and stayed one street over in the same park and I was right in between. My sister Tonya moved out there and May moved across the street from her. The whole family was in one area. When I think about all those years we was out there risking our freedom, our health from using drugs, cigs and drinking alcohol, we could have been rich but all we had was a bunch of felonies, poor health and renting instead of owning. Boy I was so tired. It wasn't worth it, but I had to keep pushing it because I do want 121 S. Carboro Rd back to give it to my grandma Lynda because she truly deserved it. So, if it's God's will, I will still do it! But we are still blessed because our conversation could be a lot worse so I couldn't complain.

CHAPTER 34

NOW I'M SITUATED and things are going well. I wake up in the morning, get out my notebook and then put on TD Jakes, and take notes on the topic of the day. I would record them on DVR so it's at my fingertips. The best thing about the family moving to Benson is, it's in the country and the kids cold stay out of trouble. I Thank God for that because we had middle school kids and lil Chico and a couple more was in high school. My cousin Candy's son Saddyq graduated high school Thank God and he started working at McDonald's so I think it's better that way until they can get use to working. See it's the little things you must Thank God for and I am very thankful because if they were in the city isn't no telling where they would be. It seemed like all the ones who were 30 plus were on drugs or alcohol so that's why I would rather see Oge in New York because in N.C. people are lost. Up there, it's a different world so he would be better. I'm guessing that's not where he wanted to be. Because he was right back down here getting on my nerves, just another soul lost.

One week before Thanksgiving 2017 I was riding to Raleigh from Benson N.C. and I parked my truck at Ms. Gail's house who stayed in the apartment right beside 412 Clark St. I walked across the street from Gail house to 409 Clark St. I was in the house, about 15 minutes sitting at my favorite spot which was the window and then I looked across the street to 412 Clark St. and I called Dino. I tell him to look because this is how the police come when raiding a spot and indeed, they were running in 412 Clark street. It was now some other niggas that moved in right after we moved out and I hoped that they didn't think it was sweet because look at them now. I saw all the traffic that was going on over there and I told Tamara to tell them that the house had just got busted right before they moved in there. I guess it fell on deaf ears, so I called Oge to tell him what happened. That's when Oge said "Tina, you think they thought you was in there?" It dawned on me like, dang, they did wait until I pulled up. OMG! So, the police locked up the two guys that was there and I looked on WRAL recent arrest on Twitter and I got their names. One guy had no bond and the other one had a $750,000 bond and I truly hated that because jail was no place for anyone. It really didn't faze me because I really wasn't thinking that they hit 412 because of me because we'd been gone from there since July. But in my gut, it was like "yea, Tina you slipped through the cracks again" Thank you Lord!

Thanksgiving came and everyone cooked something. Oge cooked oxtails, Condulace (a type of rice and peas) beef brisket, collards, oh we did it up and everyone was chilling. But I also enabled him at times to drink alcohol and that usually led to other things I was hoping for the best, but it is what it is. All my kids were under my roof and the grandbaby. Yes, Brianna came, Destiny, Layah my grand baby, lil Chico and that was a beautiful thing. Thank you, God, for making that happen for me. Thanksgiving 2017 will be a day that I'll never forget. We were deep out there and the whole family was going back and forth. I passed on the drinking that time because my kids was there, so I gave it to Oge, and he got missing. For some reason this dude started acting strange. My kids were sleeping in the living room and he could have come in the bedroom to sleep with me, but I wasn't feeling his vibe because he was getting on my nerves. I was tired because we were up early cooking, so I laid down to go to sleep and Oge came banging on the window at 4am. I get up but for some reason we got into an argument and I told him to get out. I get up the next morning, go to Clark St. and money was missing and spent. I wasn't about to

CHAPTER 34

start with that, so I brought Oge his stuff and I paid for both of them to get on the Chinese bus headed to New York City. My brother's Lamont and David had done hit rock bottom. The devil was having his way with them. Both of them was snorting heroin and come to find out, Lamont baby mother Lonette gave him heroin and told him it was powder and Lamont turned around and got Jamarcus a childhood friend and David his own brother on that shit. When I found out, I cussed Lamont out and told him God was going to handle him because why would you do your own brother like that? He's been in jail ever since! The name Gilchrist means servants of God, but these are niggas younger people looked up to growing up and now when people see them, it's sorrow. While Lamont was locked up, David came with his girlfriend Red to stay on Clark St. I couldn't see my brother outside, but what made me even more upset was because they left to follow their mother and now look at them. How I saw it, May wasn't doing nothing to help them at all. My brother Lamont barely has canteen if I don't send it to him let him tell it. May wouldn't even allow David in her house. But I know she has her reasons. I haven't been around them in years so me watching what my younger brother had done to himself hurt me to my soul! He was pimping out his girlfriend. "Lord please step in and take control of this situation". I tried to do the best I could, but I wasn't about to buy no drugs because of sickness. But seeing him go through those changes was some scary stuff and it reminds me that the devil is very busy. Lord help me come up with something but on the other hand Lord, I would rather see David locked up than to see him out here like this, Lord, your will be done!One day David came and told me that my daughter Destiny told him that Oge tried to holla at her after the 4th of July party but she didn't want to tell me because we had just started back speaking and she didn't want to jeopardize that. When David told me that, I called Destiny and asked her was it true she then said yes. I called Oge and as usual he denied it. But on the other hand I gave Oge the benefit of the doubt because at that time during 4th of July, we was staying in a hotel room so he could have easily been asking her did

ALL I HAVE

she want to go to the hotel room and she took it the wrong way. I also didn't know Destiny neither. By this time, I'd been around Oge longer than her, so I was confused. I had to sit back and see how I was about to play it. I knew Oge was a disloyal ass nigga and how things were going between us, the news that David brought my way didn't really phase me because it was over anyways. Besides, Destiny was there, and it seemed like she wasn't trying to go back home. So, I prayed and waited. Still taking things moment by moment because things do happen for a reason. All of this happening around Thanksgiving 2017 and I knew that I would have to go deeper into the word. I didn't have to go deeper because we do have free will, but I wanted to because my life seemed like it was moving way too fast. I had all 3 kids under one roof and a grand baby that I wasn't too happy about and the fact that she got pregnant and then came to me, I wasn't feeling that at all because I didn't do the babies, period. It also seemed like I was being forced back to where I first started. In my mind I was trying to find myself because at 37 years old, I wasn't getting no younger. After constantly training myself to first seek the kingdom of heaven each morning when I woke up, turning the TV to T.D Jakes at 7:30am on Daystar, that's how I would start my day. The Lord knew my struggle. I'd talk to him and try to explain to him that I'd been out in the streets since a young age as well as my brothers and sisters. My family are good hearted people, but we had no one to discipline us correctly and the streets basically raised us. From my point of view, we didn't realize we was doing wrong until it was too late, and by that time we were too far gone to turn back. How am I going to get me and my family off the streets? I had to keep seeking the Lord until he helped me find a way. I knew it was not going to be easy but as long as I humbled myself and tried to figure out what my purpose in life was, then everything else would fall into place, and that's what I did. I dug deeper into the word of God. My baby boy was 16 years old and I had a grand baby so living like I was, was getting tiring because I knew that the Lord had something better for me. I just had to figure out what

CHAPTER 34

it was. But right then, I had to think about me and my mental health because if not, I could see myself going crazy.

If it's not one thing it's another. I got someone to call the rent man to see if I could be 3 days late on rent on Clark St. and Mr. Sanja the rent man for 409 Clark St. tells us that the police called him and told him that it had been drugs sold out of the house. That kind of messed me up there because they had nothing on black and white stating that 409 was a drug house. With Sanja not taking the rent we had to move. Now those crackers were bugging out! Sanja also said that the police told him that 412 Clark & 409 Clark was connected. When they hit the 412 Clark in November, but the police lied and got this lady kicked out under false pretenses. I was tired of the police lying to get their way and ruining people's lives. So, they got that one, but as soon as 409 Clark came open, I was going to hop in it again! One monkey doesn't stop no show. FACTS! The beauty of it all was that I knew a lot of people so it was just a minor setback for a major comeback which was why it was a good thing that I had a lil change stashed for a rainy day. Now people, all that shoot em up bang, bang stuff I wasn't with at the moment. I was too old for that and getting bands on top of bands and moving bricks, I wasn't on that type of time neither. Like I said before, if I could make a certain profit a day then that to me was good money. Like Jay-Z said, He's a "business"-man and that's how I rolled. Things were definitely not like they used to be. I knew a guy by the name of Charles that stayed on Partin St. he let Tamara stay with him while I just sat at home to think because it was a lot going on at the time. I wasn't understanding where this all was coming from, but I continued to pray about it and sat back. But something in my gut was telling me that the police was following me. I didn't do hand to hand so that really wasn't bothering me, so I dismissed that. I also stayed in another county and didn't do anything where I laid my head. So, none of it wasn't any of my concern. Clark St. was closed so I was at home chilling, watching T.D Jakes but Charles was a cool smoker, he did his thang also, but he also maintained his finances. When I got

ALL I HAVE

tired of sitting at the house, I would go over to his house to play cards and drink a couple of drinks until me and Tamara found another trap house. At first, I really wasn't feeling the same house, but I had to think about the surrounding people and what was our best option. Christmas had gone by and my Birthday had rolled around but I really wasn't feeling it. I went home, fell asleep and woke up when it was 2018. My grandma would always say watch out for 2018, referring to our talks about Israel and when they had become a nation 70 years ago and how the Lord worked in 7's. So, sitting back listening to her made a lot of good points. My grandma is a Capricorn also so I'm going to pay attention to what she tells me, but anyways……. We had moved back into 409 Clark St. January 12, 2018 and my friend Tamara had went to court and had all of her charges dismissed. She told me that she's never went to court and beat anything, "Thank God!" So, the year started off on a good foot because not only did we get our house back at 409 Clark St., but her charges were dismissed. Destiny and Brianna had returned, so I still had all my kids under one roof. I couldn't complain about anything! My daughter Brie was 18 and Destiny 20. Both of them needed to find jobs and get and continue their education because I wasn't trying to hear it. My motto was Fresh spot fresh start Let's get it!

CHAPTER 35

THE LANDLORD ON Clark St. was coming to do work on the roof, so I decided not to go over that way because they knew me. But I got sidetracked and I forgot that I was supposed to get the brakes fixed on the truck. So, I called a friend of mine to see if he could take the truck to get the brakes done. I left my house in Benson and headed to Newburn Ave and I take Rock Rd exit which is exit 330. I just so happen to notice the police on the right-hand side of me like they were doing a traffic stop. It was a white car with tinted windows in front of me but mind you, my brakes are bad on my truck so I'm barely touching the brakes. I got the music blasting in my truck and while trying to get from behind this car, the next thing I know is that when I looked to the left of me, I saw a gun in my window and I instantly sped off because it all happened so quick. My mind went blank because I wasn't thinking straight, so I went down a dirt road that was in the cut. I wasn't thinking that it was the police because all I remember seeing was people dressed from head to toe in black with big guns. Once I went down the embankment (later I found out it was 40 feet). I'm glad I was in a Range Rover! But when I hoped back on Interstate 40 East, I thought about going home but I really didn't know what to think. Then I saw a few cars trying to box me in OMG! I had no gun and to me, it wasn't no telling who it was. My thoughts were, "do they think that I'm with my husband?" I had no clue and all a sudden, I looked to my left and the van said Wake Police Department! At that moment I was happy to see that it was the police but then again, I didn't because I was like if they on me like this then it's not good, they got me! "The Lord is my shepherd, I shall not want, no weapon formed against me shall prosper and at this moment, the police are a weapon! Was my prayer because I needed his guidance. This was not good. So, I pulled over and the police jump out with guns drawn and I got out and laid on the ground. First thing came out of my mouth was I needed a lawyer. One of the officers asked, "is he with her?" Another officer said "no, she is alone" and they took me to Northgate substation. Now I'm praying harder because I'm not understanding none of this because I knew my hands were clean. I was trying to figure out how they had the authority to come at me period. I knew right then the police lied to get the warrant to run up on me because I didn't do nothing. So, they sit me at a table and a white man with dirty blond hair came and sat down with his laptop. Again, I said I needed an attorney and he slam the laptop down and his face turned red and jumped up from the table. While all of this was going on, inside my head I was talking to Jesus. Then out of nowhere a lady officer came in and took me in the back room and made me take off all my clothes. She then told me to spread my butt cheeks, bend over, squat and cough 3 times, and I did, and she found nothing. After that, I saw her telling the first officer who had slammed the laptop down that I had a pad on, but she saw no blood. AT that point, I felt some kind of way because before I came out, I took a shower because my menstrual cycle was just starting to come on. While I sat at a table near the door waiting to see how they were about to play it, I saw him still on the computer and I asked him what was he doing? He said, "Getting a warrant to take you to Wake Center Hospital." I then asked him for what? He responded by saying "Because I saw you stuff something in you." Now how he saw that, I knew was impossible! Then he told me to shut up because I'd asked for an attorney. I asked him why he was so upset with me because I'd done nothing to him for this man to show so much hatred in his heart for a person that he didn't even know. So, I asked were they getting me an attorney because I felt like I was being sexually harassed. First a lady cop searched me good and

CHAPTER 35

found nothing and just because of that, he was going to fabricate another lie to take me to Wake Center Hospital. "I want a lawyer now!" I demanded. They all transported me to Wake Center even the jump out squad, I mean every officer present escorted me into the hospital like I was El Chapo's wife! While in Wake Hospital, they took me through the ambulance part and the police talked to the nurse. Now when I first got to the hospital, I knew for a fact that a warrant wasn't signed yet so how could the police be talking to nurses on my behalf already? That was the first violation because I made sure I signed no papers. I didn't want the treatment and I refused, but those people did what they wanted to do. I felt like I had no control over the situation but at the same time, I was praying to the Lord because how they were handling this situation I wasn't sure what they were capable of doing. I was seeing firsthand, how the police could do whatever they felt they wanted to do. While the cops and the nurses were out in the hallway talking, the police made it seem like they were in fear of my life which was a lie because they didn't care about me. I heard the police tell the nurse they thought I had drugs and they needed to get it out before it opened and caused severe damage. So, the nurse asked me, and I told her that I was good and that I needed a lawyer. The nurse asked could they check my vital signs and I told her sure. So, she did and said that my heart rate was 156/over something and by it being too much, they took me straight to the back and hooked me up to a heart monitor. Immediately anxiety kicked in because it's a lot going on, but I knew God was in control of the whole situation. While I was wondering where all of this was coming from. In the intake part of the hospital, my heart rate was going crazy and they thought that something had bust inside of me. But while telling these people that I didn't have anything, I guess the heart monitor said different. I figured since they weren't listening to what I was saying then out of frustration I hollered "rape" O.K. fine, there you go!" I was playing along with this game of theirs because these white people can take niggas and do whatever they please because look at what just happened to me. So, all I really had was Jesus and that was enough for me!

ALL I HAVE

Somehow my heart rate wouldn't go down and now the nurse comes back out and said that they were about to take me to the X-Ray room because if I had anything, they were going to find it. My reply was "I need an attorney" with that, the police walked in and says "The D.A. said if you give us whatever you have then they are going to be lenient on me". I looked at this dude like he was stupid. "Attorney!" I said and then I added "what about the HIPPA law?" Thank God he put that on my ear because once I said that, it opened a lot of doors because the police couldn't come back around until they got the warrant. Thank You Jesus! "The game meant to be sold, not told". So, after the police left out the hospital room, it was on and popping. But during this time, I had already screamed "Rape, sexual harassment" which I believed it to be at that time because while I was in the X-Ray room, the police officers was in there with me also. I had at least 8 police officers with me at all times and I was scared to death! The way they were moving, it was like I killed 50 people, and they never left! They took me upstairs and I was put in a room because my heart rate wasn't going down. When the officer told me that they had got my X-Rays back, it showed a mass inside me but of course it was a tampon! But O.K. whatever. So, they handcuffed me to a bed, and I spent the night at Wake Hospital. People with suits came to the hospital to talk to the police officers that looked like Internal Affairs or FEDS but there were more police than anything. People were walking by my room trying to look in to see who I was. Little old me with all this fire power and that night they took turns watching me. They had a piece of paper they passed around to each other so I'm guessing that was how they were supposed to handle me, but I still needed an attorney. Throughout that night until the next morning, if I used the bathroom, they searched the potty. I couldn't use the regular bathroom. But the woman officer that came the night of Feb 7, 2018 saw the tampon because I did the #2 in the pot and when she went through my shit not only was I full of shit but she acts like she was about to throw up! Hahaha!!

CHAPTER 35

The next day a redneck officer came right in with an attitude, snatched the remote turned the T.V. off and handcuffed me back to the bed. "You can't watch no T.V. you're in custody" He said. He had the nastiest attitude and I could tell he needed Jesus because he was miserable, so I just rolled over. I said "Lord, help me!" Something in my spirit said ask to use the bathroom so I did. The officer then steps out and the 1st nurse who attention the office got was a black woman. Good shot. He asked her to watch me while I used the bathroom and she told him I needed to be uncuffed. He uncuffed me and I went in the bathroom, sat on the toilet, flushed it two times got up and sat down on the bed after I washed my hands. "God will use the baddest of them all! Hallelujah! It was over now, and he handcuffed me to the bed, and I fell asleep. The game meant to be sold not told. When I woke up the initial officer who oversaw everything was sitting beside me and he talked to me about how he wanted to make a book and I'm like, here we go with that weak talk game. But then a lady angel with strawberry hair walked into my room and told them to uncuff me and step out of the room. She then extended her hand, I grabbed it and she told me that she was my attorney and that she had a couple of questions for me, So the officer walked out of the room and she asked me one question, did I have anything on me? I told her no, by the grace of God and she said that's all she needed to know. Then she told me that there was a lot of communication going on downtown about what had happened with me at the hospital. She then said if I didn't have anything on me then we had them, and I told her that we were good. So, she sat in the hospital with me all that day. If she had to make a run, she let me know and even then, she wasn't gone that long. But the police that was initially on the warrant sat down with me and my attorney all day Feb 8th until 11pm that night. Why did it take so long? I haven't a clue but it was time for me to go get a cat scan. Me, my attorney and the officer went, and they took me back to my room. One hour later the doctor came in the room along with my lawyer and the doctor said, "He saw nothing!" It's a miracle, she's clean and she can go! My lawyer came and shook my hand and said

ALL I HAVE

we got em! But before she left, I asked her could she come to my bond hearing because before I took the CT scan the police had told me my bond was already 6 digits. It was crazy because I couldn't understand how, so she assured me that if she couldn't make it, that she would have someone there. The officer in charge was pissed but we are one nation under God! But a 6-digit bond! I wondered what could that possibly be? So, when I was putting my clothes on, and heading out of the hospital, the police that was escorting me handed me some papers and it was the search warrant. It was an "Anticipatory Warrant". I had never in my life heard nothing of that sort so I couldn't wait to get out to find out what that meant. I learned that I was charged with fleeing to elude $100,000 bond for that and I as doing 45 in a 45 and $50,000 bond on an AWDW (Assault with a deadly weapon) of a motor vehicle on a police officer. I couldn't believe that these people could do whatever they wanted to!

On Feb 9, 2018 at 2:00pm while on the T.V. to go to court, "Thank God" for not only my lawyer keeping her word because she had sent someone down, but the judge took off $100,000 and kept the $50,000 on. Thank God for making moves for his child because the Lord worked it all out but the D.A. asked for house arrest, electronic monitoring and the judge granted that. So, I bonded out that night and when I thought I was going home, I ended up having to wait for the ankle bracelet and that took and extra 5 days in jail! I knew that calls were monitored and recorded so while upset, I let them know how upset I really was because when I was reading over the warrant they gave me, I found out that those people were crazy. They got that warrant just off my movements because the warrant said, I left my house in Benson and came to Raleigh everyday between the hours of 6am - 10am and parked my truck on Pedigree St. I walked to my friend's house and that indicated that I must have been trafficking drugs. Oh, these people had done snapped! But how they got permission to obtain the warrant was because someone had left a message on the answering machine? While reading the warrant, it said that

CHAPTER 35

all a person had to do was make a call and leave a message on the answering machine. For instance, let's say my friend's husband sells dope and 1 hour later, they could follow them for 3 months. Why I say that is because from Nov 28th, 2017 until February 2018 they had been tracking my movements. They made sure that they included my Range Rover and my whole family. Now I don't have the best family in the world, but I do love them. Look at Jacob's family in the bible. I've not been in any trouble for 8 years and these people had come at me crazy, but what I as trying to figure out was what my family had to do with me because I had not been around them in years. WOW! Those people were really bugging. They also had on the search warrant that I was the reason that 412 Clark St. had got raided in Nov 2017 and that was a lie. The police also said that I was the reason that drugs were being sold from 112 Pedigree St. but the truth was that Pedigree St. had got busted way before they said my truck was spotted there. These people were trying to ruin my life over a bunch of lies but God despises a liar, and I can prove it. Now all the pieces were coming together because now I understood why they waited until my truck pulled up before they hit Clark street. While I was across the street looking, I felt like they were following me, and the Lord also was trying to let me know but I couldn't catch it. I had a gut feeling that they were on me, but I thought I was moving in silence not thinking that I was a Gilchrist driving a Range Rover Sport. These crackers think they know everything!

You see it's the people from the outside looking in that think they know everything but they don't and come to think about it, those officers weren't nothing but a pawn to the devil to try to kill my vibe but the sovereign Lord was going to turn this to benefit him. Those people were no different in God's eyes than me! They lie to get their way. Look at what happened to me. I didn't understand what made these white people go through so much for nothing because looks can be deceiving. But, while I continued to read the search warrant, a lot didn't add up to me. The only thing they had was me leaving my house, stopping to get gas, driving to Raleigh, parking the car and walking to Clark St. on several occasions. That's it and just from that, a judge signed off on a warrant to ruin my life. A person that hadn't been in any trouble in 8 years? They did whatever they wanted by the stroke of a pen. I liked smoking weed, popping perks and sipping on Jose Cuervo Gold and I would occasionally go to a friend of mines house on Clark St. while my son was at school to chill until he got home because during that time, all my children was under one roof so I didn't want to be in that state around them. They were harassing me, and I wanted to take out harassment and perjury charges because they lied to obtain the anticipatory warrant. I wanted some answers because I feel that the judicial system shouldn't be able to lie to get their way. But Thank God for my baby father Chico once again because God used him to help me understand why all of this was happening to me however at the moment, I saw nothing happening to the police. They got to go home and sleep well after they basically ruined my life. I didn't think I deserved any of it because I'm a firm believer of karma and I couldn't see how this applied to me. Yes, I am a sinner, we all are but the bible says we all fall short and that's where Jesus come in at. On Feb. 13, 2018 I got out of jail and went to the monitoring place. My friend Alison was there, and she gave me a lift. My curfew was 5pm, so from 8am - 5pm, I could stay out. I did my house arrest at 409 Clark St., but I was traumatized because I didn't make a move for 3 months. I was posted like a light pole. But a couple of weeks after I got out, my attorney who I'm going to call Ms. Strawberry told me to come to her office. I wanted to see how she felt about the situation anyways. While there, she gave me all the paperwork and she told me that her team of attorneys advised her to withdraw herself from the case and told her to tell me to contact the NAAACP and she was going to be a witness for me. Oh snap! It was getting real. Any other time I would have been called Internal Affairs, but I asked the Lord what I should do this time, and something told me to wait. Yes, I did end up contacting Internal Affairs, but no one was in the office, so I left a voice message. Once they did return the

CHAPTER 35

call, I didn't answer so they left a voice message, but I didn't return the call. I knew I had to seek legal advice before I made that type of move because I had my freedom first to think about. I'm habitual status and these white people were already coming at me sideways, so I had to think.

At the lawyer's office, Ms. Strawberry told me the D.A. was giving me until April 21, 2018 to take 15-27 months plea for AWDW on police and if not, they were going to indict me on a habitual offender. That only gave me two weeks, but Ms. Strawberry told me not to worry because they were going to have to appoint me another attorney so that bought me extra time. So, in the meantime I was on Clark St. 10 toes down, sitting in the window, reading over the discovery material, highlighting their faults and loopholes. In the daytime I was going to the library copying things but 1st I would humble myself before praying to God. I had notebooks just about every morning while seeking the kingdom because I'm talking to Jesus even more and asking him for his forgiveness for whatever I'd done to get this type of treatment because I couldn't understand it. But I had to ask myself who am I to question God's motives. Or was this by God's hand??

Now everyone that was around me was like now look, she got her karma back. Oge was one of them of course because I'd kicked him out of the house and Tamara also because I'd told her she had to go as well. I just could not take Oge's abuse any longer and Tamara had become a straight alcoholic and I couldn't at the moment take the alcoholic tripping stuff. I needed a break from her but how about when I came home, my friends (smokers) were the only ones that showed me love. Alison the lady that picked me up is a smoker, Tamara my bestie who is also a smoker came and held the fort down and did not budge despite me telling her she had to go. My boy D was the only one that looked out for me on my bond but no one else, no sister or in-laws, blood relatives, no one and I Thank God for bringing the lawyer to the hospital because that also saved me $500 for a bond reduction. I had no friends because most of the people I used to associate with would come around me and because they were looking from the outside in, they tend to think that the game is easy and it's not. It's deeper than it looks and they would want to come and want to be down but when I saw them and if they worked anywhere, whether it was fast food, janitor or whatever I gave them the utmost respect because they were holding their family down and content. My mom's boyfriend Alamo has never had a job a day in his life and I rarely saw him with money, but I got mad love for Moe because he's always smiling and he content being broke. I dealt with Oge a while also because he was content with his smoke, food and little things here and there at first but things happen, So yea, I pay homage to all the working people because when looking back at my situation now, the reason why I believe I'm still here is because I talked to the Lord as much as I do and he shows me a lot of mercy because of that. In my mind I would just talk to him but as I'm writing this down, back then I didn't know how to humble myself and listen to him speak to me until recently, like Yolanda Adams said "Alone in this room, it's just me and you, I'm so lost because I don't know what to do, now what if I choose the wrong thing to do, I'm so afraid, afraid of disappointing the Lord" and that's what level I'm on at this very moment. Since 2016 I'd been noticing myself going deeper into the word of God because it's my freewill to find out what my purpose is in life. I was lost and mentally in a place that I shouldn't be in but something inside me had been telling me that my destiny consisted of way more than selling peanuts on the streets. So, I've been searching trying to find out what my purpose in life is, and with everything going on at the time, most definitely it was that time. I was looking at 15-27 months and I might have had one month to decide if I was going to take it or they was going to hit me with the habitual felon and if they did, the minimum that I was going to get was 5-7 years. It was real and I didn't understand why or who would call the police answering machine leaving a message saying that I was in a burgundy Range Rover Sport, trafficking drugs to Raleigh. I had to ask myself could it be Oge? Because they said the message was made Nov 28, 2017 and he left to go to New York on

CHAPTER 35

Nov 24th! WOW! Then I got to thinking that he did because he also had a video on his phone of me bagging while sitting at the kitchen table. When I saw it, he told me just in case I called the cops on him, but I would never tell the police nothing about no drugs. I am his wife and he was the one pulling out guns on me and getting my house shot up. Now that's my life he was playing with, I was supposed to come to him for protection but who was going to protect me from him? Myself, because if I had to shoot him, I was going to put the police in it and would walk after he was hurt or dead, God forbid. It's deep man! I had a few people that was suspect. I also though my brother David had done it because he had got hit with 17 indictments two weeks before Nov 28 and he was out 3 weeks later. Fastest in history! Man, everyone was suspect except my friends (smokers) and why I say that is because if they had any of them, then the police could have come in the trap house or my domain, but they dug deep to come at me. The attorney that I ended up hiring whose name was Rosemary Godwin told me that in her 33 years of being an attorney she had never seen an anticipatory warrant being used in that manner. She said, "All of this firepower for one woman!" A rare warrant for a rare woman! One of the officers even said to me "you are a smart woman, why won't you do something with it?" My reply was "I am, right now I need an attorney" Facts! So, yea, when I saw the extent that they went through to come at me that right there told me that my people was loyal, but I did say, no new friends!

So now I'm on a mission to figure out what was God's plan behind all of this. I knew that there were consequences for our actions, but this was a far reach for the Lord to allow the devil to come at me. All of my kids were under one roof and a Grandbaby, my husband was about to be sitting nice and that might have been over with because if I had to do 15 months, Oge most definitely was not going to be there when I got out. But God got me and that's good enough. The Lord also made it possible for my baby father Chico to hold me down mentally and that's really what I needed at that moment. I needed to read the bible so I could get the knowledge so it could open my heart and eyes to understand with wisdom to be able to come out on top of this. I had no choice but to be 10 toes down for 3 months, but I also had a lot of thinking, praying and humbling myself to do. I had to finish paying the bondsman which I did that but bills, bills, bills! I was also trying to hold out on paying for an attorney but the following week after I went to see Mrs. Strawberry, I had a new attorney, Mr. Petro. This dude's attitude was that he didn't care and wasn't trying to hear or feel anything I was saying. Right then I knew he was going to be a dub (joke). I then called Rosemary, set up an appointment and prayed to God to help me and to show me how he wanted me to handle this situation. "Lord, I know I'm a sinner but God you know the lies these police told to obtain this warrant to come at me." I was talking to God like that because like I said, I knew I was a sinner, but the Lord knew my struggle and my heart. I wasn't going to shut my Lord out because I needed him more than ever! The judicial system was no different from me and the ones reading this in God's eyes. The police had no right to bring up fake charges, or giving people get out of jail free cards for lies. Because of it, all a person had to do was tell the police what they wanted to hear and because we have been in the streets for over 20 years that's all they needed whether people were drug addicts or not. It's not what it seems and not one time have they found any drugs on Lamont Gilchrist, David Gilchrist, Latonya Gilchrist or May Gilchrist. Just tell the police a Gilchrist did it and they got out of jail. Boom that simple! It's sad and I was getting tired of these people (Judicial system) getting away with it. My brother Lamont is sitting in jail right now with no evidence period and I think the only reason why he is sitting in jail is off the word of a police officer. Police are humans also, so they are no saints. "Lord please forgive me if I do tend to get out of hand. I'm a sinner living in the flesh in Jesus name - Amen"

CHAPTER 36

AFTER MY LAWYER withdrew herself and after I went to check out Petro and fired him, I went to talk to Rosemary. I was telling her how I was trying to go about the case and how I wanted to do a suppression of evidence because they lied to obtain the Anticipatory warrant, but Rosemary told me that I not only had to do a Frank's motion and hire a private investigator to go inside the prison to talk to the two guys they took out of 412 Clark St; but the investigator had to go to the landlord to get proof of the phone call and the rental agreement. So, the two franks motions were $2,500 apiece and $2,500 for the private investigator for the suppression and $5,000 for her. My attorney fees came to $12,500 and I'm not about to sugar coat anything, I didn't have it like that at the moment. But after talking to my baby father Chico, I began to learn a lot and what he advised me to do is to continue taking it moment by moment and "Believe" that God would work it out. It was real because it seemed like every white person that rode by the house was the police and if I walked to the store, I thought I was being followed. When I looked at the warrant, I saw a picture that the police took, and it had an UBER sticker on the picture. So, people, the police do drive, Lyft and UBER watch out! I wasn't going to put nothing past them and because of it, I was afraid for my life. I was going to have to spend $17,500 off the police lies and now if they knew their job might be on the line, there was no telling what they would do. I was scared to death! I made sure I kept minutes on the phone so Chico could talk to me all day long. It was like he was everywhere I went but it did cost me $60 a day. If I had a question about anything whether it was prayer, bible study, spirituality, he was a lot of help. I really did Thank God for making him available to do it. The only place I went to was the gas station that was on the corner because that's where I'd go to play the machine or play my numbers, just to get out of the house. Chico would ask me to pray with him because if 2 or more went to the Lord, the Lord was in the midst and it began to amaze me how the Lord will use the baddest person to accomplish his goals. One day I heard Chico say "Tina, everything that's been happening this far is all about you!" At first, I didn't know how to take that because I'm nobody! But then I started to replay different situations that I'd been through and I started to think about it a lot. My initial thoughts were O.K. so what's next? But I couldn't really get off into what was next when I had so much going on mentally in the NOW. The only thing that felt right for me was humbling myself, being myself and trying to figure out what move the Lord wanted me to take. However, every day that I talked to Chico, I would understand the word of God more and more. I also had the king James app on my phone that did 3 verses a day to help me. When I was home with the kids, I would lock myself in my room and watch T.D Jakes until 3pm and I would get my Aunt Nita to come picks me up at 8am and she would drop me off. I had to pay her $40 because no one did nothing for free, but my boy D. I didn't want him to think nothing crazy about me because I'm a loyal female! So, I gave him all my paperwork and told him to read everything because I had nothing to hide. I was still sending money to Oge in New York, but I was the one that just got out. I had no problem with it because I knew he was safe, and I really couldn't take any more problems right then. I was willing to do just about anything just to keep him away from me. I Thank the Lord for making it possible for me to be able to pay for the rides and to be able to send Oge the money I did send him. Oge also got locked up and I had to send him bond money to get out, but I didn't believe he got locked up in the first place. Yet the Lord allowed me to be able to also send my brother Lamont, Chico,

CHAPTER 36

my brother David who got locked up also and my cousin Wayne that stays locked up canteen money whenever I could. But the Lord didn't just stop there. I also had to pay two rents at two households with everything that came with them on top of a car note Etc. Yes, the Lord made sure I was able, "Lord how should I play my situation because in my mind I knew the police lied to come at me and now I was the one that was facing prison time behind a bunch of lies and I feel that they need to be punished also because on the search warrant it was several lies that was on the paperwork. I'm heated because they did me dirty and I'm not budging at all. I just knew now I must play chess. But one thing I do need is Mrs. Godwin (lawyer) and Lord I need your help" Shortly after that prayer, I walked to the gas station. I would always go two hours before 5pm because I had to be in by 5pm so I went there, got on the machine and was there 20-30 minutes give or take and I hit for $3,600! Thank you, God, I got right up out of there, but I had to come back to get $2,500. So, the next day I caught a ride to pick up the rest of the money and went straight to Rosemary office and gave her every dime! The next day I went back to the gas station and hit for $1,200. Thank you, God, Again I called Rosemary and made another payment. I knew that the Lord felt I needed some help because he was providing for my needs. I was on fire! I also hit the pick 3 numbers a couple of times, so I had $5,000 to Rosemary quick! I then made another appointment to go talk to her to see how things were going and she wanted to talk to me also but not over the phone. Now I wasn't feeling well because something told me that this wasn't good. So, I go to her office and she tells me that the district attorney that was handling my case came to her and said that the FEDS was interested in me! WOW! I knew it was some fishy stuff going on because no way was the FEDS supposed to be interested in me because I was not on that type of time! Now they were really trying to play me because I didn't know what was going on. I had to pray and tell the Lord make it stop and to take the wheel. I then asked Mrs. Godwin did she believe in Jesus and she told me "yes" and when she did, that's all I needed to hear because when I told her that something wasn't right, that's when she told me about a trial that was going on in Charlotte with the blood gang members that had gotten arrested. When she said that that's when this all made sense because the police came at me hoping Oge was with me because of the last time Oge got shot and those three were the ones responsible of the shooting, Tink, her brother Jimmy, Tommy, who were involved with an 83 man blood gang indictment. I believed that they wanted to catch us together slipping so we could flip on them. But they were coming at the wrong one sideways. At the time when Rosemary said that to me it didn't register to me until recent but after that visit, I couldn't believe the FEDS was interested in me. OMG! They were trying to ruin my life! I personally didn't believe the FEDS came to the district attorney, but I did believe they went to the FEDS and it was way out of my league. So, I asked the Lord "What shall I do? All of this is crazy to me, first they lied and came at me with a rare warrant and now they threatened me with the FEDS. At first they said if I didn't take 15-27 months they were going to indict me on a habitual felon and I would have to make a $100,000 bond and have to pay more money to get a lawyer but if I lose, I will be facing a minimum of 5 years all over some lies and a stroke of a pen. Jesus help me please!" And the crazy thing about all of this is everyone was telling me to take the 15-27 months. Even Chico my baby father told me to take it but I never stopped praying to God so I told Chico he had such little faith, My Uncle Rodney was the only one telling me to take it to trial but I continued to talk to my Lord and also Chico. In those past couple of months of me talking to Chico, I'd come to the realization that I still loved him just as much as I did 17 years ago. It was amazing to see how he's matured. Chico was 26 years old when he left me and he's 42 now and I've learned a lot about him that I didn't know and Vica Versa. Chico rarely judged me, always listened to me and gave me good advice, but I realized that I'd learned a lot and matured mentally also because as the months slipped away, I came to look at life different. The Lord does things for a reason and in my heart, I thought it was a reason behind all of this and that there's no such thing as coincidences. Yes, there's

CHAPTER 36

consequences to one's actions but I think it's a spiritual meaning behind all of it. Was this all a test of my faith? But whatever it was I would say "Lord, whatever it may be, I don't think prison time will help the situation none because I was seeking the kingdom before all of this" I always said that when people get locked up the 1st person they call on is the Lord but I was still young and I didn't fully understand him as I do now. I would pray for knowledge, wisdom and understanding and I Thank God for allowing me to understand his word more and more each time I seek him, but sometimes it seems so hard to me for some reason. It's like "how do you know what to listen for?" Yolanda Adams said, "What if I choose the wrong thing to do" But I did know that if it's anything contrary to God's word, it's not from him. A couple of months before I didn't understand that Jesus was tempted by the devil mentally but now I know that the devil is going to try to tempt you to sin mentally but it's not a sin until you react on the temptation! So now I have a better understanding, but I also know that it's not going to be that easy and it's a continuing progress because nothing happens overnight. So, yes all this that I'm writing is because the Lord allowed Chico to help me mature spiritually. I knew in my heart that my life consisted of something better than what I was living but I hate that it had to come down to me fighting for my freedom again to make me come to grips on reality. I just needed a little more time because Oge was about to get straight and I had in my mind that I was going to get me a rental car service and a house Etc. but I didn't believe that he was going to hold it down for 15-27 months so all of this would be for nothing. I came to see why my son and myself was still holding on and it was because Big Chico was praying for us continually as well as myself. Maybe others but I know Big Chico did. I learned also that Chico held onto every memory that he had about our relationship. Every little detail down to the color shoes I had on when we first met, down to the holes that was in my pants leg between my thighs 17 years ago. That was amazing to me, and I felt so bad because I had tried to erase every memory of him because it hurt me so bad to think about him, knowing it's a blessing that I have someone like him as a friend. And the whole time I thought it was his fault that he left me because if he would have done right by me, then the Lord wouldn't have intervened. But it was deeper than that. After talking to him and listening to his struggle, the Lord had saved him because he knew how much I loved him and he knew that one day he would come in handy or maybe it's bigger than I could possibly imagine because anything is possible through Christ Jesus. But I would ask myself am I ready for it mentally but then negative thoughts would tell me "what am I thinking about, I'm going to jail!", but then I'd have to tell myself "wake up Tina, do you think that you would be going through any of this for no reason?" But I still felt that I'd messed up somewhere with God and I needed to figure out where, but there was no telling where this was coming from. Since all of this happened I'd spent many nights crying to the Lord as to why, and what kept popping up in my head was when Oge would say "you out here giving your people poison, and you think God loves you more than me?" I personally wouldn't never think that I was better than someone. I hate that he thought that way about me because I'm the total opposite of that. I just thought that believing in the Lord and talking to him as often as I did give me a little lead way. If the United States of America could tax cocaine and heroin it would be legal today as weed is now, so I really didn't think I was doing nothing wrong in God's eyes because cigarettes and alcohol are legal and they kill more people than anything else. Big Chico would tell me that I had a long run and maybe it was God's way of saving you from something so he would tell me think about it because he didn't want me to play with my life because of my record but I was pleading with Chico and the Lord to hear my side also because I believe that I tried my best with the cards I was dealt. But here the police were saying they knew for a fact that trafficking charges were going to come in the immediate future and that was some scary stuff! So, they were going to plant drugs on me now I thought. Man, it was too much for me to handle and as the days ticked by, my faith grew stronger but I'm a sinner living in the flesh. "Lord, please forgive me for if and when I waiver but

CHAPTER 36

know that I love you regardless Lord, you know my heart." I had to realize and accept that tomorrow isn't promised and yesterday was gone so at that point it was moment by moment. My first superior court date was April 27, 2018 but that was just an arraignment. They had continued my court date for a later date, but I had to wait for it to come in the mail or through my attorney when she called me. I did also contact N.A.A.C.P and left a message. They ended up sending me a pack of papers to fill out and I turned them back in. They returned my call, but paranoia overcame me to the point that I changed numbers every week because due to the mental state that I was in, I had to handle one situation at a time. But, check it out, my lawyer called me and told me that the district attorney that was handling my case had left the D.A. office and we had to wait on a new D.A to come in. It caught me off guard with that one, so I asked her if she knew why and she said "no", but she didn't think it was behind my case. I don't believe in coincidences, but I was putting my trust in The Lord because he was the one in control and even if I did take the 1527 months, my situation could have ended up a lot worse. But my lawyer also said that she liked the D.A. that left because she'd won a lot of cases against him. She thought she could have intimidated him so now she had to figure out someone new. I also asked my lawyer about the judge that signed off on all those warrants and she told me that the judge had just got into office in 2017 and she was the D.A. for drug and vice for 25 years. Right then, that's when it all hit me, she had to be on one of my family members paperwork as a district attorney because my whole family had been out there longer than that and if it was true, then it would be a serious problem. Everything just seemed to get deeper and deeper. Man, I felt it was a conspiracy going on and it was with the largest gang in the history of America, the judicial system and all they had was an ink pen and a military to back it up. Something wasn't right because they went through a lot of trouble, but I was going to let the Lord handle it because he'd reveal it to me when the time was right. Another thing that I came to understand was that the devil was trying to keep me confused or busy to throw me off what the Lord had in store for me. Chico would tell me, regardless of the turn out "Tina, you know one day you're coming home so just know that the Lord does things for our own good and whatever I decide to do, just know it's a minor setback for a major come back. "But I swear I didn't want to do 15-27 months in prison. So Chico and myself would pray together and sometimes he would start it off and sometimes I would start it off and we would ask the Lord to help us better understand the meaning of all of this because I was feeling like Job in the book of Job in the bible, and I know that I was nowhere near as rich as he was but Thank God for not letting the devil go to the extreme with me as it was with Job. But, yes I was still trying to figure out what was going on because I still didn't know which way I should go with this because the evidence and the picture that I was trying to paint to the jury was very compelling and you all know it's on who paints the best picture. Yes, from how I was going with it, I was almost willing to take that gamble because I wasn't going to take 1527 months for assault with a deadly weapon of a motor vehicle on a police officer when no one was hurt. Those people were just upset because they had me in the hospital for 37 hours for no reason. It wasn't my fault and now because I was vulnerable, they all were trying to play me. My attorney showed me the video and on the video it had them coming at me with an assault rifle and me pulling off and since the D.A. was saying that when the officer moved his hand out of the way, he was in fear of his life, they were really coming at me sideways. But one thing I did know, something was going to have to give. But, just so happened, I'd received a call from my lawyer and paper in the mail stating that my court date was July 26, 2018 at 9:30am in courtroom 701. It was a little over a month away and my attorney told me that she had an appointment to go speak to the D.A. about my case. She also said that she loved the way I had everything organized for her and both of us looked at the video the police had, and we looked at it in slow motion. It showed that the officer's hand only went back as I speed off. Simultaneously, she also said she heard the voice recorder and it was a male's voice that sounded like

CHAPTER 36

whomever it was, was reading it off a piece of paper. The police claimed that it was an anonymous caller, but it sounded scripted. She went onto explain the law and it stated that if a person have to move out the way in fear of their life, then it's assault and the deadly weapon was my car. She said that if we took it to trial and I lost, I'd be looking at a minimum of 5 years and would be hit with habitual felon on top of that. She also told me that I needed to think about it. So, she told me that she was going to call me after the meeting. This was on that Friday before court and the meeting was on that Monday at 3pm. It felt like the longest weekend ever! With it almost being before my court date, I'd began to be at peace with the whole situation. It had been 5 months since I went to jail and I'd been on house arrest since then wearing a monitor with a fee that went from $160 to $300 because it was out of the county since I'd switched it from Raleigh to Benson. I'd already talked to the kids and explained the situation to them and it was like it all took me back from when I first had my girls because going back and forth to jail was the reason why they were taken in the first place. And now I had them back in my presence and now they were going to be gone again. I just couldn't seem to never be happy and Layah my Grandbaby, I was going to miss her getting on my nerves so I hated I couldn't enjoy her because my mind had been all over the place. First my marriage and now my freedom! "Lord please have mercy on me. I need your strength because a person can only take but so much!"

CHAPTER 37

I GOT MY mind made up and I'm content with the court situation. I'm going to get all my affairs in order with pertaining to my children and I'm going to try to keep the house going while I'm gone. I know I will have to call on Oge and help me out until I get back home where I belong. It's a hard pill to swallow 15-27 months but like I said before it could be worse. Besides money isn't an issue it's all about maintaining what is already coming through. It's easy to say and every time I think about doing 15-27 months for a crime I didn't commit. I get pissed. Matter fact if I have to do 15-27 months for a crime that I didn't commit I want everyone that is responsible for this Anticipatory Warrant to feel my pain. If I have to go, they have to go period!! I'm tired of these white people doing whatever they want to do with misfortunate people and getting away with it. Deep down in my heart trial seems like the way to go, and matter of fact if they not coming off that 15-27 months Trial is what it's going to be. We are one nation under God and God do despises a liar and lies they did tell so now mentally I'm preparing myself for trial and now Lord I need your help with posting $100,000 bond for a habitual felon charge. I also need an extra $5000.00 for trial. I'm not going down without a fight. I called and talked to Oge and as I already knew he's willing to come and help me hold the fort down just in case the district attorney not talking the way I want them to. I also told the kids once I go to court I might not be coming back home. I told them to call their Foster parents and use them as a steppingstone to get themselves in a better position to take care of their own. I told them don't never depend on no one. They must spoil themselves and if when they get a man that's willing to help them out then that's and extra bonus. Hurts my heart because I have them all under one roof and now that was short lived. My grandma Lynda said Chico was more than welcomed to stay with her. I love her life!! And that took a lot off my chest. Business wise, I'm a Hustler if Oge don't hold up his end of the bargain then so be it. I'm not going to think that far ahead. One thing I do know is that you can't depend on no one to look out for you with pertaining to canteen and for me at this very moment in my life I have absolutely no one to help me financially. But God is doing a good job holding me down so basically, I don't need no one. I'm going to miss my buddies out here and looking at their actions I know they're going to miss me also. I think about my buddies well-being because they've been here holding down the fort! And once I'm gone where would they go? They will say "Tina I don't want you to go" and I know they don't because they have absolutely no worries no rent, lights, water, food and they get paid well! Spoiled rotten! But now I'm forced to put everything in a disloyal negro that I know for a fact that ain't worth it but deep down in my heart I look at it like I held him down so it don't hurt to try. He the only one that I feel well at least try not to forget about me! Sad situation. Now N.A.A.A.C.P (national association for the colored people) I've been waiting on that call back. I'm going to literally raise hell and now I have all my ducks in a row, now it's time to fight!

June 25th, 2018, this is the day that my lawyer Ms. Rosemary had gone to talk to the district attorney to see if they're willing to come off that 15 to 27 month. I've been anxiously waiting on her phone call because June 28th is my court date. The whole time I'm praying and talking to Jesus Christ because I know he is going to the father on my behalf. Jesus you know my heart, he knows my struggle, please Lord soften their hearts. Finally, around 4 p.m. my attorney called me and said "Tina he not coming off the 15 to 27 months, I'm sorry" I told her it was okay because the Lord knows best and I asked her was she be willing to take my case if it goes to trial and she said that I was her last case because she was going to be a federal attorney! That let me down because we need people out here like her! But she said if I'm willing to do a speedy trial then she will. I then told her I will let her know once we go to court in three days. I looked up in the sky and I told the Lord that I still love him, and as my father I will accept my punishment. But at the same time, I'm trying to make Jesus feel my pain because if they didn't never tell lies on me in the first place I wouldn't even be in this situation. Okay, I can understand that they thought they knew what they knew but it's all about the truth. Lord please take that into consideration. And it was all of them that played a part in coming at me sideways. Everyone I'm talking to said Tina you better take that plea but that ain't right! Why should I? I didn't attempt to kill no one, especially not an officer. Forget this, I'm going to trial!

Tuesday June 28th, 2018

I called Rosemary up and told her I was taking it to trial. Of course, she broke the law down to me and asked was I sure? Because if I do take it to trial, she would have to call me on the stand and once she does then my prior perjury conviction going to come into play and that would not be a good look for us. It's deep now because she right. She also said that if they could beat you more than likely you're going to get the worse end of that sentence and that will be 7 years. But she also said we have a 50-50 chance of winning but knowing the state they're going to call up a bunch of police officers that's going to throw me under the bus just to look out for one another and what if the jury that was picked love police officers then it can be a major problem! Are you willing to take a 7-year gamble for 15 to 27 months? She had a serious point there, if I was habitual felon status then I would take the gamble, but is it worth it?

CHAPTER 37

June 28th, 2018 9 a.m.

Heart coming out my chest as I walk into the courtroom and it wasn't packed at all like it used to be. My friends Tamara and Bobby came with me to court because Bobby will always say support from people always look good in court. Just think about it. When a judge and the jury see that you have back up most of the time, they be a little lenient on you. So, I walked in and as I walk in, I see my lawyer Rosemary talking to the district attorney and her facial impressions not looking too good. I'm thinking about the Bible verse Chico and myself read the night before and it said in the final hour you will know what to do. Follow your gut instinct. I turned and I told Tamara that if I have to go today the Lord does what he does for a reason, and I hope that nothing will happen to no one by the time I get out because the Lord is my shepherd! I'm covered! Tamara said I hope not either Tina so my lawyer walks over my way and tells me to meet her in the hallway so Bobby, Tamara, and myself walks out Rosemary said they not coming off the 15 to 27 months, the DEA said if you not taking the plea today then he is going to indict you on a habitual felon but she also said you won't be going to trial no time soon and don't worry about jail today if you don't take the plea they will come back and serve the warrant for the habitual felon Bond first which will be $100,000 and after that be looking to go to trial.

Damn that hurt and everyone looking at me like Tina it ain't worth it just take the 15 to 27 months but every bone in my body told me to tell Rosemary we going to trial so I did and I asked her will she'd be willing to take my case and Ms. Rosemary asked me am I willing to do a speedy trial and I told her let's do it and she said okay Tina let me go inform the district attorney of our decision and I will come right back to you. We will talk further. So, she goes and talk to him with both of their backs turned and I couldn't even read lips or see facial expressions. But while they're up there talking, I look to the judge and to my surprise it's the same judge that signed off on the Anticipatory Warrant, now I'm feeling my life is being threatened. I'm looking at it like it's a conspiracy why would they have me in front of the same judge that was in this in the first place, talking to Jesus what should I do I feel like I'm trapped this is just a nightmare that needs to come to an end, now what are the odds of me coming in front of the same judge that first sign the Anticipatory Warrant that was built upon lies, and now I'm looking at it like they all trying to cover their tracks, is this your way of telling me to go ahead and take this plea, talk to me, talk to me what should I do? Tamara and Bobby look worried, I am especially worried because I don't know if the Lord wants me to take the plea or go to trial. Sweating bullets I then look up and see Rosemary coming my way she nods her head towards the door, so I get up and goes out. She said Tina, good move and she smile! OMG! What did they say Rosemary? He said he's willing to do a split plea, what that mean I asked Ms. Rosemary, she said are you willing to take two years of supervised probation and 90 days active sentence! Yes!!! Thank you, God,

The final hour! I'm going to take it give it here but I'm not pleading guilty, I'm taking an Alford plea meaning I'm not admitting guilt, but I accept the plea agreement. Yes! I gave my girl a big hug! She said this all you! With a little help from me of course this is what Ms. Rosemary said. We gave each other a big hug when she asked what I was going to plead guilty to I had two choices, attempted trafficking, or attempted assault on a police. I wasn't pleading guilty to no drugs. So attempted assault on a police officer. So, she went back and talked to the DA got the paperwork and I signed it and I waited on the judge to call me.

They finally called me to come up in front of the judge. Now I'm in front of the same judge that signed the Anticipatory Warrant, also the same judge that signed on the hospital warrant. On top of the police and their lies and obtaining these warrants I'm heated but I also know that things could have been a lot worse. I looked at Rosemary and she said let's get these papers signed by the judge first because she doesn't have to agree to this arrangement. So the judge asks what

CHAPTER 37

this matter was about like she didn't already know what was going on I mean you was the same judge that signed off on all this paperwork but the D.A starter it off with saying the police attempted to approach Mrs. Gilchrist vehicle as she sped off which resulted in this charge. Now once the district attorney said the police attempted to approach that statement alone right then and there, I knew that I had them. But once it was Ms. Rosemary turn she came back with it's a lot of things that went wrong with this case Judge. And she was looking at my rap sheet and she said she a level four in sentencing and you are offering her probation? That's when the DA said something that got her attention yes, it's a lot of holes in this case. Then the judge said I shouldn't be doing this but I'm going to side with the state and on this one and Rosemary asked could I get some time to set my affairs in order and she gave me until August 23rd 2018 but she didn't take the ankle bracelet off once I turn myself in for the 84 days. The judge gave me credit for the six days that I was in jail and the 37 hours they had me in the hospital. I had the biggest Kool aid smile on my face they weren't even supposed to consider probation but I'm a force to be reckoned with. Thank you God one thing for sure I know for a fact after the judge that signed off on all this was the last one I seen, they're trying to cover their asses and once I get out I'm going for their jobs, I'm going for badges, I have to go down for this for their lies and then they must go down also a lot can happen in 84 days but one thing I do know God is good!! Vengeance is his!

www.ingramcontent.com/pod-product-compliance
Lightning Source LLC
Chambersburg PA
CBHW030239170426
43202CB00007B/50